Tool-Making Projects for Joinery and Woodworking

D1289942

Tool-Making Projects for Joinery and Woodworking

A Yankee Craftsman's Practical Methods

Steve A. Olesin

Cambium Press
Bethel

TOOL-MAKING PROJECTS FOR JOINERY AND WOODWORKING

ISBN 10 1-892836-23-8
ISBN 13 978-1-892836-23-6

First printing: October 2005
Printed in the United States of America

Published by
    Cambium Press
    PO Box 909
    Bethel, CT 06801
    www.CAMBIUMPRESS.com

Library of Congress Cataloging-in-Publication Data
Olesin, Steve A., 1949-
    Tool-making projects for joinery and woodworking : a yankee craftsman's practical methods / Steve A. Olesin.-- 1st ed.
        p. cm.
    Includes bibliographical references and index.
    ISBN-13: 978-1-892836-23-6
    ISBN-10: 1-892836-23-8
1. Woodworking tools. 2. Woodwork--Equipment and supplies--Design and construction. 3. Joinery. I. Title.
    TT186.O44 2005
    684".08--dc22
            2005023059

Acknowledgements

When I think of all the people who have taught me about tools and woodworking, the list would include all of my students, instructors, and especially the many fellow woodworking guild members who give freely of their knowledge and time to aid others.

My appreciation for help with this book must first go to my wife, Jane, who read every word and encouraged me faithfully.

The book was content-reviewed by Eastern Massachusetts Guild of Woodworkers members Chris Kovacs of Chris Kovacs Designs in Groton, Massachusetts, and Peter Wilcox; by Lexington Arts and Crafts Society Woodworkers Guild members Jeff Chatfield, Rod Cole, Jim Dorsey, Dave Eaton, Josh Haines, Dan Power, and Myron Rosenblum; and by Guild of New Hampshire Woodworker Dave Anderson of Chester Toolworks, in Chester, New Hampshire. All of these wonderful woodworkers graciously accepted the challenge of reviewing and improving the material herein. Their contributions were valuable to me and hopefully made the text that much more valuable to you.

John Kelsey, editor and publisher, was a guiding light throughout this project, helping to focus the subject matter and sharpen the descriptions as well as providing a wonderful education in publishing.

Back in a time when we hadn't yet sorted out what we were to do in life, a dear childhood friend, Will Moyer, and I used to talk about someday. To him I offer my thanks for providing the seed for this writing project.

Special thanks to Dan Power for allowing the use of his turned mallets for a picture in that section.

Table of Contents

Striking Tools 125

Part II   Making the Joints 137

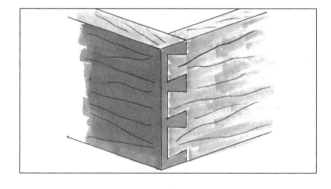

Appendices

Introduction

I'm a tool junkie. Sitting down with a tool catalog is a visit to a candy store. Over the years my workshop has added many new motorized cutters. But nowadays many of them have returned to their boxes. My journey in woodworking was from power-tool mania to hand-tool tranquility. The transition was one of increased knowledge and decreased tool count.

The turning point came when a friend and I went to a tool show – you know, one of those gatherings where every conceivable vendor sets up a booth in a room the size of a dirigible hangar. We wandered around for hours looking at all the machinery marvels. I had a bag full of new "must haves" when he casually mentioned that it would take me a month just to read the instructions for all of the tools.

Something clicked, and I started to think of all the tools I own, and began to assess just how many I really knew how to use well. When I arrived home that afternoon, I placed my cache in a box at the corner of my workshop and stared at the great unknown sitting all around me: chisels, planes, table saw, band saw. My tool passion had overtaken my woodworking passion.

Since that day, I have done some humble making-up to those pieces of fine tool steel by learning their ways and allowing them to show me their real value. I started with the power tools I enjoyed so well and became increasingly curious about my hand tools and what they could do. Though I have much to learn, I've found that many of the quiet tools are the most powerful. Knowing every one of our tools and what they can do teaches us a lot about what we can do.

Tools and the methods of using them must be of interest to all craftsmen. Without the knowledge of what tools are available and how to use them, the craftsman is at a serious disadvantage.

In this book, we will explore how to make tools, how to use them, and how to apply our knowledge to specific tasks. We need tools that will mark, measure, hold, hit, and cut. The goal is to stimulate the reader's creativity to think beyond the catalog offerings, and to explore the opportunities that materialize when you can make the tools you need.

Wood is a material that is harder and tougher than our skin and fingernails, resulting in the need for a tool that is harder and tougher than the wood we are working. To shape balsa wood, we could probably use a piece of hard maple. To work maple, we need to graduate to steel. We will not attempt blacksmithing techniques, but we will form steel to our purposes.

Methods within these pages expose the reader to techniques that are good practices in general woodworking. The things I learned while making stringed instruments helped me become a better cabinetmaker. The same was true in the opposite direction. Tools are, for the most part, just oddly shaped wood projects. They will provide insight into ways of doing other projects.

How to proceed with building a tool

Before building a tool, read the section about that tool completely and observe the illustrations as an aid to the text. Gather all of the parts required for the project prior to starting any portion of the tool, since part sizes may vary and affect the details of construction. It is extremely valuable to re-read the section once you have all the parts in hand.

On all but the simplest tools, there are exploded views of the parts, a condensed build procedure, and a cut list for quick reference. Each section of the book contains a separate tool, but many of the procedures or techniques are common, so I encourage you to read the cross-references within the book.

A note of caution: Woodworking safety is your primary objective. A book can only give overview directions due to the limitations of pictures and words. When reading these pages, you may find some operations unfamiliar. Seek help from a knowledgeable woodworker for instruction or for a clearer explanation. When attempting any type of operation, double-check that everything is in working order and that the work area is safe. If you are not entirely satisfied that the operation you are about to perform can be done safely, please don't attempt it.

—*Steve A. Olesin, Acton, MA, July 2005*

Steve Olesin employing his bench plane.

1. Single-beam cutting gauge (page 12).

2. Dual-beam marking gauge (page 21).

3. Mortising gauge (page 30).

4. Joinery check gauge (page 40).

5. Wooden squares (page 46).

6. Marking knife (page 35).

7. Case-squaring stick (page 42).

Marking and Measuring Tools

On my journey from power tools to hand tools, a curious change in work methods took place. Instead of setting machinery to exact measurements that were calculated in advance on my detailed work plans, I began to make approximate measurements which were then cut with hand tools. My work soon became far more accurate and my joinery began to fit extraordinarily well.

How could this be? I might call it awareness of the theory of relativity. What became clear was that it did not matter if a mortise and tenon were positioned slightly to the left or right or up a bit. What mattered was that the parts were perfectly aligned and square.

The marking gauge allows accurate layout of mortise and tenons joints and dovetails with or without the use of a ruler. For example, in the half-blind dovetail joint, the height of the pins is exactly the same as the length of the tails. It doesn't matter what the exact dimensions are, as long as they match. The marking gauge enables us to replicate an exact marking several times on different pieces of wood.

The dovetail marking gauge, the joinery check gauge and the case squaring stick all operate with relative accuracy versus exact measurement.

The small squares we build will be powerful well beyond their size in contributing accurately squared markings to joinery success.

Starting a project with flat surfaces, squared edges and

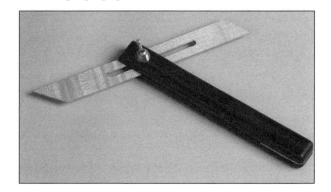

8. *Dovetail gauge (page 38).*
9. *Bevel gauge (page 50).*

accurate markings immediately improves our chances of success. Therefore, marking and measuring tools are the logical place to start in building our tool set. The tools described here are specifically scaled for furniture and interior joinery, but it is easy to see how they can be made for larger work. Let's start our toolmaking journey with tools that enhance accuracy.

CHAPTER 1

Single-beam Cutting Gauge

10. The cutting gauge uses wedges to retain the cutter and to lock the fence to the beam.

A marking gauge is used to scribe lines on your project wood to give guidance in cutting joints. The cutting gauge is a marking gauge with a chisel-shaped cutter, so that when scribing a cross-grain line with it, you are actually making the first chisel cut on your joint. In Part II we will see how this allows us to accurately cut joints by hand.

The single-beam cutting gauge described here is based on a tool used in colonial America that features a wedge for securing the moveable beam. A nice feature of this wedge design is that the beam can be set and secured in place with one hand.

The components of a gauge

The marking gauge consists of the fence, beam, wedge, and cutter. The fence is a glued lamination made of at least three layers of wood. If you like, for decorative appeal, use contrasting colored woods. The

wedge and beam may also be laminations but they will be assumed to be solid wood for this discussion.

The overall dimensions of the fence may be anything you desire. I tend toward a fence of 3 inches x 2-1/4 inches x 3/4 inch, which works out nicely when using wood of 3/4 inch x 3/4 inch cross section. The fence must be wide enough to provide a steady reference for the cutter, yet not overly wide and unwieldy. Plan on a beam length of no more than three times the width of the fence.

The central section of the fence and the beam should be cut to the same cross-sectional dimension, which allows the beam to fit in the fence exactly. I usually cut them from the same piece of wood. The beam is generally less than 9 inches long. If you make it longer, increase the beam profile for improved rigidity, and increase the fence size to stabilize the longer beam.

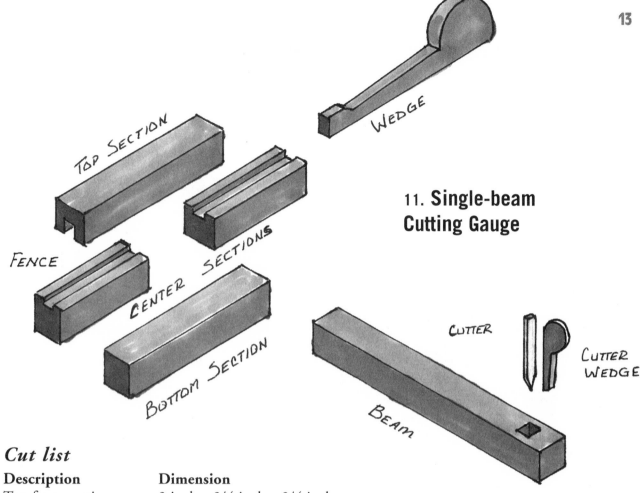

11. Single-beam Cutting Gauge

Cut list

Description	Dimension
Top fence section	3 inch x 3/4 inch x 3/4 inch
Bottom fence section	3-1/2 inch x 3/4 inch x 3/4 inch
Center fence section	2 each 2 inch x 3/4 inch x 3/4 inch
Beam	8 inch x 3/4 inch x 3/4 inch
Wedge	6 inch x 3/8 inch x 1 inch
Cutter wedge	2 inch x 1/4 inch x 3/4 inch

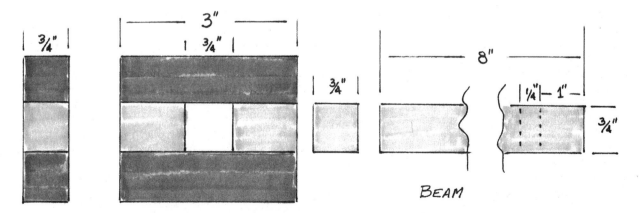

FENCE

BEAM

Building a single-beam wedged cutting gauge

Procedure	Tools	Materials
Cut wedge slot	Table saw or router	Hardwood
Cut parts to length	Table saw, miter gauge	
Cut ramp ends on slot	Chisel	
Make the wedge	Bandsaw, coping saw	Hardwood
Glue fence	Clamps	Glue
Fit wedge	Plane or sandpaper	
Make cutter and cutter wedge	Hacksaw, coping saw, bandsaw, sharpening stones	Scrap circular saw blade, Hardwood
Square fence	Miter box, table saw, chopsaw	
Finish		Oil and wax

The wedge has a central ramp with a prominence on each end. For a 3-inch wide fence, the wedge will be at least 6 inches long. The prominence on the smaller end ensures the wedge will not fall out when in use. The prominence on the larger end provides a finger grip and gives the wedge visual appeal.

Make the Fence

We will make the fence out of a stack of 3/4 inch x 3/4 inch sticks ripped from wider boards, but first we need to figure out a safe way of handling the workpiece.

Many of the following operations require cutting fine details into the component workpieces. Since there is real danger when handling small pieces near spinning blades, we will minimize risk by milling in the details on the edges of a large board and only after the details are installed will we rip the board — thus severing the needed workpiece from the large board.

Putting the milling details into the edge requires holding the board on edge against the table saw fence. To improve safety and accuracy during this operation, attach an auxiliary tall fence to the normal saw fence .

(12)

Start with a large board

Starting with a 3/4 inch thick board (or two boards if using contrasting woods) at least 12 inches long by at least 4 inches wide, we will first install the slots into the top and central fence sections.

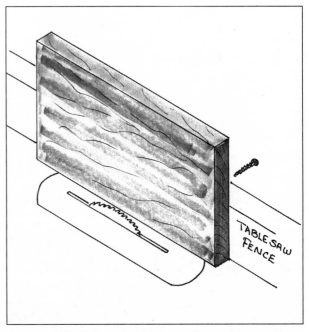

TABLE SAW FENCE

12.   A tall fence can be screwed into the normal table saw fence.

Safely ripping thin pieces

Thin pieces of wood can be ripped out of a wide board by setting the table saw fence the desired cut-width from the blade, but it is unsafe. Fitting a push stick to guide the workpiece in that narrow space is difficult and unstable.

A safer cutting method that produces a cleaner cut is to remove the piece from the opposite edge of the board. To cut our required 3/4 inch sticks off a 5 inch wide board, the fence would be set to 4-1/8 inches from the blade. This allows for the width of an 1/8 inch blade kerf and yields the 3/4 inch stick from the outer edge of the board.

Use a feather board as both a safety device and a dimensioning index. Set the feather board so it just touches the edge of the workpiece. Locate it just shy of the front edge of the blade so it cannot push the wood into the blade. Cut the first piece.

Now slide the fence into position with the board again just touching the feather stick. Make a cut and compare the two pieces. Adjust your technique to achieve consistent results.

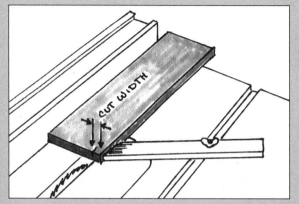

13.   To rip thin pieces use the feather board as an index as well as a safety device. Note that the off-cut is the width to which you are cutting .

Cut the wedge slots

If you are going to add any decorative layers beyond the three described, now is the time to do it. Add them to the top and bottom fence sections, which won't affect the fit of the central section and beam.

To add a decorative layer, edge-glue the desired layer onto the workpiece board and clamp. When the glue has dried, the decorative edge can be worked as if it were a single board following the instructions below.

The top and center fence sections have slots cut at the center of their lengths to receive the wedge. To cut the slots with a normal blade, we will have to make multiple cuts. Set the fence so it is 7/16 inch from the saw blade. To cut the slot in the top section, use a normal blade set to a 3/8 inch cutting depth with a zero-clearance table saw throat plate. Run the 12 inch x 4 inch board through the blade with the board held on edge so the slot is cut into the 3/4 inch edge. **(14)** Then turn it end-for-end and run it through again. This will result in two 1/8 inch kerfs with an 1/8 inch vane of wood between them. A corresponding slot is cut in the central section piece to a depth of only 1/8 inch. If cut

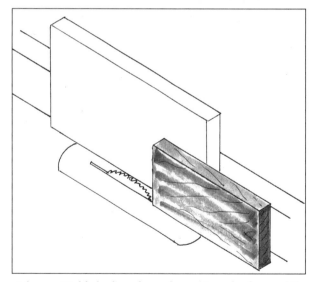

14.   Hold the board on edge against the fence while cutting the wedge slot into its edge.

at the same table saw fence setting, the two slots will automatically align. With a 1/4 inch chisel it is easy to remove the thin vane of wood between the two cuts, leaving a 3/8 inch wide slot. When the fence sections are held slot to slot, the resulting 1/2 inch high slot will accommodate the wedge.

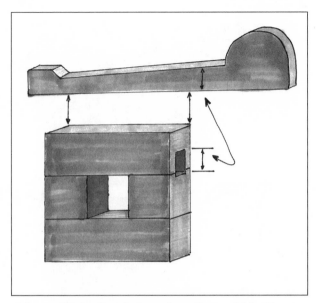

*15.   Cutting the slot ramps requires paring 45°
wedges off the outer ends of the upper slot.*

*16.   Wedge length depends on fence width. The
wedge ramp at the thick end should be no thicker than
the height of the slot.*

Once the slot detail has been cut, the 3/4 inch x 3/4
inch fence sections can be ripped off the larger
board(s). The top section can be ripped from the edge
with the detail installed then the bottom section, with
no slot details, can be ripped from the board next.

Finally the pieces can be cross-cut to length using a
sliding cutoff sled, or a miter gauge with an attached
length of wood to fully support the small pieces. Note
that the bottom fence section is longer than the top
section. This will be trimmed later.

Now with the miter gauge set at 90°, crosscut the central fence section into two roughly equal lengths,
which will be on either side of the beam when the
fence is complete. The bottom section needs no further machining.

Chisel a 45° ramp about 3/16 inch from both ends of
the upper fence section slot by firmly paring the bevel
while the top fence section end is supported against a
bench-hook fence (refer to page 117). **(15)**

The 45° bevel on the wedge and fence are important
because they reduce the shearing force when the small
end of the wedge prominence hits the fence during

loosening. Without these bevels, the small end would
soon be knocked off. Further care can be taken when
loosening the wedge by lightly tapping the small end
on a hard surface. **(17)**

Make the wedge

Saw a wedge blank to 6 inches x 3/8 inch x 1 inch or
more. Measure 1 inch in from one end and draw a
vertical line, marking the large (1) end. To mark the
small end, measure in 1/2 inch from the other end of
the blank and draw a second vertical line. From the
bottom edge of the wedge, mark a point 1/2 inch up
on the first of the lines and 1/4 inch up on the other.
Using a ruler, draw a line (4) between the two points
to define the ramp. From the narrow end of the ramp,
mark a 45° line (3) upward toward the end of the
wedge. **(16)**

Using a band saw or handsaw, cut down to the ramp
line on the line (1), defining the large end. Next saw
the line (2) 1/2 inch from the bottom of the blank,
starting the cut from the small end. Cut the 45° line (3)
down to the ramp on the small end and to within 1/4
inch of the bottom edge of the wedge.

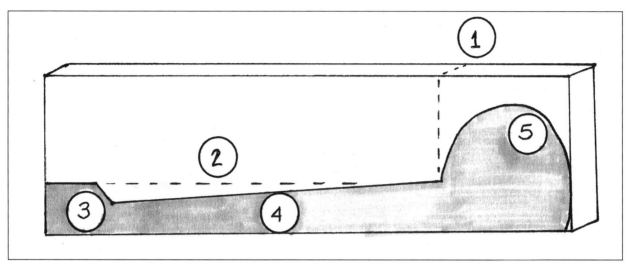

17.   Shape the wedge ramp (4) after removing excess wood with cuts 1 and 2, allowing the bandsaw blade to start the cut from the thick end.

Then starting from the large end of the ramp, cut along the ramp line (4). With a mill file or sanding block, smooth and straighten the ramp. Fine-tuning of the wedge will be done later. **(17)**

Finally, cut the large end to rough shape (5). The wedge's large end is an artistic opportunity so don't be restricted by the shape suggested here.

Test setup and glue-up

The first step in gluing-up is a dry run. Place all the fence sections on a piece of waxed paper with the wedge slots aligned. Lightly clamp the three sections and spread the central section apart enough to allow the beam to set in place. Snug the central sections around the beam. Check that the beam is captured squarely, approximately in the center of the fence. **(18)**

Now do the same with glue spread on all mating surfaces except those touching the beam. Wipe the glue on thinly, since any squeeze-out will interfere with the beam or wedge. Snug the central sections around the beam and clamp the fence. Extract the beam and use a 1/4 inch stick to remove any glue squeeze-out from the beam hole and wedge slot.

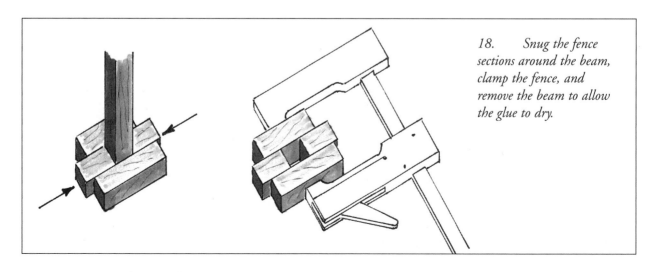

18.   Snug the fence sections around the beam, clamp the fence, and remove the beam to allow the glue to dry.

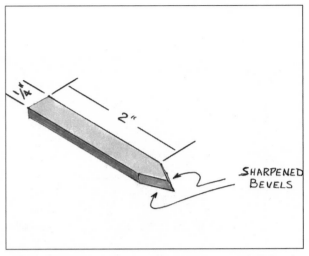

19.   The beam must be able to slide through the fence with the wedge installed. Turning the fence upside-down will make it easier to see if there is interference.

20.   The cutter has a point with two angled chisel edges to allow slicing in either direction.

Fit the wedge and beam

Once the glue is fully set, fit the wedge and beam in their slots and ensure that they move smoothly.

If the wedge does not fit into its slot, check for glue squeeze-out. Clean it out with a 1/4 inch chisel. Ensure that the wedge small end is no taller than the slot, and trim as needed. If the beam does not fit in the fence opening, check for squeeze-out and with fine sandpaper backed by a wooden block, chamfer the corner edges of the beam.

Now turn the marking gauge so the wedge slot is below the beam hole and insert the wedge. Slide the beam through the hole. **(19)**

If the wedge obstructs the hole when you try to insert the beam, the wedge may be too thick. Trim wood off the bottom of the wedge until the beam slides through with the wedge in place. Check the fit frequently when trimming, so the wedge tightly captures the beam when pushed from the big end. If you go too far and it has become too narrow to capture the beam, glue a strip of veneer to the wedge bottom and try fitting again.

The chisel cutter

The cutter and its wedge will be installed in a 1/4 inch square hole through the beam about 3/4 inch to 1 inch away from the end. Cut the hole using a 1/4 inch hollow chisel mortiser or by drilling a 1/4 inch hole and paring the walls square with a 1/4 inch chisel. If working by hand, pare the hole from both openings because this will result in the cleanest squared opening.

Make a cutter from a junk circular saw blade by hacksawing a 1/4 inch x 2 inch section out of it. The rough-sawn cutter blank can then be smoothed, squared, and ground to a chisel point. **(20)**

Cutting up an old saw blade sounds ominous but a new hacksaw blade will make quick work of the task. You can use a circular saw blade of any thickness. Refer to page 84 for hacksaw technique suggestions. **(21)**

Clamp the saw blade flat on a bench with a portion hanging off the edge. Start cutting in a tooth gullet for about 2-1/2 inches. Make another cut of equal length from the next tooth gullet. Now cut at right angles to

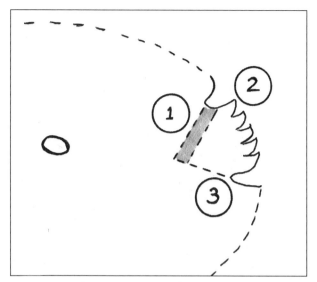

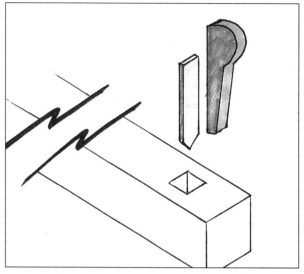

21.   *Hacksawing sequence for removing the cutter blank from a circular saw blade.*

22.   *The beveled face of the cutter faces the fence and the wedge is installed on the side away from the fence.*

those to sever the cutter from the blade and square its end. This won't take more than 10 minutes with a good hacksaw blade.

With a file, clean up the edges of the cutter blank so that it will fit in the square hole in the beam. Once it fits, start filing a chisel end on the blank. The chisel should have two beveled surfaces intersecting at the point. Use a sharpening stone to bring the tip to a sharp point by first flattening the back of the cutter, then honing the two bevels. **(23)**

The cutter is installed with its flat back facing the end of the beam. A wedge is shaped to snug the cutter in place while itself not extending below the beam. Look at the drawing **(22)** to estimate the wedge shape you are trying to create. Once again, this is an artistic opportunity.

23.   *Shaping the cutter point is easily done with a flat or triangular file, eliminating the risk of overheating the small piece of metal.*

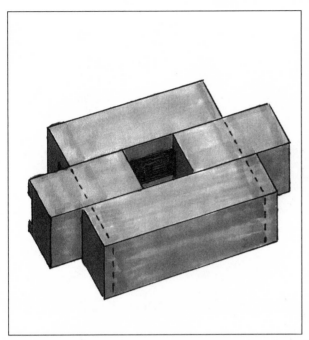

24.   Squaring fence can be done with a miter box, or on the table saw or bandsaw using a miter gauge.

Finishing steps

The marking gauge is now functionally complete but it probably looks rather rough. With a miter box, chop saw, or table saw and miter gauge, square the two sides of the fence with the top fence section. Do not cut off the angled slot ramp at each end of the wedge slot. Sand the faces of the fence smooth. Sand the beam and lightly round over its edges. **(24)**

Finishing is a personal preference. Whatever finish you choose, ensure that the finish does not get into the beam hole or wedge slot because this may interfere with the smooth movement of the assembly.

A low-risk finishing suggestion is to rub on a light coat of linseed oil. Let it dry for a few days, apply paste wax, and buff it out.

25. A knurled screw locks each beam to the gauge fence.

CHAPTER 2
Dual-beam Marking Gauge

I wrote earlier that you can never have enough marking gauges. Maybe that was an exaggeration. Too many gauges lying around on the bench will sooner or later become an accounting problem. The dual-beam marking gauge consolidates two marking gauges into one tool.

In comparison to the cutting gauge's wedge-style fence, this fence uses thinner wood laminations, has no wedge slot, and incorporates screw pads and screw holes to secure each beam independently. For this fence, we tap threads directly into the wood and depend on the strength of the wood to hold the screw. If you are uncomfortable with this approach, using a threaded metal insert is an option.

Cut the fence pieces

Start out with a couple of 12 inch long x 3/4 inch boards that are wide enough to rip strips off of safely. Use differing species for cosmetic appeal, such as one light-colored and one dark colored wood. You can even laminate some wood layers together to form a fence section, as was done in the center section of the gauge depicted above.

Rip a 3/8 inch stick and a 1/2 inch stick from each board. Refer to page 15 for suggestions on ripping techniques for small pieces of wood.

Set your table saw miter gauge to exactly 90°. Cut two 4 inch lengths from each of the 3/8 inch sticks for the upper and lower fence body. Cut two 2 inch lengths

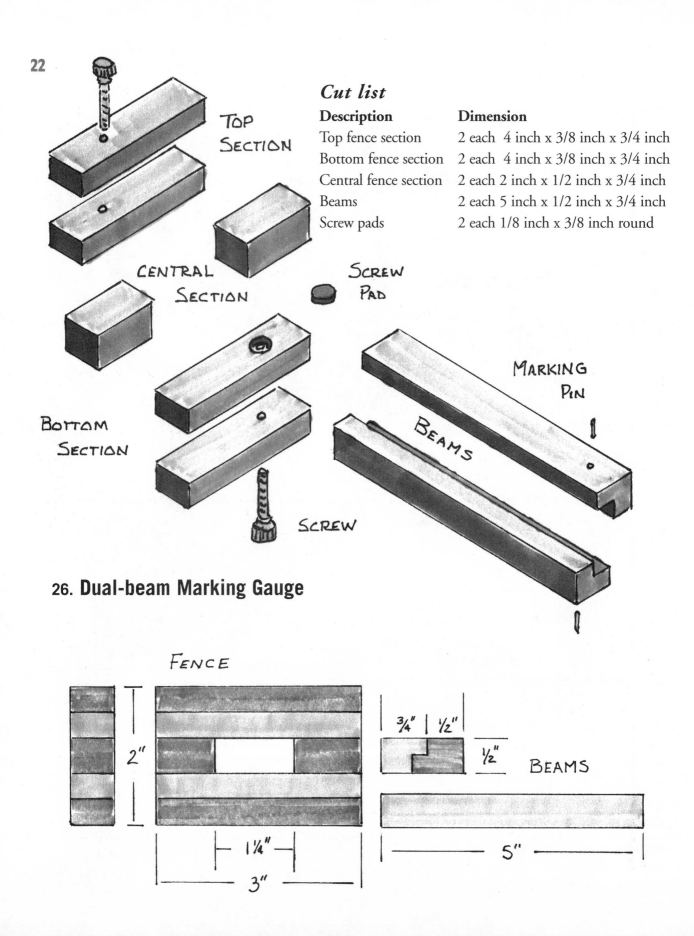

TOP SECTION

CENTRAL SECTION

BOTTOM SECTION

SCREW PAD

SCREW

BEAMS

MARKING PIN

Cut list

Description	Dimension
Top fence section	2 each 4 inch x 3/8 inch x 3/4 inch
Bottom fence section	2 each 4 inch x 3/8 inch x 3/4 inch
Central fence section	2 each 2 inch x 1/2 inch x 3/4 inch
Beams	2 each 5 inch x 1/2 inch x 3/4 inch
Screw pads	2 each 1/8 inch x 3/8 inch round

26. Dual-beam Marking Gauge

FENCE

2"

1¼"

3"

¾"   ½"

½"

BEAMS

5"

Building the dual-beam marking gauge

Procedure	Tools	Materials
Create mating surfaces	Router bits and table saw	3/8-inch and 1/2-inch thick boards of various wood species
Cut the fence pieces	Table saw	
Drill pad hole	3/8 inch brad point	
Drill screw hole	3/16-inch drill	
Tap hole	10 x 24 tap	
Glue up fence	Glue and clamps	
Install cutting points	1/16 inch drill	Finish nail
Make screw pad	Hacksaw and metal shears	Scrap metal
Square fence	Table saw	
Finish	Rag or brush	Shellac or oil and wax

from one of the 1/2 inch sticks to become the center sections of the fence.

Make the beams

My dual-beam gauges are diminutive tools that are most frequently used for marking half-blind dovetails, therefore the beams are only 5 inches long. We will use 12 inch x 1/2 inch boards that are at least 4 inches wide to make the beams. This will allow us to machine the edge details safely, and only after that will we rip the beams from the larger board. Here is a chance to make two gauges at once out of those longer boards, allowing you to try different details as you perfect your techniques. Now we will fashion the interface of your choice between the beams.

The beams fit against one another with either mating tongue-and-groove, matched rabbets, or open dovetails, depending on your visual and mechanical preference. The rabbeted interface is the easiest with a table saw and the open dovetail is the easiest with a router. The tongue-and-groove is very stable but requires the greatest cutting accuracy.

Both beams must be the same thickness for the following descriptions to be valid. Read on to decide which interface you prefer.

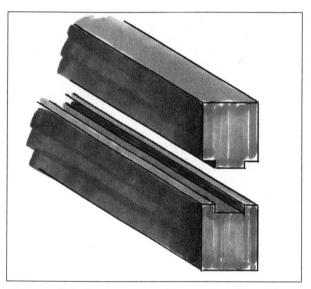

27.   *A shallow tongue-and-groove interface will keep the beams stable.*

Tongue-and-groove the beams

The tongue-and-groove joint for the beam interface is a two-setup operation. First, we set up to cut the groove in the center of one workpiece edge. Second, we cut the shoulders off the other workpiece edge to create the tongue. (**27**)

I would only attempt this cut using a table saw where

28.   Once the groove is cut, align the tongue cut by using the actual grooved beam as an alignment tool.

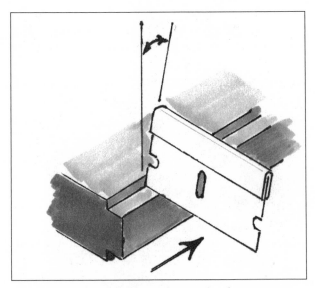

29.   Scraping tongue with a single edge razor is a way for final fit the beams.

the measurements can be taken direct from the workpieces being machined, as described below in **(28)**. Start by making the groove in the 1/2 inch side of one workpiece edge. Attempt to make it about two saw-kerfs wide. To do this, with the saw switched off, slide the workpiece edge up to the table saw blade, which is raised around 1/4 inch above the zero-clearance throat plate, and set the fence to cut the workpiece edge on or near its centerline.

Cut the shallow kerf along the length of the workpiece edge in one direction and then run it through again in

the other direction to center and widen the cut. Measure the width of the groove. If it is around 1/4 inch, you are done except for scraping the groove clean of any stray wood fibers. If it is not wide enough, move the fence away from the blade by about half the thickness of the short fall and repeat the cuts. A successful groove is between 3/16 inch and 5/16 inch wide.

Leave the saw blade at the previously set cutting depth. Our next objective is to make a tongue in the other workpiece edge to fit the groove. With the saw switched off, adjust the fence so the blade is aligned slightly outside the groove in the grooved workpiece edge. Set the grooved piece aside.

Feed the uncut board through the blade in both directions as before. It is now developing a tongue. Hold the tongue against the groove and estimate how much the tongue is oversized. Move the fence toward the blade by half the amount and feed the board past the blade as before. Approach the correct dimension incrementally. Overshooting this cut creates scrap wood.

When the tongue and groove are too close in size to trust the saw any longer, use a cabinet scraper or a single-edged razor blade to scrape the tongue shoulders until the two slide smoothly against each other. With the detail completed, rip a 3/4-inch beam from the edge of the workpiece. **(29)**

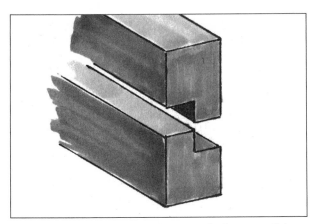

30. A rabbet interface between the beams will be easier to cut and almost as stable as the tongue and groove.

Rabbet-jointed beams

To cut the alternative rabbet-joint interface, find the centerline of the workpiece on its 1/2-inch side. Mark that point on the end of the wood. Now the challenge is to cut to that line. **(30)**

I generally approach fine fitting by cutting shy of my objective line on the first pass. The error in fitting will indicate of how much to move the fence to achieve a perfect cut. The rule of thumb is to move half the error width. As in the tongue-and-groove description above, using a single-edged razor to fine-tune the surfaces may be your best option when you are really close. Over-cutting the line is again irreversible. **(31)**

With the saw switched off, raise the blade 1/4 inch above the zero-clearance throat plate. Set the table saw fence so the blade is cutting to the outside of the workpiece, creating a rabbet. Make a single-pass cut on each of the two mating boards. Now shift the fence incrementally closer to the blade and make another cut. Check to see how the pieces mate. A perfect fit is when the two sides of the boards form a smooth, continuous surface. Toward the last few cuts, check the fit after each pass through the cutter.

Once the pieces have been fitted side to side, use the cabinet scraper or razor blade to smooth the tooth marks from the top edge of the rabbets.

31. The rabbet beam interface is cut by making multiple cuts with a regular blade and creeping up on the half-thickness dimension.

This same cut can be done using a router mounted in a router table, using the same technique as above. Take very small cuts and creep up on the line, since the router is prone to grab the wood aggressively. Use a 1/4 inch diameter straight router bit so the bite of the cutter is minimal. With the detail completed, rip a 3/4 inch beam from the edge of the workpieces.

Open dovetail beams

The final alternative beam interface is an open dovetail, which can be visualized as a half pin. This cut is practical only with a router mounted in a router table, and a sturdy fence to guide the wood. **(32)**

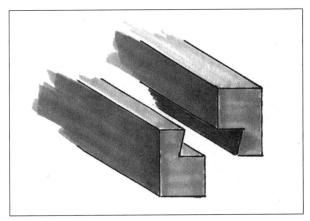

32. Open dovetail beams add a little pizzazz to the beam interface.

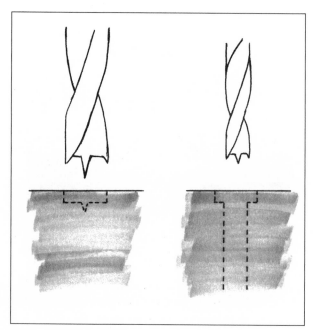

33.   When drilling the hole for screw pad and screw start with the larger bit so the smaller bit can be re-centered into the large bit brad point hole.

Mounting a small-diameter dovetail bit in the router and a small diameter insert in the router table opening, raise the bit to 1/4 inch above the surface of the table. Set the fence so that the bit barely makes a cut in the beams. Stand the board upright with its 1/2 inch edge resting on the router table.

Shallow multiple cuts are safer and create less chip-out than taking deep cuts. Make incremental shallow cuts until a smooth continuous surface is formed across the two workpieces. Toward the last few cuts, check the fit after each piece goes through the cutter. With the detail completed, rip the 3/4 inch beams from the edge of the workpieces.

Top and bottom fence sections

Glue the 3/8 inch sticks into two 3/4 inch x 3/4 inch x 4 inch long fence sections, alternating the woods for a dramatic effect.

Screw pads installed in the completed fence will keep the screw end from marring the beam surface. The

screw pad holes will be oriented toward the beam opening in the fence. Mark a line for the screw hole 2-3/8 inches from the end of both pieces. We will rotate one of the fence pieces end-for-end to position the screw holes diagonally opposed to each other after assembly.

Before drilling the screw holes in the fence pieces, we must drill the screw pad holes to a depth of 1/8 inch using a 3/8 inch brad point bit. Using the center left by the brad point, we next drill the 3/16 inch screw holes. To avoid splitting out as the drill exits the hole, either support the fence piece with some scrap, or stop drilling just shy of emerging on the rear side and flip the workpiece over to complete the hole. **33**

Create the screw pads

The screw pads can be made out of a thick piece of plastic or scrap metal, but my favorite material is 1/8-inch MDF or hardboard. Place your chosen material on a bench hook and cut a 3/8 inch x 3/8 inch square from one corner, using a 1/2 inch chisel or a fine-tooth saw.

Shape the small square into a rough circle using sandpaper or a file. Loosely fit it into the hole. If needed, redrill the screw-pad hole to a depth where the pad does not protrude above the surface of the wood. Remove the pads until final assembly.

Glue the fence together

With the beams mated, it is time to assemble the fence and fit the beams. On a piece of waxed paper, assemble the fence pieces so that the three layers of fence create a beam hole in the center. Alternate the wood color layers for visual appeal.

Orient the top and bottom fence pieces with their screw-pad holes diagonally across from each other in the beam opening. Place the mated beams in the opening and slide the two center sections inward to capture them. Without glue, clamp the top and bottom fence pieces so the assembly is stable. Extract the beams and make sure that the screw-pad holes are entirely within the beam opening. **(34)**

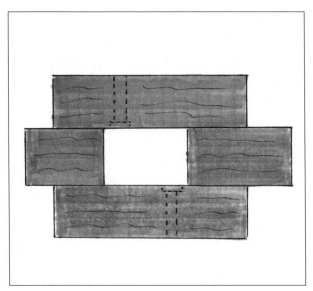

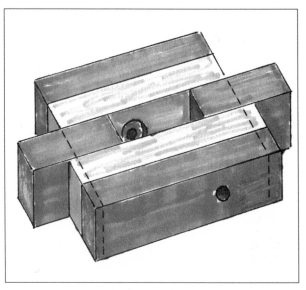

34.   Screw hole orientation is offset so each screw will secure one of the two beams. Note the top and bottom pieces are identical – just turned end for end.

35.   Squaring the fence is done after everything is glued and the beams are tested for proper fit.

Make orientation marks across the clamped fence pieces. If the beams are too tightly captured between the top and bottom fence sections, the beams will have to be trimmed so that they do slide through the hole easily.

Repeat the above procedure, except this time use glue on all the surfaces that do not face the beam opening. Align the orientation marks and insert the beams for just enough time to size the hole. Set the clamps, recheck that the beams fit and the face of the fence is flat, then remove the beams and let the assembly dry overnight.

The fence can be squared on the table saw using either a miter gauge with an extended fence attached, or a cross cut sled. Leave at least 3/4 inch of wood around the beam hole to ensure a solid fence structure. **(35)**

Another way to square the ends of the fence is to use a hand saw followed by a shooting board (see page 120) and hand plane.

Fit the screw

Once the fence has been glued up, tap the two screw holes using a hand-held 1/4 x 20 tap from the hardware store. When tapping wood, turn the tap inward for about four turns and then back it out two turns. Repeat that sequence until the tool emerges into the beam hole. Back the tool out slowly when done. If tapping more than 1 inch deep, back the tap out after it has gone about 3/4 inch into the screw hole. With

36.   Decorative screw choices.

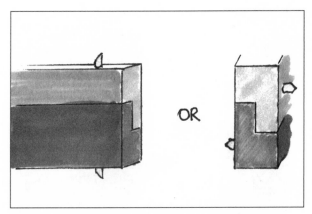

37.   Pin installation can be done on either set of opposing faces. Ensure that the chisel shaped cutter is at right angles to the beam with the bevel facing the fence.

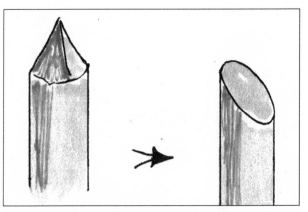

38.   Starting with a typical nail point use a file to shape it into a chisel-faced cutter.

the tap removed, you can clear out the wood fiber debris and then finish tapping the hole.

Any 1/4 x 20 screw will do but you may wish to dress the tool up with a brass thumbscrew or some other decorative screw (**36**, previous page). For a perfect fit, it is likely that the screw will have to be cut to length using a hacksaw. Insert the screw pad, insert the beam and thread the screw into the hole. Determine how much is to be trimmed off by measuring how much of the threads remain exposed. Remove the screw and

hold its tip in a metal vise, and cut to length. Buff the threads and screw end with a wire brush to remove any metal debris.

Install the marking pins

Decide on which surface of the beam you wish to install the marking pins (**37**). Find a nail and a drill bit that makes a hole that is just about the same diameter as the nail. Grind the nail point into a chisel point — one side straight, the other side beveled (**38**). Cut

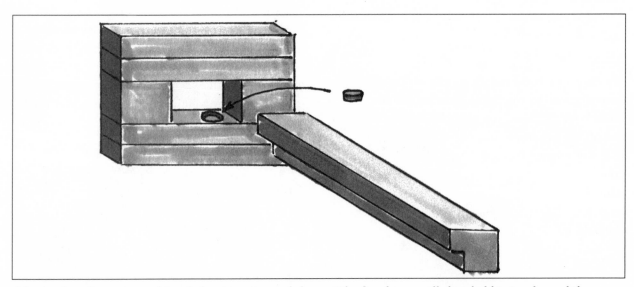

39.   Install a screw pad just before inserting each beam. The first beam will then hold it in place while installing the second beam and screw pad.

Threaded wood is strongest when the hole is drilled cross-grain.

A note on drilling and tapping wood

The orientation of the drill holes in wood will affect the strength of the threads. Drilling a hole across the grain produces a hole that will have stable threads when tapped. Drilling into the end of a piece of wood creates a hole that will have weak threads.

Cross-grain drilling cuts perpendicular to the fibers and leaves both end-grain and long-grain edges within the hole. Viewed as a cross section, the fibers jut into the hole and form strong threads.

A hole drilled into the end of a board, along the line of the grain, produces all long-grain edges which, when tapped, leave many short-grain fibers holding the threads in place.

the nail to about 3/8 inch in length using pliers with a wire-cutting notch, or using diagonal cutters. Drill a hole 1/4 inch deep about 1/2 inch to 3/4 inch from the end of the beams.

Place the nail in the hole such that the chisel point is perpendicular to the beam and the flat side of the chisel is facing toward the near end. On the nail, place a drop of fast-setting cyanoacrylate glue (super glue) that will migrate into the hole. Allow it to set for a couple of minutes. Alternatively, you can use yellow or white wood glue but you must place a small quantity of glue on the blunt end of the pin before placing it in the hole.

Final assembly

Finish the marking gauge prior to final assembly. If you choose a thick finish like polyurethane, avoid coating the beams and beam hole heavily or the beams may not move freely within the hole. I prefer oil finishes followed by a buffed coat of wax.

Assemble the gauge by first installing one screw pad in its hole and sliding in one beam to cover that pad. Turn the tool over, install the other screw pad, and install the other beam. Install the screws and lightly tighten. The wood threads will eventually fail if the screw is twisted too hard. You will find it takes very little pressure to secure the beams in position. **(39)**

CHAPTER 3
Mortising Gauge

40. The mortising gauge has two sharp points with adjustable spacing.

Making a mortise-and-tenon joint with hand tools is straightforward with the help of a mortising gauge. The idea of the gauge is to mark two parallel lines on both pieces of wood to be joined. When cutting to the inside of the two lines, you are making a mortise. Cutting to the outside of the two lines, you are making a tenon.

An alternate beam style to the single-beam cutting gauge fence, described in Chapter 1, is the mortising beam which consists of a beam routed with a T slot and a slider shaped to fit that slot. Since this is a variation on the cutting gauge, the following explanation will be directed largely at the differences in making the beam and the details of how the beam is held.

Choose the fence style

We have made both the wedge and the screw fence and either one will do as long as we pay attention to detail in how the mortising beam works. (**41**)

The beam is essentially a U-shaped piece of wood surrounding a sliding bar. If the sides of the open portion of the U are crimped when the wedge or screw is tightened, it will tighten around the slider and both the beam and slider will be secured in place.

When planning the fitting of the beam to either fence, mark the beam surface that is going to be slotted and observe that it will be properly crimped.

The mortise beam can be used with the wedge-style fence because the wedge is capable of exerting enough pressure to crimp the beam and slider. If you desire to

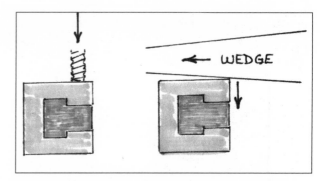

41.   The crimp mechanism for a mortising gauge beam slider depends on the wood flexing slightly at the open end of the slot and a snugly fitting slider.

Cut list

Description	Dimension
Beam	5-1/2 inch x 3/4 inch x 3/4 inch
Slider	7-1/2 inch x 1/2 inch x 3/8 inch
Top fence section	3 inch x 3/4 inch x 3/4 inch
Bottom fence section	3 inch x 3/4 inch x 3/4 inch
Central fence section	2 each 2 inch x 3/4 inch x 3/4 inch

42. Beam and slider for mortising gauge

Task	Tool
Slider slot	3/8 inch keyhole router bit
Slider slot	1/4 inch straight router bit

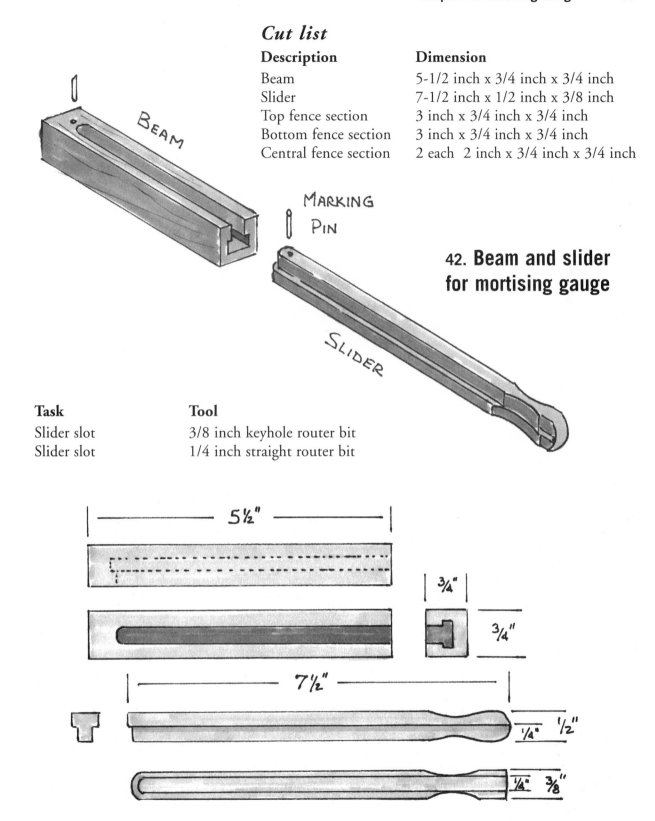

Building the mortising gauge

Procedure	Tool	Material
Rout beam	Router, 1/4 inch straight bit, 3/8 inch keyhole bit	Hardwood
Shape slider into a T	Table saw, router	
Cut beam off board	Table saw, band saw	
Cut slider off board	Table saw, band saw	
Fit slider to beam		Paste wax
Install cutter pins	Small drill bit	Cyanoacrylate glue, nail

use the screw type fence, it's better to forgo the tapped threads in wood and instead use a metal threaded insert. This will provide ample crimping strength without the risk of stripping the wooden threads. Be sure to allow for a screw pad to avoid marring the beam with the screw end.

Make the beam

Two tools are required to rout the T slot in the beam: a 1/4 inch straight or spiral up-cut router bit, and a 3/8 inch keyhole router bit. The keyhole bit has a 1/4 inch shank with a 3/8 inch wide cutter head. It is sometimes referred to as a T-slot cutter but pay attention to the size when looking for one. **(43)**

I use a dial caliper to check dimensions and set up my cuts. It is near impossible to use a ruler for objects as small as the slider and T slot.

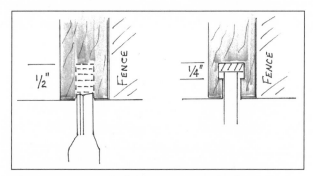

43.   *Routing the beam requires multiple passes. Feed the wood slowly and don't move the fence.*

The board edge will be routed 90% of its length with a 1/4 inch straight or spiral-cutting router bit, to a depth of 1/2 inch. This must be done in multiple depth passes on a router table, starting with the bit raised no higher than 1/8 inch above the table through a small diameter table insert. Raise the bit 1/8 inch on each pass until it reaches the 1/2 inch height.

The router bit is then changed to the keyhole bit, the bit is recentered on the existing groove before turning the router back on, then the wood is routed with the bit raised to 1/2 inch to match the height of the existing groove. Next, lower the keyhole bit until there is a 1/4 inch tee routed at the top of the slot.

Once the T-slot is completed, rip the milled edge off of the board making a 3/4 inch x 3/4 inch beam. Refer to page 15 for a safe method of ripping thin strips.

Less desirable alternatives

A less desirable alternative is to just cut the 1/4 inch straight slot and omit the T-slot. This results in a functional mortising beam but the slider is capable of flexing out of the slot if the fence-hole fit is at all loose.

Cut the slider

To make the slider, start with a 3/8 inch x 12 inch x 4 inch board held on edge against the fence. Trim off 1/16 inch on each side to a height of 1/4 inch.

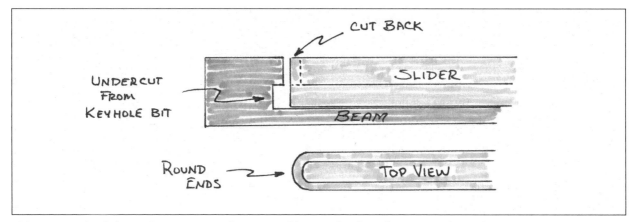

44.   *Fit the slider so the pins are as close as possible to each other allowing marking of narrow mortises.*

If done on the table saw, you will need to attach a sacrificial fence to your normal fence since only part of the blade will be exposed. Position the fence so that 1/16 inch is exposed past the sacrificial fence and raise the blade to 1/4 inch. (**45**)

If using a router bit and router table, set the bit at a height of 1/4 inch and set the fence to allow the bit to cut 1/16 inch of the side of the slider.

Once the slider has the recesses milled into each side, it must be ripped off the board as above. Care must be taken to leave 1/4 inch beyond the milled recesses creating the 1/4 inch thick top of the tee. Be aware of the saw blade thickness and which edge of the blade will be cutting the valuable part of the rip operation. The slider should be very close to 1/2 inch high.

45.   *The slider can be cut on a tables aw by using a sacrificial fence to hide part of the blade thickness.*

Round over and shape edges, and paste-wax the entire slider. Attempt to slip the slider into the T slot. If it is tight, determine where the binding is occurring and sand or scrape the slider to remove the binding while leaving a friction fit.

A way of determining the binding points is to retract the slider from the slot and look for shiny spots on its sides and top. These spots are created by the wax being buffed by the over-tight interface. Trim at the shiny spots as needed. Re-applying paste wax to the slider will immediately improve the sliding motion, so don't trim too aggressively.

If the slider is loose, it will not hold a setting. There may be no recourse but to get another slider blank and make the slider again.

Once the slider operates smoothly, if it protrudes out of the bottom of the beam use a block plane or scraper to trim the slider flush with the beam's bottom surface. Remove the slider when trimming so you do not remove any wood from the beam,which has already been fitted to the fence opening.

When the router bits cut the slot, they left rounded ends. Before we are done with fitting the slider, we must round the leading end on both the large and small width of the slider. The small-diameter section must be cut back 1/16 inch before rounding. This can all be done with a chisel and sandpaper. (**44**)

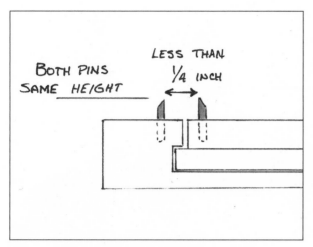

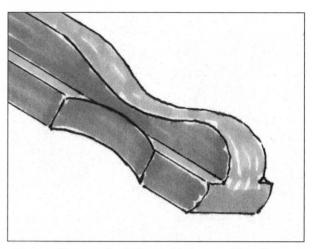

46.   *Equal pin height installation facilitates even marking, otherwise the gauge will have to be tilted to mark both lines simultaneously.*

47.   *Shaping the slider end helps provide a finger hold. Let your creativity run wild if the mood strikes.*

Install the pins

Next install the marking pins. One marking pin will be installed 1/8 inch away from the end of the slider slot on the main beam while the other marking pin is installed on the slider about an 1/8 inch or less away from its end. The goal is to have the points slightly less than 1/4 inch away from each other at their closest adjustment. This will allow the gauge to mark 1/4 inch mortises. (**46**)

Locate a small-diameter drill bit and finish nails that are very close to the same diameter. Refer to page 28 for details on pin shaping. Drill holes 1/4 inch deep in the locations directed above.

Orient the chisel points back to back so that they are as close to each other as possible. Take care to get the points of the pins level with each other. Place a single

drop of cyanoacrylate glue (super glue) on the shank of the point and allow it to run down into the hole, or place a drop of wood glue on the blunt pin end before sliding it into the hole. Wait for the glue to fully set.

Contour the free end of the slider to a pleasing shape that will assist your fingers in pulling and pushing it into position. The finish on the slider should be paste wax only. The beam may be finished with oil and paste wax. (**47**)

CHAPTER 4

Marking Knife

48.   *The marking knife is an asset in the joiner's tool kit.*

Layout tools such as squares and dovetail gauges could be used with a pencil or a marking knife. Since these tools are made of wood, using a marking knife is a somewhat risky proposition. However, a marking knife is among the traditional marking tools and cannot be ignored as an asset in a joiner's tool kit. We will see in the section on cutting dovetails that an alternate purpose of the marking knife is that it can be used as a skew chisel.

When marking with a knife, you are not only laying down a reference for future cuts, but you are also making your first cut into the workpiece. When cutting across the grain as in a shoulder marking operation, the knife line becomes a stop cut, and it also remains as the visible cut line for the completed joint.

Marking in line with the grain can be difficult in some woods because the knife may start to follow the grain lines instead of the intended line. This is when

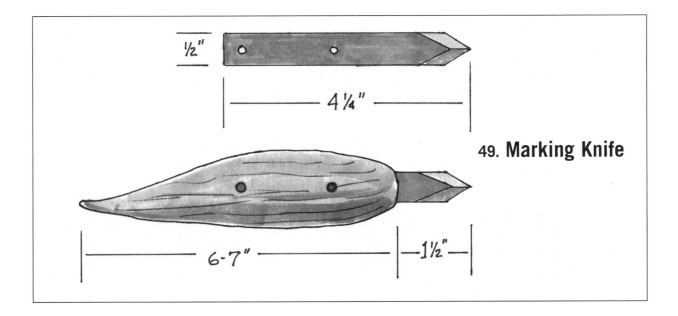

½"

4 ¼"

49. Marking Knife

6-7"

1½"

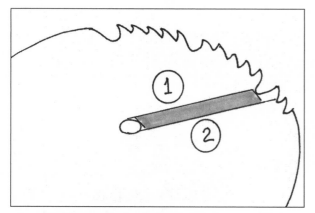

50.   *Cutting the knife blank out of a scrap blade can be a bit more efficient if the cuts are made into the arbor hole.*

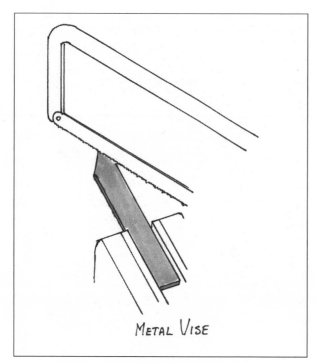

51.   *Shape the knife blank to a point with a hacksaw to save time. Filing to a point is an option but a tedious one.*

the best technique is to observe in which direction the grain is tending and position your square such that if the knife falls into a grain pattern, it will be pushed up against the blade of the square. This will restrict the knife's tendency to wander.

If you made the single beam cutting gauge, you have essentially made a small version of the marking knife without a handle.

Making the blade

We will start with the blade and then size the handle to fit it. Using a hacksaw and scrap circular saw blade, cut a 4-1/4 inch x 1/2 inch rectangular knife blank. The 4-1/4 inch value is the typical distance from the center hole to the bottom of the tooth gullets on a 10 inch circular saw blade. Refer to page 84 for hacksaw technique. **(50)**

With a file, smooth and straighten the long sides of the knife blank while it is held horizontally in a metalworking vise. Next, clamp the knife blank by its edges in the vise with one end extending 2 inches beyond the vise jaws. Saw the knife blank to a V-shaped point. Using a file, grinder, or stationary disk sander, bevel the point so both bevels are on one face of the blank. Refer to page 85 for grinding instructions. **(51)**

Hone the bevels to a sharp edge using the techniques described on page 86. At this point you can decide to use the knife as is, or install the blade in a wooden handle. The bare marking knife is nice since it will get into smaller, deeper places than the handled version, but it is a little less comfortable.

Making a handle

With the blade fully shaped and sharpened, we can size a handle to fit. The easiest approach is to laminate a handle using three layers. The middle layer will be sized to a thickness equal to the knife blade, while the outer layers will make up the bulk of the handle thickness.

To make the middle layer, rip a strip, the same thickness as the knife blade, off the outer edge of a 1-1/2 inch thick board that is 7 inches or longer. We can cut the strip to length later. Refer to page 15 for a safe way of cutting thin strips.

With the saw turned off and unplugged, align the 1

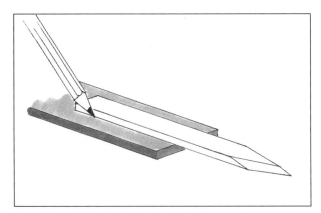

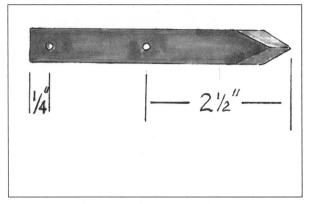

52.   *Cut the knife outline into the middle layer after tracing the blade outline onto the wood blank.*

53.   *Drill locations for the two holes using a carbide tipped or solid carbide drill bit. Masonry drills are low cost and do the job.*

1/2 inch thick board with the edge of the table saw blade furthest from the fence. Lay the knife blade up against the outer edge of the saw blade and re-align the fence so the outer edge of the board is even with the outer edge of the knife blade. Make a test cut and compare the strip to the thickness of the blade.

Place the knife blank centered on top of the middle layer with 1-1/2 inches of the pointed end of the blank overhanging the end. Trace the outline of the knife onto the middle layer. **(52)**

Now clamp the middle layer on a sacrificial board and saw on the inside (waste side) of the marks through both the middle layer and sacrificial board using a hand saw. With a chisel, sever the waste.

Cut two 3/8 inch thick pieces of wood to the same size as the middle layer. These can be of the same or contrasting wood.

Glue and clamp the middle layer to one of the pieces, using waxed paper to ensure the clamps do not stick to the wood. When the glue is set and dry, lay the knife into the slot and adjust as needed.

Next we will drill 1/8 inch holes through the knife blank using a masonry bit or a solid carbide bit. When drilling in metal, never hold the metal with your hands. Clamp the blade to the table or in a machinist's vise while drilling. With a hardened center

punch, mark one or two hole locations within the handle area. One of the holes should be 1/4 inch from the blunt end of the knife. If you wish to drill a second hole, it should be 2-1/2 inches from the point of the blade. **(53)**

Using the holes as a template, drill two holes through the partially built handle, being careful to minimize tearout with a backing board.

Now dry-assemble the knife handle and blade, turn it with the holes on top, and drill through the handle once again. Remove the blade and reassemble the handle with a copper nail placed in each hole to maintain orientation.

With a coping saw, band saw, rasps, or other shaping tools, shape the handle to an attractive, comfortable fit for your hand. Smooth and sand the edges.

Disassemble the handle, install the knife blade, and glue the handle together using the copper nails as locators. Once the glue has set, remove the copper nails, cut the heads off and cut them to a slightly greater length than the thickness of the handle. On an anvil or piece of hard metal, peen the copper nails into the handle holes. The copper will mushroom out and form a permanent retainer for the blade.

Using sandpaper, smooth the handle and sand the copper nails flush. Apply a finish and let it dry.

54. The dovetail gauge can include a right angle along with a slope.

CHAPTER 5

Dovetail Gauge

When making dovetails, a line must be drawn to indicate the bevel angle of the pins and tails. This is commonly done with a sliding bevel gauge. Though it is an adequate tool, it's large and cumbersome so I've made simple dovetail marking gauges that are scaled to the size of my work.

The simplicity of the dovetail marking gauges allows you to make several gauges of various designs and angles and determine which you like the best. They are great for speeding up the marking of the tails or pins when used in conjunction with a small wooden square.

Make the gauge body

Set the table saw miter gauge to an angle between 7° and 14° and cut off one end of a 12 inch x 1-1/2 inch x 1/4 inch board. Flip the board over and cut another 1-1/2 inches off the end to create the body of the dovetail gauge. **(55)**

From a 1/4-inch thick board, rip a long piece 1/4 inch x 1/4 inch to become the fences. Cross-cut it to the approximate length of the top and bottom of the gauge body. Using a bench hook or tabletop and a piece of waxed paper, glue the two pieces of wood to

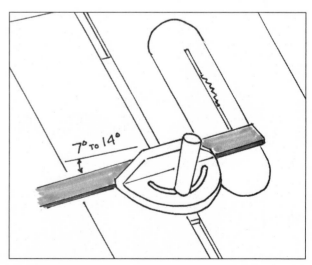

55.   Cut the angles with the miter gauge set to your chosen angle then flip the board over and cut it again at the same angle. The cutoff is part of the gauge.

56.   Glue the edge references by using some waxed paper and table as your alignment surface.

opposite sides and ends of the gauge body, using the flat surface to ensure they are parallel to the edges. **(56)**

After the glue has set, trim, sand, and finish the assembly. Hmm, not much to this one! I kind of like that. Make a few and hand them out to your friends as gifts during their next visit to your shop. Keep at least one for yourself, because we will need it to lay out the dovetails in Chapter 25.

Alternate Designs

The above gauge is my favorite but it has one drawback. It marks only the angled cuts of a dovetail. The alternate gauges below have both beveled edges and 90° edges.

One alternate gauge marks both the angled and right-angle markings, but you need to flip it over frequently. The second alternate design is a gauge that has two angled edges and two right-angle edges. Experiment and discover your own improvements or other alternatives. **(57)**

To make the alternative gauges, square-cut a 12 inch x 1-1/2 inch x 1/4 inch board and then saw the ends at an angle as instructed above. You now have a short piece of wood with one angled and one squared end. Square-cut again, and you have the parts for the second alternate design.

Glue pieces of 1/4 inch x 1/4 inch stock so that one is on each side of the top edge of the gauge. Make a few gauges at different angles between 7° and 14°.

57.   Alternate gauge designs, which include edges at 90° as well as at the dovetail angle.

CHAPTER 6

Joinery Check Gauge

Many woodworkers use a combination square for checking the squareness of the walls of their joints. This works well as long as you can get the blade into the hole at an angle you can observe. I've found that is not always possible so I developed the joinery check gauge.

This is a deceptively simple tool that can improve the fitting of joints that require squared sides. The essence of the tool is a vertical 3/16 inch rod that fits in the small recesses of a joint to check if the walls were cut squarely. When checking a tenon, the tool can identify if the tenon cheeks have been trimmed flat and square to the board face.

All you have to do is drill a squared up hole.

On a 3 inch x 1-1/2 inch x 3/4 inch block of wood, locate a hole about 1/2 inch from one end of the block centered on its edge.

Drilling a 3/16-inch hole that is truly perpendicular to the reference surface of the gauge is the greatest challenge to making this tool. Using a drill press, square the table to the drill, checking all the way around the drill to ensure squareness in all directions.

If your drill press table is not square, there is a convenient tilt adjustment from side to side on all tables but there is no tilt adjustment forward to back. If the drill press table sags toward the front, try propping up the front edge of the drill press table. Don't apply so much force that the machine destabilizes. **(59)**

Building a joinery check gauge		
Procedure	**Tool**	**Material**
Cut body blank	Table saw, band saw	Hardwood
Drill hole	3/16-inch drill	
Cut notch	Table saw, band saw	
Square bottom	Sandpaper	

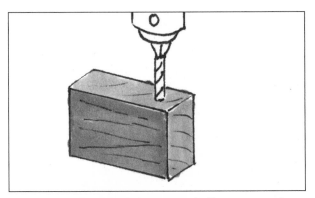

59.   *Drilling the hole using a drill press starts the tool off with an accurate perpendicular hole.*

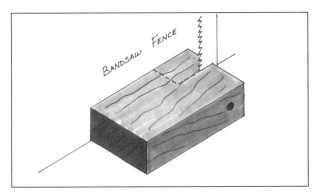

60.   *Cut the corner off after the hole is drilled. This is necessary so you can see all the way around the sliding rod.*

Another method of squaring the drill press table is to place a 12 inch x 12 inch flat board on top of the table and shim until the board surface is square to the drill. I used folded printer paper and got excellent results. Drilling by hand is also fine but the reduced vertical accuracy will require more squaring effort.

Cut off a 3/4 inch x 3/4 inch corner of the block where the hole was drilled. This allows you to see the rod inside a mortise or dovetail joint. **(60)**

Check and tune the tool

To check the squareness of the gauge, use a 2 inch thick test board that has squared edges and flat surfaces. Check the edges of the test board with a combination square or wooden square (see page 46) to verify squareness. **(61)**

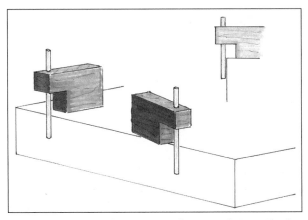

61.   *Checking for square is the critical step. Check the tool to the edge of a reliably squared board at a wide variety of angles.*

Slide a 4-inch long, 3/16 inch diameter metal rod into the drilled hole and check that the rod is firmly held and at right angles to the bottom surface. With the notched corner down, extend the rod down the side of the board while the bottom of the gauge sits flat on the surface. Notice if the rod is parallel to the board edge when the gauge is oriented at several angles.

If the rod is too tight in the hole, ream it with the drill. Be sure not to wobble, however, since an oval hole will introduce errors in alignment. Apply wax to the rod and slide it back and forth through the hole using a board as a push point. If it really won't succumb to these efforts, sand the rod lightly with 220-grit paper and wax it again.

If the rod is not square, correct minor errors by using a piece of 150-grit sandpaper adhered to a piece of 3/4 inch MDF. Lay the sandpaper block on a known flat surface and carefully hone the bottom of the block to squareness. Ensure that you maintain a totally flat bottom surface by holding the block at both ends and not rocking the gauge while sanding.

To use the tool, slide the rod into the joint so that the rod is visible through the cut off corner of the gauge. Notice if there is a gap between the rod and the walls of the joint. A gap at the top or bottom of the joint wall indicates that additional squaring of the joint walls is required. Correct the joint and check again.

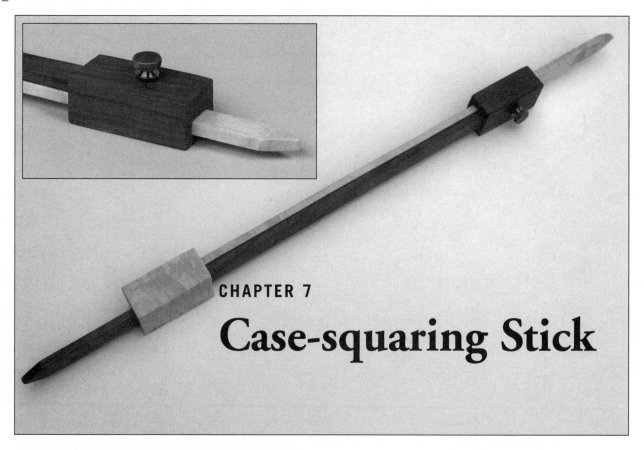

CHAPTER 7

Case-squaring Stick

An important detail when building case pieces is squaring the case prior to final glue-up. Checking the diagonal distances of the case is the only reliable means of testing for squareness. The case-squaring stick, sometimes called a bar gauge or story stick, does not have graduations to do measuring but instead is a comparative measurement device.

The four sides of a rectangular case or box do not make a rigid structure since it can be turned into a parallelogram by pushing on any corner. Unlike the rectangle, a triangle is rigid, meaning you cannot change the angles of the joints without changing the length of at least one of the three sides.

A diagonal line between opposite corners of a rectangle, in effect creates two triangles. The line is the same length no matter which diagonal pair of corners it was drawn to. Knowing this, we can square a case by making the diagonals the same length. **(63)**

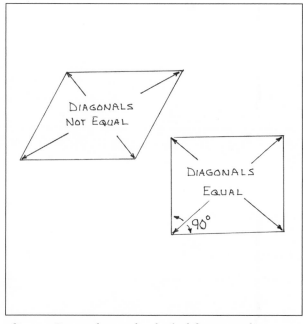

63.   *Rectangles can be checked for square by comparing their diagonals.*

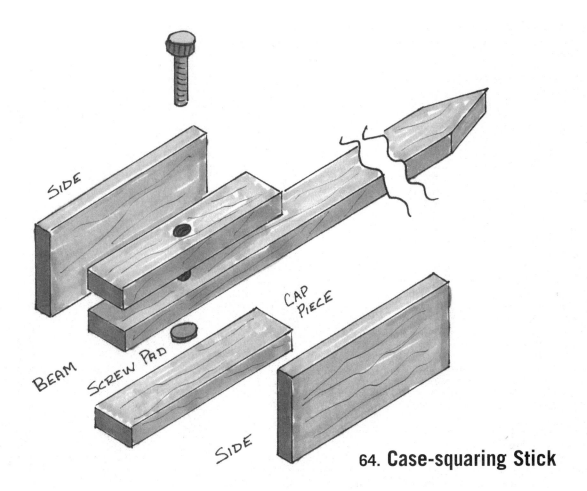

64. Case-squaring Stick

Stick length (case diagonal)	Beam length	Holder length
12 inches to 18 inches	11 inches	2 inches
16 inches to 26 inches	15 inches	2 inches
18 inches to 30 inches	17 inches	2 inches
24 inches to 42 inches	23 inches	2 inches
30 inches to 54 inches	29 inches	3 inches

Building the case-squaring stick

Procedure	Tools	Material
Cut beams and holder pieces	Table saw, band saw	Hardwood
Shape beam points	Chisel, knife, or spokeshave	
Drill screw pad and screw holes	3/8 inch brad-point bit	3/16 inch drill bit
Tap screw hole	1/4 x 20 hand tap	
Make screw pad	Hand saw	1/8 inch metal, plastic, hardboard, MDF
Make beam holders	Clamps	Glue
Install screw		1/4-20 thumbscrew

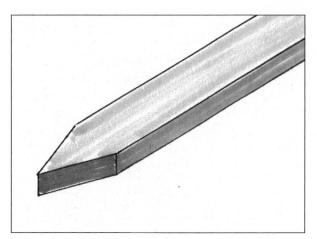

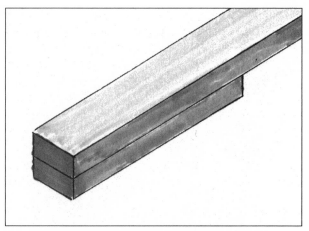

65.   Shaping the beam ends to a point will allow them to get right to the corner of a case piece.

66.   Beam with glued-on piece of the eventual beam housing. The extra layer ensures the screw has good purchase while leaving space for the screw pad.

The case-squaring tool consists of two beams with beam holders that slide through each other, in order to extend or reduce the total length of the tool.

Rough-cut the stock

Building the tool starts with selecting the beam sizes. Select a size that suits the type and size of projects you tend to make.

I have one case-squaring stick that extends from 16 inches to 26 inches, and another overlapping from 24 inches to 42 inches. Smaller tools are as easy to make but I find that a steel ruler works just as well for small boxes. The instructions that follow apply to the 16-inch to 26-inch version. (table, previous page)

Starting with a straight-grained 1/2 inch x 15 inch hardwood board that is at least 4 inches wide, rip three 1/4 inch sticks from it. Refer to page 15 for guidance on ripping thin stock. Two sticks will serve as the beams. Cut four 2 inch lengths from the extra stick to serve as the cap and additional thickness piece of the beam-holders. When the pieces are cut from a single board, their widths will be identical.

From a 1-1/4 inch thick board of at least 10 inches length, rip a 1/4 inch strip off the outer edge. Cut that strip into four pieces 2 inches x 1-1/4 inches x 1/4 inch to serve as the side walls of the beam holders.

Shape the beam ends

The beam ends can now be shaped to a 30° point with a chisel, plane, sandpaper, spokeshave, or any other slicing tool. Smooth the beam points and round them over so they are not fragile. **(65)**

Make the beam holders

At the blunt end of each beam, glue on one of the 2 inch x 1/2 inch pieces to increase the beam thickness to 1/2 inch. Allow the glue to dry. Sand or hand-plane the sides of the beams, beyond the holder only, to take off less than 1/64 inch in width. Reducing the width of the beam very slightly ensures it will slide easily through the opposite holder. **(66)**

Next, we need to drill a screw-pad hole and screw hole centered on the blunt end of one beam to accept a pad that will keep the screw end from marring the beams. Drill a hole 1/8 inch deep using a 3/8-inch diameter brad-point bit. Centered on that hole, drill a 3/16 inch hole through the beam. Tap the screw hole with a 1/4 x 20 tap. **(67)**

Make the screw pad

A piece of 1/8 inch hardboard or MDF is shaped into a rough round that fits loosely into the pad hole. Start by cutting a 3/8 inch square off one corner of a sheet

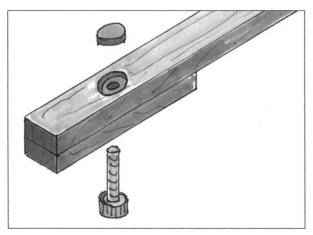

67.   Screw pad and screw hole. Drill the larger hole first – then center the smaller bit in it.

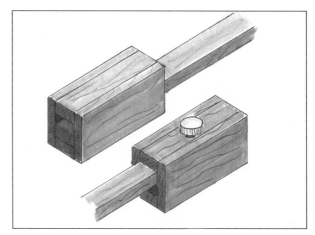

68.   Glued beam holder before insertion of the opposing beam.

of 1/8 inch hardboard, and then round it with sandpaper or a file. The pad hole may need to be deepened to ensure that the pad does not extend above the wood surface. Remove the pad until final assembly.

Glue the beam holders

Glue-up of the beam holders requires fitting them with the opposing beam. Waxing the shaped ends of the beams will reduce the risk of gluing everything into one useless mass. Work all the way around the beams with paste wax for at least the end four inches. You can wax the whole beam but you must leave the last several inches of the blunt end unwaxed since that is where the glued-up beam holder resides. You may wish to dry-fit everything so you get the orientation correct before committing your wood to glue.

Place one beam down on a piece of waxed paper with the glued-on piece down. Apply a fine line of glue to the two sides of the thickened section. Slide the 2 inch x 1-1/4 inch side pieces in place and lightly clamp. Now slide the waxed shaped end of the other beam into the cavity. It should slide back and forth with little resistance. Apply a fine line of glue on both edges of a 2 inch x 1/2 inch piece. Without totally releasing the clamps, wedge open the beam holder assembly and slide the cap piece of the beam holder assembly in place. Tighten the clamp a bit more and check that the

beams slide relative to each other. Remove the other beam from the holder and allow the glue to dry overnight. **(68)**. Perform the same operation on the remaining beam when all the glue has dried.

If the ends of the holders are uneven, you can cut them square with a table saw by setting them against the miter-gauge fence. Insert a 1/4 inch piece of wood behind the unsupported beam to stabilize the holder while it is being sawn. Sand or plane the outer surfaces until all of the wood interfaces are flush.

Assembly

If wax was applied as suggested, the only finish that will adhere to the wood will be thin shellac. A better idea is to just wax up the rest of the beams and consider that the final finishing.

Buy or cut down a 1/4 x 20 screw to a thread length of 1/2 inch. If the screw is too long, clamp the end of the screw in a vise and hacksaw it to length. With a wire brush, de-burr the cut end and threads, and reinsert the finished screw into the holder.

Install the pad in its hole and carefully slide the beams into their beam holders. Clear away any glue squeezeout. With the pad held in place by the beams, install the screw that will secure the beams while in use.

CHAPTER 8

Wooden Square

69. The blade of the wooden square can fit flush with the base, or it can protrude (left and second from right).

In woodworking, knowing when something is at right angles to something else is paramount in the pursuit of accuracy. Squaring the end of a board, joining two boards at right angles, cutting a mortise to accept a tenon… the list is endless. So you go out to the store and pick up a square for a few bucks and say, "I've got it and I'm all set." Not so fast. Many squares sold in retail stores are accurate to within a degree or two and are often too flimsy to make repeatable settings. That won't do in fine joinery.

The CD square

In my search for the common man's square, I've asked, "What in my everyday life is reliably square?" Since I have a known accurate combination square, I went about checking everything in my house. Besides making my wife very concerned about my mental stability, I found only one item that was always square. The music CD jewel case – slimline CD cases won't do.

The music industry CD case has smoothly molded

edges with no protruding features to interfere with making measurements. Looking carefully at a case, you notice that the edges around both wide surfaces are smooth and nicely rounded while the edge between frequently has a recessed rippling detail. The slim-line cases are not as usable due to molded features being closer to the edges of the case.

Use the protruding edges to check the squareness of your project but avoid using the hinged corners. When checking an outside corner, make sure they are both on a smooth flat surface when doing so. This may actually be hard to find in some houses. Age and house movement notoriously warps kitchen counter tops. Use your table saw top or jointer table if you have them.

Armed with our new international squareness standard, we can use it to evaluate the purchase of a square or to make a few from wood. You may be wondering, "Why are we making a square when we just got hold of the ultimate in squares?"

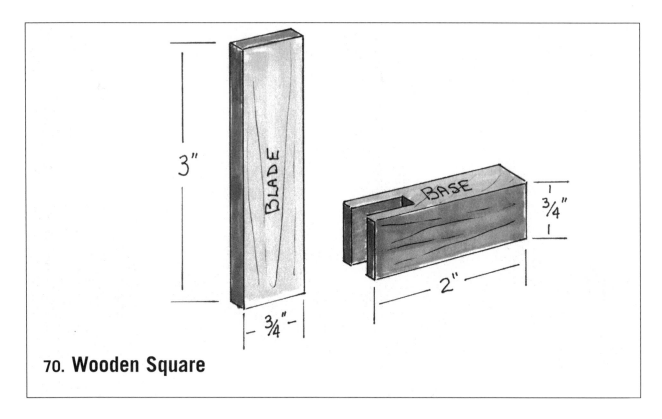

70. Wooden Square

Features of a wooden square

The squares we build are going to have body features that make their usefulness in joinery well worth the effort. CD cases don't make the grade when it comes to everyday practical use.

Our wooden square is small and light. It has a thick arm to hook over the edge of a board when marking joinery. The L shaped body provides inside and outside reference corners. If the tool is made from straight grained wood, it will remain stable and accurate.

We will make a small square designed specifically for joinery but squares as big as 6 inches are just as easy to build using these instructions.

Making the tool is the ultimate in simplicity as long as we maintain accuracy. The short, thick leg of the square, called the base, has a kerf cut made in it that accepts the long, thin leg of the square, called the blade.

A safety note: We are venturing into the realm of working with very small pieces of wood. This requires an extra margin of safety when using powered machinery. Use jigs or devices to keep your fingers away from moving blades.

The square base

The base piece of wood must start out longer than the intended length in the completed square since we don't want our hands near the saw blade. The tool described has a 2 inch long base and 3 inch blade. To make the base, we will start with an 8 inch long stick approximately 3/4 inch x 3/8 inch.

To make this stock, start with a 3/4 inch thick board that is at least 3 or 4 inches wide and rip a 3/8 inch strip off the outer edge. Refer to page 15 for suggestions on ripping techniques for small pieces of wood.

The slot in the base must be cut using a tenoning jig for the table saw. It is impractical to cut this slot with any other tool. The table saw must be fitted with a zero clearance insert to keep the material being cut from being pulled down into the machine.

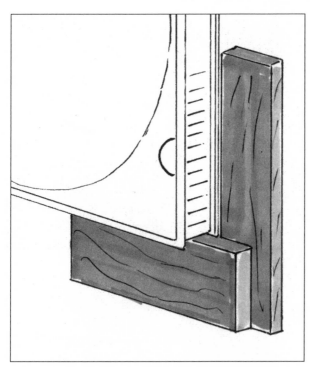

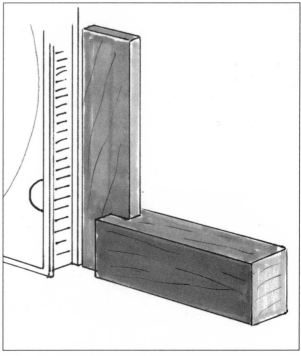

71.   *Checking for inside square using a CD case as a standard. Take care to use the outer edge of the case as the reference only.*

72.   *Checking for outside square must be done on a flat surface such as a table saw top or thick piece of MDF.*

With the saw turned off, set the table saw blade vertical using the CD case as a check. Raise the blade to about 2 inches above the table and slide the case, with hinged edge up, up to the blade and adjust it to vertical. Once set, retract the blade to a height of 1/2 inch.

Clamp the piece into the jig and advance it past the saw blade. While you are at it, do the same to the other end of the stick and you can make two squares. Square-cut the base piece to 2 inches using a cut-off sled or miter gauge.

To make a quick version of a tenoning jig, plane a 12 inch x 6 inch board flat on both sides and clamp the workpiece vertically to the board. Optionally, you could glue on a vertical backer support to reduce exit chipping during the cut.

Hold the backer board up against the fence and align the blade to the workpiece for your cut. Keep your hand well above the blade when making the cut.

The square blade

Rip the blade for the square as you did the base except this time cut an 1/8 inch strip off a 3/4 inch thick board. The 1/8 inch dimension is assuming you have a standard 1/8 inch wide blade that made the kerf in the base. If you have a thin-kerf blade, the strip should be 5/32 inch thick. Using a cut-off sled or miter gauge, square the end of the strip and cut it to a length of 3 inches.

Are you feeling these exacting dimensions are a bit much when using a ruler? I agree. When working to this kind of tolerance, use a set of dial calipers to make your measurements and set up machines. You will be impressed with how much better you can make these precise cuts.

Take practice or setup cuts with scrap wood before cutting your final stock. That allows you to make fine adjustments before risking your best wood.

Checking a square

I would be negligent if not including the accepted means of checking a square. It is valid for any size square but one caveat is the smaller the square, the less accurate this check. Another critical factor is that the straight edge of the below-described board must be accurately straight.

Using a board that has just been jointed to have a straight edge, lay the base of the square over the edge and trace a line along the two edges of the square's blade. Use a sharp pencil or fine lead mechanical pencil.

Now flip the base over right to left so it is aligned with the lines that were just made. Check both edges of the blade of the square against both lines. The blade must align exactly with both lines for it to be considered totally square.

If an angular error is detected, determine the means of correction from the preceding text and repeat this test by marking two new lines and checking again with the flipped-over square.

If the blade is too thick for the square base slot, sand or scrape the thickness down so it just fits. Place a drop of glue in the slot and slip the blade in until it seats at the base of the slot.

Using your CD case, adjust the square inside angle until it is perfectly aligned with the edge of the case corner. Allow the glue to set overnight. **(71)**

Check the square against the CD case when the glue has set. If inner angle is correct and the outer is off, lightly sand the outer edge of the square blade on a piece of sandpaper adhered to a piece of MDF. Ensure that your blade edge remains perfectly straight by sanding slowly while holding the blade at mid-length. Repeat until it registers square. **(72)**

To correct the inside angle, use a well-sharpened bench chisel and pare the edge to correct the error. The chisel back must be truly flat for this to work. **(73)**

Add a light coat of oil and wax, and you have a marvelous tool.

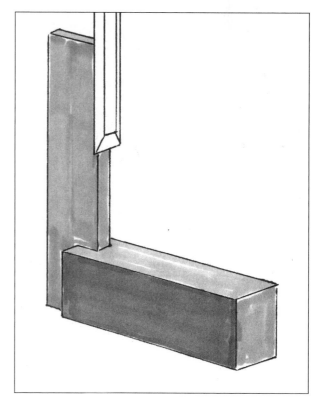

73.   Paring the square blade requires a sharp chisel with a very flat back and a steady hand.

74. This sliding bevel gauge locks with a brass wing nut.

CHAPTER 9
Sliding Bevel Gauge

The bevel gauge can be set to any angle for dovetail marking plus a myriad of other angled woodworking tasks. When building a Chippendale style chair, you encounter angled tenons and compound angled shoulders. Marking them out is the task of the sliding bevel gauge. Note that the gauge does not measure angles, but rather it transfers them from drawing to wood, or from one workpiece to another.

It consists of a laminated clamshell body around a sliding blade that is captured and secured with a thumbscrew or wing nut.

Make the blade

Start with surfaced and planed 1-inch thick hardwood stock about 12 inches long and at least 4 inches wide. Two contrasting woods can make it into a real show piece. We will be using very little wood but we are ever-cautious about getting fingers near blades so we begin with oversized stock.

Mark the flat surface of one board with two marks — one at 3-1/2 inches and the other at 7-1/2 inches from one end of the board. Make the marks visible when the board is standing on edge because you will

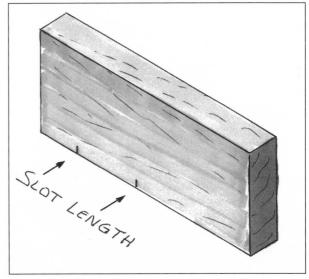

75.   Mark the location and extent of the edge routed slop to guide the blind cut.

use them to guide a blind router cut. **(75)**

Install a 1/4 inch straight plunge bit in a table mounted router and adjust the fence to center the bit 1/2 inch away. Raise the bit 1/4 inch above the table surface.

Turn the router on and lower the board edge down into the bit at the mark nearest the end while holding

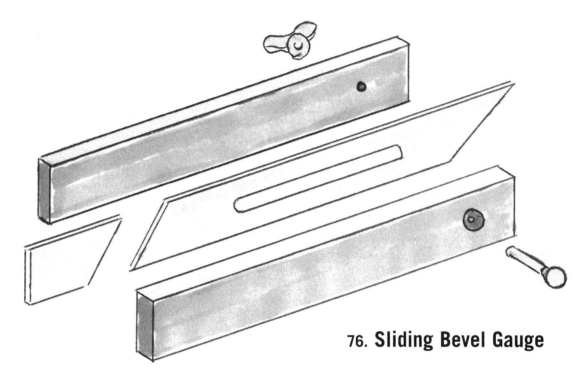

76. **Sliding Bevel Gauge**

Cutting list

Blade	1 each	1/8 inch x 1 inch x 12 inches
Body	2 each	3/8 inch x 1 inch x 8 inch
Fastener	1 each	1-1/4 inch 1/4 x 20 flat-head screw (brass or steel)
	1 each	1/4 inch washer (brass or steel)
	1 each	1/4 x 20 wing nut (brass or steel)

Building the sliding bevel gauge

Task	Tool	Material
Route slot on board edge	1/4 inch plunge router bit	Hardwood
Rip blade from edge	Table saw	
Cut 60° cutoff	Miter gauge and table saw	
Cut 45° length	Miter gauge and table saw	
Rip body sides from edge	Table saw	Hardwood
Glue body sandwich	Clamps	Glue
Drill screw clearance hole	1/4 inch brad point bit	
Drill countersunk hole	1/2 inch countersink bit	
Round-over corners	Sandpaper, rasp, or round-over bit	
Install screw and nut		Flat-head screw
		Wing nut and washer

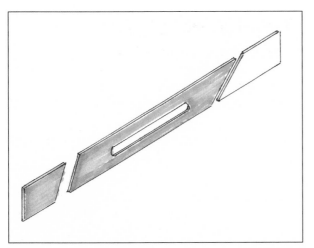

77.   *Cross cut the blade blank into two short end pieces and a blade. One will become the spacer between the gauge sides.*

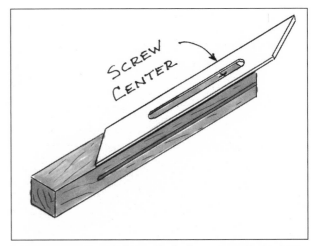

78.   *Lay the blade on the body and mark the drill center for the securing screw.*

the workpiece snug against the fence. Move it forward until reaching the other mark. Hold the workpiece steady and turn the router off. Allow the spinning bit to come to a complete stop before releasing your grip on the workpiece.

We now have a board with a 4 inch x 1/4 inch slot cut in its edge. We will now sever that edge from the board to create the bevel blade.

Using the method described on page 15 for sawing thin stock, we will cut off a 1/8 inch blade from the large board. Install a zero clearance throat plate on the table saw and adjust the saw blade to perfectly vertical. Place the slotted edge of the board toward the fence and rip the opposite edge by removing minimal stock in order to make the edges parallel.

Set the saw fence so the waste piece from the next cut will be 1/8 inch thick. Cut the waste piece off – thus making the blade blank. The exact dimension is not of great importance. The important thing is that it is consistent in thickness with straight grain. **(77)**

Now that we have the blade at the right thickness, use a miter gauge set at 60° to guide cutting 2 inches off of the end nearest the slot. Save the cut-off waste.

Finally, set the miter gauge to 45° and cut the blade so

the tip of the cut will be about 3 inches away from the other end of the slot.

Make the body

The body is made up of two 1 inch by 3/8 inch x 8 inch sticks glued together with the above 60° cutoff placed between them at one end.

I make body blanks by ripping a 3/8-inch strip off a piece of 1-inch planed stock that is 18 inches or so long and at least 4 inches wide. I like keeping my fingers away from the saw blade. The 18-inch strip is then cross-cut into two approximately equal lengths forming the body blanks.

Spread some glue on one side of the 60° cutoff and glue it to one of the body blanks with the squared end aligned to the end of the blank. To complete the sandwich, spread glue on the other side of the cutoff and align the other body blank. Clamp the three layers together while they are resting on edge on a piece of waxed paper. This will align the two halves of the body so they are parallel, which is important for this tool. Note that the blade is not installed at this point. Use a thin piece of wood to scrape any glue squeeze-out out of the slot. Let the glue set.

Install the securing mechanism

The blade must be captured between the two large body blanks and to do this we will use a thumbscrew or wing nut. First we must locate the position of the screw hole. **(78)**

Lay the previously made blade within the body slot to ensure that it fits. Keeping the blade in the same orientation, lay it on top of one side and mark an X about 1/2 inch from the far end of the blade slot centered on the slot. This is the location of the screw hole which will be around an inch away from the end. Predrill this hole all the way through to the other side of the gauge body with a 1/16 inch bit. This established a center on both sides for our next operation.

Determine what form of screw is going to be used to secure the blade. For this gauge, I will use a flat-head screw, with washer and wing nut. Because I don't want the head to stand proud of the gauge body, I'll drill a countersunk hole to allow the head to recess into the body. We could have used a carriage bolt or connector bolt and then the recess for the bolt head would have been a 1/8 inch flat-bottom bore about the same diameter as the bolt head.

For the flat-head screw, we place a wooden spacer between the two sides so they do not flex while drilling. First, use a brad point bit to drill the 1/4 inch clearance hole down into the other side of the body but not completely through. Turn the body over and finish the hole from the other side to minimize chipping on the surface. Countersink one side of the tool body to allow the screw head to rest below the surface.

Place the blade in the body with the slot aligned to the hole. Insert the screw and place a thin washer on the protruding end. Thread the wing nut on and tighten until the screw has receded below the surface. Re-drill the countersink if needed.

Final steps

The gauge is functional but rough so here is where we clean it up. Remove the blade and screw mechanism.

The joy of making tools

For every tool and most operations described in these pages, I attempt to give a reason for what is being done. Picking the body size for the bevel gauge should be no exception.

The size was determined after painstakingly searching for a piece of scrap wood that would work for joinery and look good. Many of the projects herein can be made with the cutoffs that haven't yet made it to the woodstove or trash barrel. Many projects are quickly made and yet totally functional regardless of the source of wood.

Experiment with shapes and details. Make more tools than you need just to practice some of the methods that are new to you. Be inventive and think about problems that need solving in your woodworking experience, and see if a creative new tool may be the solution.

The joy of tool-making is to become unbound from the tool catalogs and unbounded in your thinking about what a tool really is. It is an aid, a jig, a cutter, a spacer, a way of keeping your hands safe, and most of all, part of the challenge called woodworking.

Slide a scrap of wood into the end of the slot to keep the two sides parallel and cut off both ends squarely.

Use a block plane, rasp, or sandpaper to round over the sharp edges of the gauge body. Reassemble the tool. If the blade stands proud of the body when in the closed position, you can sand it flush to the body if you make certain the two edges of the blade remain parallel. To check for parallel, set a marking gauge to the blade width and slide it along the edge.

Sand both the gauge body and blade surfaces smooth. Disassemble and apply your finish of choice. Reassemble the gauge and go build a Chippendale chair.

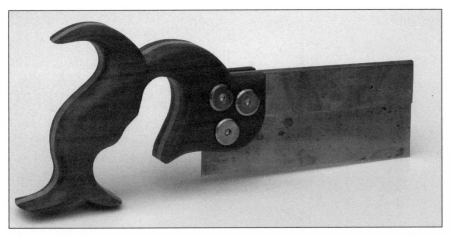

79.   Backsaw, page 56.

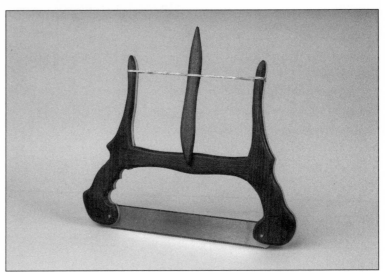

80. Bucksaw, page 68.

81.   Shoulder plane, page 93.

82. Bench plane, page 78.

Cutting Tools

If a woodworker were asked what they do most, the answer would be cutting. We cut to length, cut square edges and ends, cut flat surfaces and, of course, cut joints. To do these things by hand, we need saws, planes, and chisels.

I remember the drudgery of trying, as a youth, to do like the books said in trimming and surfacing a board. My early experiences were hamstrung by dull, barely functioning tools. I have learned that handling a well-tuned tool is not drudgery, it is a pleasure.

The satisfaction is mesmerizing of seeing a shaving curling out of the throat of a plane and hearing the hiss of the edge cutting several thousandths of an inch off the board from one end to the other. So much so that on a bed I was making for myself years ago, I became so infatuated with the elegance of cutting that I took nearly twice as much wood off the edge as I intended and spent a good part of the day figuring a way to salvage my project.

The joy of a good tool can not be underestimated, the elation of an excellent tool borders on decadence.

In the prior chapter, we made the marking tools to give us guidance and in this chapter we make tools that excel at cutting to those lines.

The backsaw and bucksaw described are intended specifically for joinery by being sized to the task and built to provide maximum control of cut. We will see that the more accurately a saw cut is made, the less work is needed in fitting a joint.

The one-handed bench plane and shoulder plane are a time saving duo for fitting joints to perfection. The hand plane's place in woodworking is in making those last few surfacing passes that will give a snug slip-fit to a tenon or leave an almost polished surface around a through dovetail. We will learn that while the principles of plane-making are common to all planes, the shape of the body and the blade are the differences that define which task a plane is built to accomplish.

A full compliment of cutting tools for joinery includes chisels, which require blacksmithing skills that we are not covering.

83.   The backsaw can have an open handle or a closed one.

CHAPTER 10

Backsaw

All handsaws consist of a steel blade with teeth filed into the edge, which will cut on either the push stroke, pull stroke, or both push and pull strokes. Western handsaw design evolved a push-style saw, while Asian cultures evolved a pull saw.

Blade thickness has a significant effect on the ease of sawing. When pressure is applied to the rear-mounted handle of a Western push-style saw, the blade tends to bend. The thinner and longer the blade, the more bending. The backsaw solves this with a rigid, soft-metal reinforcement on the blade's non-cutting edge.

The handle helps the hand transfer muscle power to the blade efficiently and its shape is a major factor in comfort and control of cut. It spreads the force of cutting over a large area of the hand, and if designed well, enables natural body mechanics.

In fine joinery the backsaw is held in high esteem and the dovetail saw is the most revered of backsaws. Dovetail saws have a short, thin blade and finely spaced, minimally set rip-cut teeth and a rigid back, attached to a well designed pistol-grip handle. You will get a greater appreciation for that description as we progress through saw design and construction.

Materials and tools

Part	Material
Blade	Card scraper
Blade back	16-gauge brass or steel
Blade attachment	3 connector screws with nuts
Handle	7" x 5" x 1" board

Tool	Purpose
Fine indelible marker	Marking teeth
5" XX slim triangular file	Sharpen saw teeth
4" metalwork vise	Bend blade back
Saw set	Set saw teeth
Metal shears	Cut gent's saw blade

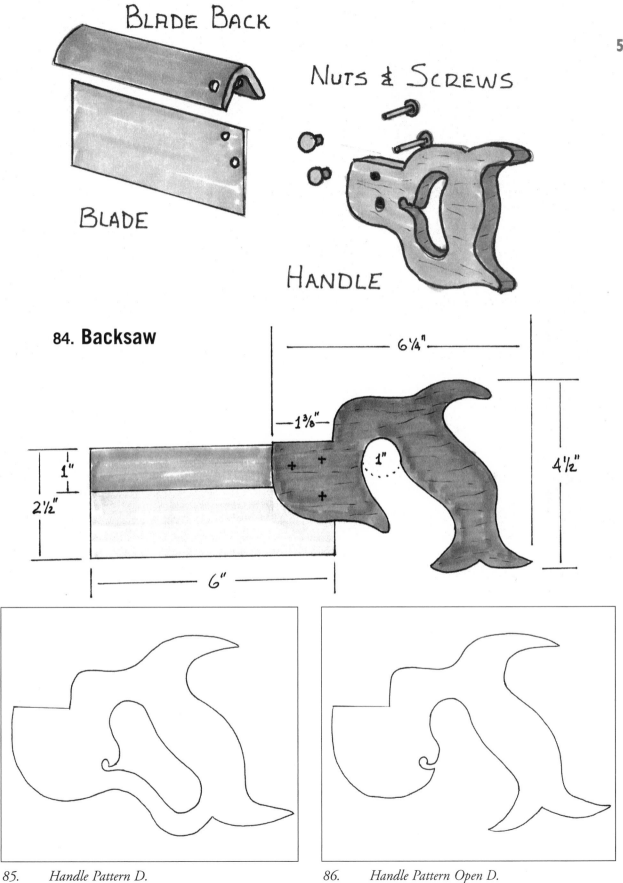

BLADE BACK

BLADE

NUTS & SCREWS

HANDLE

84. Backsaw

6¼"

1⅜"

1"

4½"

1"

2½"

6"

85.   *Handle Pattern D.*

86.   *Handle Pattern Open D.*

Building a backsaw

Procedure	Tool	Material
Mark blade blank for teeth	Fine-point marker and ruler	Card scraper
File tooth locations	5" XX slim triangular file	
File teeth	5" XX slim triangular file	
Make blade back	Hacksaw	6 inch x 2 inch x 16 gauge common sheet steel or brass
Attach blade back	Drill press and vise	
Size handle	1 inch dowel and ruler	Pencil and paper
Cut blade slot	Table saw	7 inch x 5 inch x 1 inch board
Shape handle	Band saw, router, rasp	
Shim blade slot	Glue	Veneer
Fit handle for blade back	Chisel	
Drill attachment holes	1/4 inch twist and masonry drills, countersink	
Attach handle to blade	Screwdriver	1/4 x 20 screws and nuts
Finish handle	Rag	Oil and wax

Make the Blade

Making a backsaw starts with the blade. It can be made from any thin sheet steel, but tool steel (also called spring steel) is more durable and stronger than mild steel. Steel with greater strength allows for a thinner blade, which cuts with less work. In tool steel blades, the ratio of length to thickness should be less than 300:1. That means for a .020 inch thick blade, the maximum length is 6 inches.

We'll use a card-style cabinet scraper as the blade blank. This readily available spring-steel rectangle is 6 inches long and 2-1/2 inches wide. It is thin and strong, and will retain a sharp edge. The short blade is excellent for sawing dovetails and tenons in casework and chairs. My shop-made dovetail backsaw has an ease of control that I simply don't experience with any name-brand production backsaw.

This saw's small size is not the right choice for hand-cutting a 15-inch sliding-dovetail case mortise, but if you can lay your hands on a 4-1/2 inch x 14 inch piece of thin spring steel, you can also build a larger tenon saw.

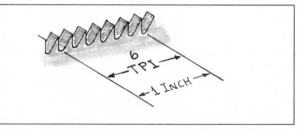

87.   *TPI is measured by counting the number of teeth or points per inch.*

Realizing that not everyone is going to want to make a backsaw blade from scratch, a later section describes how to convert a low-priced gent's saw into a backsaw.

Prior to cutting the teeth

The first step in making the saw blade is to file the teeth. A count of 12 to 14 teeth (or points) per inch is a good balance between fast sawing and smoothness of cut surface. **(87)**

Marking the tooth locations with uniform spacing makes the teeth easier to file and sharpen, so a little care now will save a whole lot of time later.

Obtain a very fine point indelible marker such as the Sharpie "Ultra Fine Point" by Sanford. Next we need to find a ruler with 12 to 14 marks per inch. A metric ruler has 25.4 mm (millimeters) per inch. If we mark the edge using every other millimeter mark, we will end up with just shy of 13 points per inch, a convenient compromise. Another way is to find a ruler graduated in 64ths of an inch and mark the edge every five 64ths. This will yield bleary eyes as well as approximately 13 points per inch. **(88)**

Clamp the ruler and blade together in a vise with the long edge horizontal and the ruler behind and slightly above the blade, with its markings as close to the edge as possible. With the fine-pointed marker, just touch the blade adjacent to the mark on the ruler. Be sure your marks are evenly spaced. After marking all tooth locations, remove the ruler and re-clamp the blade in the vise with its edge protruding 1/4 inch above the vise to provide stability.

We next need a 4-inch X Slim or 5-inch XX Slim triangular file. The 6-inch triangular file that's readily available in most hardware stores is too big for this task.

Going directly from marking to cutting teeth is a risky business because all you have is a smudge for guidance. By lightly scoring a nick at the location of each mark, we can improve accuracy.

Position the file with a flat side down next to a mark. Rotate the file toward the mark so its triangular edge is directly on the mark. Lightly push the file forward with a long smooth stroke to score the steel. One stroke should do it. **(89, 90)**

Continue along the entire blade then look over the marks to be sure that they are evenly spaced. Small variations in teeth per inch are not an issue and will slowly be corrected in future sharpenings. If there are skips or gaps in the markings, place the file midway between marks and make a light cut. In the unlikely event you really messed up, you can flip the blade over and start again on its other edge. Or you can draw-file the edge square and clean, as you would when sharpening a scraper.

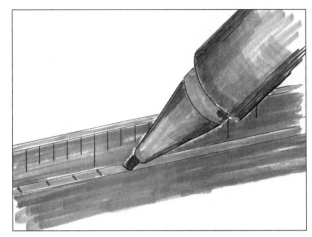

88.   Mark the tooth locations with a extra-fine-tipped marking pen.

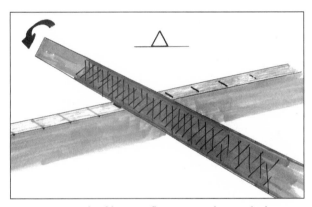

89.   Lay the file on a flat next to the mark then rotate the file on edge over mark.

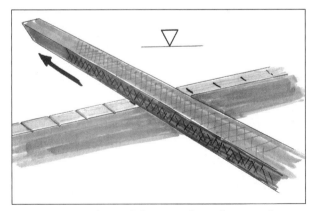

90.   Score the tooth locations by making one long light stroke using file corner – once a small detent is has been established at each mark, accurate tooth filing is easy.

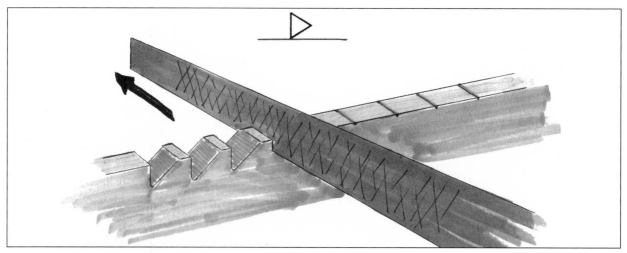

91.   With one face of the triangular file vertical, file the tooth location.

Cut the teeth

Files work in one direction. Dragging them backward does no good for your cut and great harm to the file. I do not lift the file on the backstroke, but I don't put any weight on it either.

Whether you chose to make a rip saw or a crosscut saw, the teeth are initially shaped the same. Set the file on a mark near one end of the blade. Tilt the file so one of its three flat faces is vertical and facing the near end of the blade. Keep the file square to the steel edge and start a light, forward stroke running most of the length of the file. Repeat that stroke until the sloped edge of the cut falls three-quarters of the way between the vertical cut and the next mark. Repeat the cut along the entire edge, rotating the file every few teeth so it wears uniformly. Don't press too hard so you do not distort the blade and dull the file. **(91)**

When you make it to the other end, you have completed the most tedious blade-making operation. To finish the backsaw blade, we will set and sharpen the teeth, but after we have attached the back and handle.

Attach the blade-back

The blade-back is a stiffening and vibration-damping element, but it also adds weight to assist with your sense of vertical balance. It must be made from a strong, malleable metal several times thicker than the blade. My personal favorite metal is brass, though common-grade mild steel of around 16 gauge thickness is just as good.

First cut the back metal to 2 inches wide and slightly longer than the saw blade. Have your supplier shear it if you can. Otherwise, clamp the steel to the bench so that it overhangs the edge 3 inches. Score the layout lines with a utility knife or felt tip marker. Set the hacksaw blade on the mark and start sawing very lightly. Keep the pressure light until you have progressed about 1/8 inch into the metal. Now increase the pressure, but resist bearing down really hard.

You will find that it is easy to cut a straight line in the metal by keeping the angle of the saw very low. The hacksaw frame encourages a low angle because it allows you to cut further into the sheet before it tangles.

Next, we need to make a bending jig. The jig is nothing more than two pieces of 3/4 inch thick wood, longer than the blade-back, spaced 1-1/2 inches apart. Glue them to a third board to keep them stable while bending. We also need a bending caul, which is a piece of hardwood, such as hard maple, that is longer than the blade with one long edge beveled to a V-point.

With a utility knife, score the blade-back twice near its centerline to create a weakness for the bend to fol-

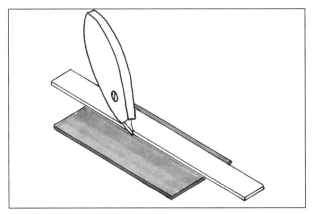

92.   *Scoring the middle of the metal plate used for the saw back will keep the bend on track.*

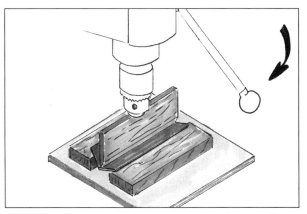

93.   *Start bending the back metal with a simple jig used with a drill press. A board trimmed to a pointed edge can be used as the caul to apply pressure.*

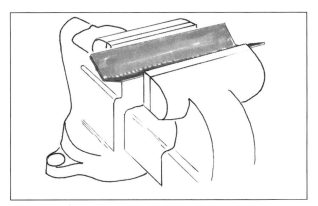

94.   *Continue bending the back in a vise once the initial bend has been started.*

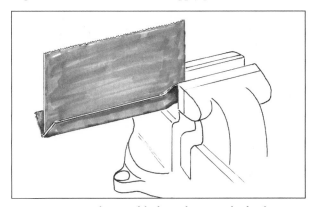

95.   *Insert the saw blade and crimp the back onto the blade. Start at one end and work along.*

low. Lay a straightedge just off center and score the blade-back several times. Now move the straightedge over a blade thickness and score the metal again. **(92)**

Bend the back

We use a drill press and the bending jig to start the bend in the blade-back, then we finish the bend in a metal vise.

Place the bending jig and the blade-back, with the score lines visible, under an unplugged drill press without a drill installed. Open the drill chuck all the way to retract its teeth. Place the bending caul between the drill chuck and the metal and align it with the scribed lines. Slowly crank the chuck down to bend the metal as far as it will go. **(93)**

We will complete the bend over the blade using a 4-inch or larger metal vise. Place the partially bent blade-back between the vise jaws. Close the jaws until they are about an inch apart. Insert the saw blade in the bent back and continue closing the jaws. **(94)**

When the jaws won't close any further, reposition the back and blade so that only 1/2 inch of the back is held between vise jaws. Close the vise jaws until the back crimps the blade. Repeat this step at the other end of the blade-back. To keep from marring the blade-back, cover the vise jaws with a smooth piece of metal. **(95)**

Incrementally walk the crimp down the entire blade-back. There is no adhesive or other binding other than the crimp of the back. If you notice small gaps in the exposed edge of the crimp, don't be concerned. For large gaps, crimp in the vise again.

To straighten a bent blade, lightly hammer the blade-back with the arch of the blade up. Check it with a straightedge. (see drawing 163, page 102)

You can remove tool marks from the blade-back by buffing it with fine sandpaper. Heck, you can send the thing out to be engraved if it warms your heart! The blade is now complete other than final sharpening.

Now skip to the section describing making the handle — unless you want to read about a simpler way to get a respectable blade. It won't be as sturdy, nor have that custom look, but it will be quicker.

Using a gent's saw blade

The gent's saw is a lightweight backsaw that sports a dowel handle and a respectably thin blade. I find these saws difficult to use because they have an inferior handle design and a blade that is too long for its thickness. **(96)**

The solution is obvious: Cut the blade to a more suitable length and install an improved handle. A wonderful by-product of this solution is that you could wind up with two saws. The 10 inch gent's saw I used to make this 6-inch saw blade also gave me a 4 inch gent's saw which is just right for light work. To make this miraculous transformation, we hacksaw the leading 6 inches of the blade off and proceed to the next section on making a handle.

Mount the gent's saw blade, as seen in **(97)**, in a vise so that there is only 4-1/2 inches of blade clear of the vise. Lightly start a hacksaw cut 6 inches from the end and cut until the back has been severed. Remove the gent's saw from the vise and use metal shears (tin snips or aviation cutters) to complete the cut. **(98)**

If the blade is too thick to be cut with shears, clamp the saw flat on the corner of your bench and cut with the hacksaw at a low angle. De-burr the cut ends.

96.   *The gent's saw.*

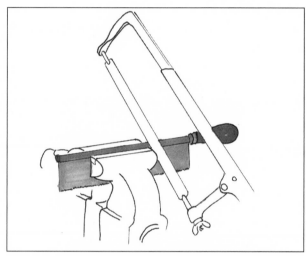

97.   *Cut the blade-back by holding the a hacksaw at a glancing angle to the gent's saw blade. This improves the squareness of the cut.*

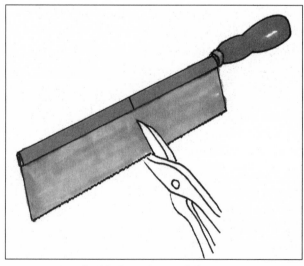

98.   *Cut the blade with metal shears.*

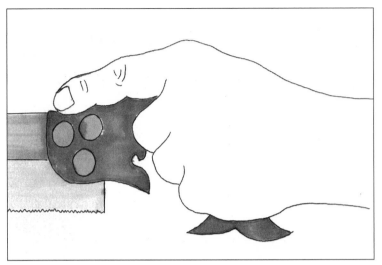

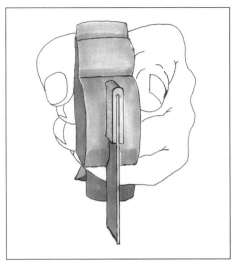

99. *When holding a saw, point the index finger along the handle toward the blade and three fingers grip the handle stock.*

100. *Another view of holding the saw.*

Making the Handle

Design the handle

The handle is where you can exercise your artistic tendencies and create a personalized tool. Let's first explore the functional requirements.

The handle attaches to the blade with screws. Forces of sawing transfer to the palm of the hand, so the back part of the handle must be shaped to distribute these forces across the palm. The fingers curl around the handle to hold the saw. Of course, the saw must feel comfortable in your hand.

Before getting into handle sizing, let's discuss the way to hold a D-style handle. The index finger extends forward along the side of the handle pointing at the cut, while the remaining fingers wrap around the grip. With the wrist in a neutral position with respect to the arm, the muscle action of the arm is directed straight through the handle and into the blade. If the wrist was bent or stressed, you would be likely to wander off the line as well as cause repetitive motion damage to your wrist. **(99, 100)**

For the first handle, let's stay near the industry norm.

Examine the drawings on page 57 and choose your preferred handle style. Both the D-style handle and its close cousin, the open-D handle, are pistol grips. Also see page 71, sizing the handle.

With your hand in a neutral position, grasp a dowel or stick that is big enough so your fingers don't wrap around to touch your palm. Note the angle the stick makes to the wrist and arm. This is the angle of the grip in relation to the top edge of the blade. Adding an extra couple of degrees of tilt increases the downward force on the blade and increases cutting speed, but too much tilt will harm your wrist. **(101, next page)**

Extend your index finger forward, as in pointing, while still holding the stick. Measure the distance along the stick covered by three fingers. This plus 1/4 inch is the width of the forward face of the grip and the size of the interior D-hole. The extra room will increase comfort. Too much room will decrease comfort

Measure the distance across the knuckles of your hand. This plus 1/4 inch is the width between the horns of the handle. A female craftsman's hand generally ranges from 2-1/2 to 3 inches wide at the knuckles, while most male hands are 1/2 inch wider. The

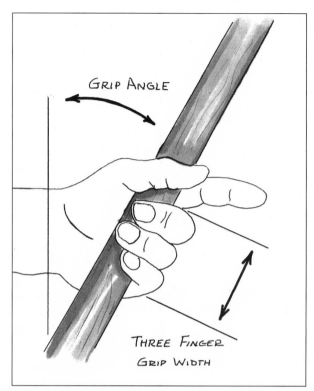

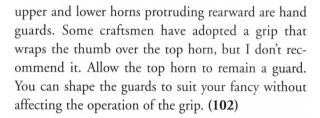

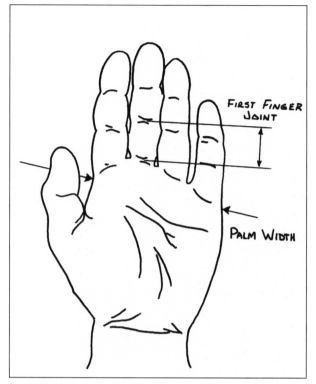

101.   Sizing the handle requires measuring the width of three fingers while gripping a large dowel or stick. The angle made with the stick when your wrist is straight will determine the angle of grip to blade.

102.   Palm width establishes the distance between the upper and lower horns of the handle. The finger measurement helps determine the depth of the grip.

upper and lower horns protruding rearward are hand guards. Some craftsmen have adopted a grip that wraps the thumb over the top horn, but I don't recommend it. Allow the top horn to remain a guard. You can shape the guards to suit your fancy without affecting the operation of the grip. **(102)**

Measure the length of your middle finger, on the inside of your hand, from knuckle joint to the first finger joint. That is the distance from the top of the grip rear edge to the top of the grip front edge across the side. The grip must conform to the palm shape while allowing the fingers to comfortably wrap far enough around the handle for a firm hold without squeezing. Notice how the handle smoothly widens in the center of the grip. This widening allows for the slight cup-shape in your palm and informs the hand of slippage. The first joint of the fingers will be just

even with the front edge of the grip, before the edges are rounded off for comfort.

Measure the distance from the first finger joint to the second finger joint. That is the thickness of the handle.

Finally, the part of the handle in front of the handhold is where the blade will fit. The top straight section will align to the back of the blade. The sharp angled corner will align to the rear of the blade and blade back. Be sure your handle design allows for a slot at least 1-1/4 inches deep.

After all this, if you are uncertain about sizing and shaping, use the dimensions of the example handle pattern. Use a copying machine to enlarge the picture until the distance between the horns is 1/4 inch larger than your hand measurement. There is your pattern. **(85, 86, page 57)**

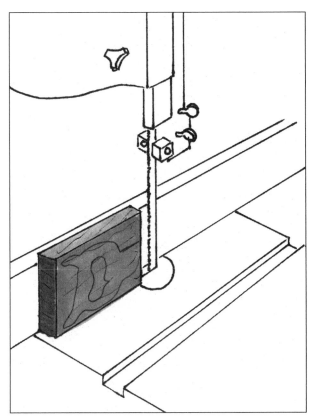

103.   Cut the blade slot in the handle while the handle blank is still rectangular.

Shape the handle

For my hand, the handle blank will be 5 inches wide, 7 inches long, and 1 inch thick. Trace the paper pattern onto the workpiece aligned with the grain. Mark approximate centers for a 1 inch drill that will cut the top and bottom rounds of the D-hole. Mark the centers of the holes used to define the upper and lower extents of the handle between the horns.

Cut the blade slot

The slot logically would be cut with the blade that is going to be installed. If you created a blade from a gent's saw, you may be able to cut the slot with the shortened saw. Attempt this only if you have confidence that you can saw to a line because the blade must be in line and centered in the handle.

Start your hand-sawing by marking a centerline on the front edge and one side edge of the handle blank. Set your saw at a 45° angle to the corner of the wood so you can cut the line on two edges at one time. Start the cut slowly, trying to cut the lines in half. Keep guiding the saw until it has penetrated the corner about 1 inch. As you cut, slowly decrease the angle of the saw so that you are following the top line more than the side line. By the time the saw is 3/4 inch deep into the top edge, the saw should be doing the guiding and you are left to do the pushing. Don't be discouraged, cutting to a line is no first-timer's joy. So practice.

Cut the blade slot with a band saw

If you custom-made a blade, the slot will be have to be cut with another tool since we are at a chicken-or-egg state. The choices are to cut with the band saw or the table saw and shim the slot when fitting the blade. I prefer the band saw because it cuts a thinner kerf.

On the band saw, align the blade with the fence and cut to the desired depth. A 1/4 inch or 3/8 inch blade will typically cut around a .030-inch to .045-inch wide kerf. This may be a bit fat for your blade but if needed, the slot can be shimmed. **(103)**

Setting up to cut the slot on the table saw is easy while the workpiece is still squared. Just raise the blade to the desired depth of cut and mount the blank in a tenoning jig. Shimming will be necessary.

Cut out the handle

To shape the handle, start with the cuts that will be most shock-intensive to the workpiece. Shock, like hitting the wood with a hammer, can fracture the grain structure in thin areas. There will be drilling, band-sawing, and coping, then either router rounding-over, or rasping with a coarse file. You can't do the routing before the drilling but you can do the drilling before the band-sawing.

For clean holes, drill almost through the workpiece from one side until you see the drill point emerge.

104.   *Pre-drilling holes in the handle will ease forming of smooth transitions and provide a place to start saw cuts.*

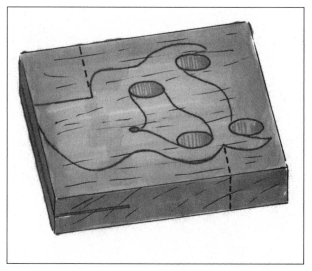

105.   *Short waste cuts simplify cutting sharp angled transitions.*

Flip the board over to finish the hole. **(104)**

Following the outline scribed on the workpiece, scrollsaw, jig saw, band saw, or cope along the line to form the outside shape of the handle.

To have a reasonable chance of following the curves when using the band saw, mount a 1/4-inch or narrower blade. Make short, straight, relief cuts from the edge of the workpiece. This way you can back out of tight turns without the risk of pulling the blade off its drive wheels **(105)**

The interior of the D-handle needs to be removed with either a scrollsaw, jig saw, or coping saw. If you have chosen to add the decorative detail in the example, be sure to drill the terminus hole prior to sawing. If you miss this hole by a small amount, clean up the cut by boring the hole out to a larger size.

Use a 3/8-inch radius round-over bit in a router to dress the edges down to a comfortable fit. With scarcely more labor, and a lot more freedom to become artistic, the edges could also be rounded with chisels, rasps, files, sanding pad, card scraper, or a hand-held knife. **(106)**

Round over with a router

I use a router table and start with the bit retracted slightly, so the initial rounding pass is done with minimal risk of danger to myself and minimal shock to the wood. Then I make several progressively deeper cuts. Start routing on a long-grain edge and move the workpiece against the force of the cutter.

Shaping the inside of the D-handle is risky with the router so chose a tool you are confident in using. If you wish to use the router, remember that the cutting direction is reversed on inside cuts.

Attach the blade

The blade slot must be widened to accept the thicker back of the blade. Mark where the back will enter the handle from the front. Slide the blade into the slot from the top of the handle and mark where the widened slot ends. At the same time, mark the width of the cut needed for the back to fit.

If the blade slot is oversized for the blade, slide two pieces of veneer, one on each side of the blade, into the slot. Add veneer layers as required.

Using a small chisel, mortise the slot to fit the blade-

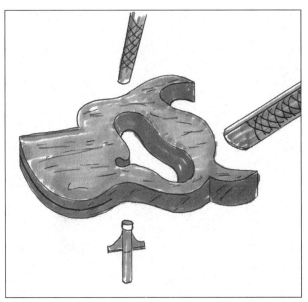

106.   Shaping the handle can be done with a router, round file, or curved-face rasp.

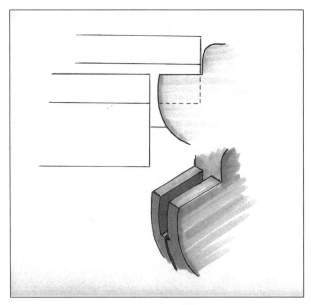

107.   Use a small chisel to mortise a blade-back slot into the handle. A 1/8 inch width chisel would help.

back. Slide the blade into position and ensure that the blade aligns with the handle as planned. **(107)**

We will be using 1-inch long 1/4 x 20 flat-head screws with hex nuts. A dressy alternative is brass or steel connector bolts with cap nuts. Mark two or three hole-centers with one piercing the blade-back and one or two piercing only the blade. Space locations as widely as possible while leaving a minimum of 1/2 inch to the handle edges.

Remove the blade and drill pilot holes through the handle at the marked locations. Use the smallest drill available and drill squarely.

Reinsert the blade. Once again drill into the holes with the pilot drill to mark the blade. Remove the blade and set it on a hard surface, and lightly center-punch the markings to guide the drilling.

You are about to drill into tool steel. That stuff is hard and tough and only slightly softer than regular drill bits. A carbide drill is one solution, and another is to buy a carbide-tip masonry bit. My local hardware store carries 1/4 inch masonry bits, which work nicely to make the hole for a 1/4 x 20 screw.

Clamp the blade down before drilling. Do not try to hold it with your hands. If the drill were to catch it would spin like a lawn-mower blade. Drill the holes accurately and file any ragged edges around the holes.

The handle needs receiving holes drilled for the head and nut of the screws. Use a countersink bit for the taper of the flat-head screw. On the opposite side, use a brad-point bit to drill a recess for the nut. After doing that, re-drill the handle holes all the way through with a 1/4 inch bit.

Slide the blade into the handle and align the holes. Insert a screw in each hole to ensure that everything fits. Tighten the screws fully and check that the blade is entirely stable within the handle. At this point the screw ends will protrude. Power-sand or file them flush. Clean up any undesirable marks and final-sand before finishing.

As with the other projects in this book, an oil finish is recommended, but you are the captain of your ship, so sail on and choose the finish that suits you best.

The saw still needs to be set and sharpened, refer to page 101 for those instructions.

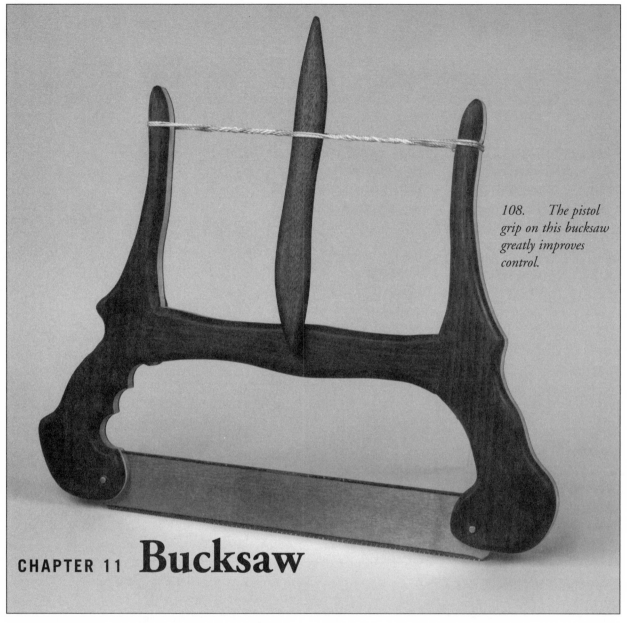

108.   *The pistol grip on this bucksaw greatly improves control.*

CHAPTER 11 Bucksaw

The bucksaw is typically associated with log cutting, not furniture joinery. After seeing an article where Tage Frid, one of the luminaries of woodworking instruction, used a large framesaw to cut dovetails, I started to experiment. This little bucksaw, designed specifically for cutting joints, is the culmination of my efforts.

All framesaws, which include bucksaws and bowsaws, consist of an H-shaped frame with a blade between the lower arms and a tensioner attached to the upper arms. The significant advantage of the framesaw is that a tensioned thin blade, which reduces sawing effort, is able to cut through a piece of wood without bending. The horizontal frame piece (fulcrum) is tenoned into the arms to allow the frame to pivot for tensioning while keeping the blade in alignment.

Bowsaws are traditionally made with a narrow blade that can be angled to the frame. A bucksaw has a wide blade at a fixed angle that guides the cut straight in the kerf. The unique pistol grip on this bucksaw resembles the D-handle for improved blade control.

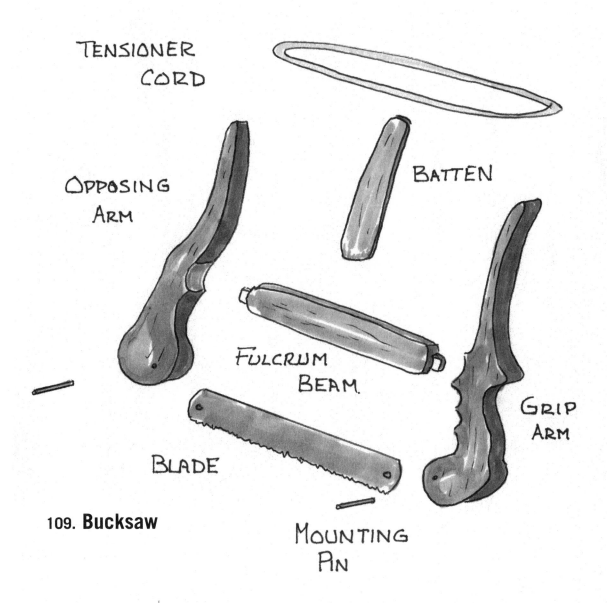

109. Bucksaw

Cut list	
Purpose	**Material**
Blade	12 inch x 1-1/2 inch 14 TPI blade
Arm laminations	6 each 14 inch x 3-1/2 inch x 3/8 inch hardwood
Fulcrum beam laminations	3 each 10 inch x 2 inch x 3/8 inch (same wood as above)
Batten	9 inch x 2 inch x 3/8 inch (same wood as above)
Tensioner	48 inch cotton cord
Blade pin	3/16 inch metal rod

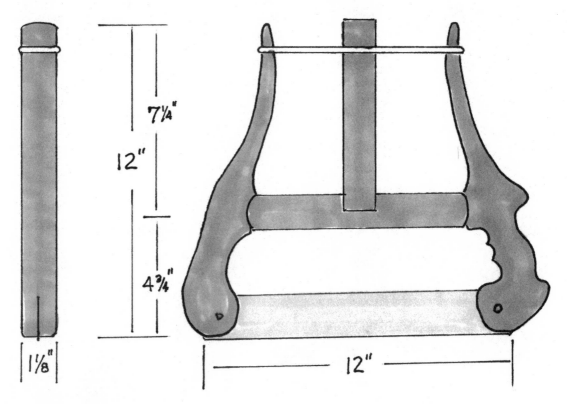

110. **Bucksaw**

Building a bucksaw

Procedure	Tool	Material
Make or buy blade	Metal shears 1/4 inch masonry bit	See appendix for blade sources
Size handle	1 inch dowel	Pencil and paper
Cut lamination layers	Table saw, planer	6 boards @ 3 1/2" x 14" x 1/4"
Mortise, glue up arms	Handsaw, chisel, glue	
Cut blade slot	Band saw	
Contour grip and horns	1-inch Forstner bit	
Drill blade retainer holes	3/16 inch drill bit	3/16 inch x 1 inch rod
Shape arms	Band saw	
Cut fulcrum beam laminations		3 boards @ 10" x 3/4" x 1/4"
Size fulcrum beam	Pencil, hand saw, chisel	Sizing board 10" x 3/4" x 1/4"
Shape fulcrum beam	Stationary disk sander, sandpaper, chisel, knife	
Laminate fulcrum beam	Glue	
Fit beam and arms	Chisel	
Make batten	Band saw, table saw	8" x 2" x 1/4" board
Make tensioner	Knife	Cotton cording
Apply finish	Rag	Oil and wax

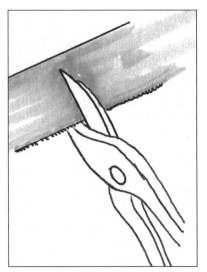

111.   *Cut the blade in half if using a 2-foot long blade version – that is unless you want a really long-bladed bucksaw..*

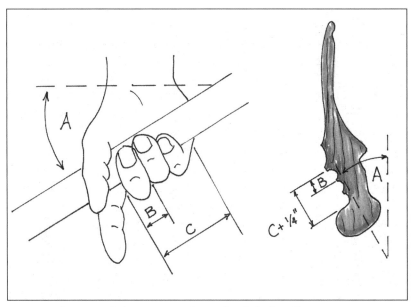

112.   *Sizing and determining the angle of the handle grip requires taking measurements using your own hand for a custom fit.*

Making the blade

If using the 2-foot long blade, cut it to half-length using metal shears. File the new cut so no sharp corners can injure your hands. **(111)**

You now have two bucksaw blades, each with only one hole. Align the two blades on top of each other so the two holes overlay, and drill a 1/4 inch hole through the far end. File off any rough edges around the hole. Whenever creating new blades, use an old blade as a template to drill the hole so the new blade will be correctly sized to the frame.

Designing the frame

The frame consists of two vertical arms separated by a horizontal fulcrum beam. The fulcrum beam is tenoned into the two arms without the use of glue. If we create the frame as a lamination of three layers, we can create the loose tenon joint with minimal work, plus produce an appealing tool by using decorative woods. That means the most decorative construction method is the easiest, a nice combination.

Sizing the handle

The bucksaw handle has a rippled grip to provide distinctive positioning of each finger. Bucket seats for fingers! It is held with three fingers curled around the handle and the index finger pointed along the side of the fulcrum beam. Using this method of holding the saw, we will now determine the angle and width of the grip.

Let your arm fall to your side comfortably while holding a 1 inch dowel or square stick in your cutting hand, with your index finger extended straight down. Have an assistant determine the neutral angle of your grip by measuring the angle the dowel makes to the floor. That is the desired angle the grip will have in the finished saw. **(112)**

A method of determining the slant is to start by measuring the length of the dowel, measure the height of each end from the floor, and calculate the difference in height. For example, if the dowel was 36 inches long and the ends were 21 inches and 39 inches from the floor, the slant is 18:36 or 1:2. That would mean for a 3 inch wide grip, the final slope of the grip would slant 1-1/2 inches from the top to bottom of the grip area.

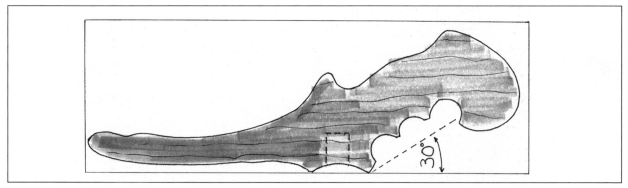

113.   *An example of the bucksaw grip arm layed out on a handle blank.*

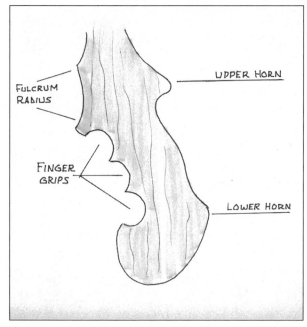

114.   *Features of a bucksaw grip.*

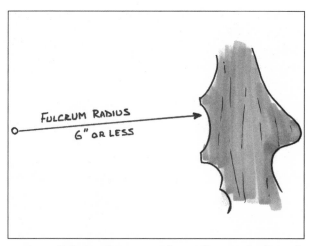

115.   *Fulcrum bearing surface radius can be formed from 3/4 inch to 6 inches depending on the tools available.*

Have the assistant measure the width of your three fingers wrapped around the dowel. Add 1/4 inch to the measurement to determine the width of the grip. Please refer to page 63 for another discussion on making a comfortable handle.

If you chose to use the example pattern, use a copying machine to enlarge (114) until the distance across the three-finger grip area is 1/4 inch larger than your measurements. The example design uses 30° (2:1 slope) as the neutral grip angle.

Extend the blade mounting area below the grip a total of the width of your blade plus 1/4 inch. I extended

the arm 2 inches below the grip because my blade is 1-3/4 inches wide.

When the fulcrum mortise is horizontal, the tip of the arm must be vertical or bent back slightly to prevent the cord tensioner from slipping off. A small indent can be shaped into the arm where the cord is to be located, though it should not be required. (113)

Finally, the fulcrum bearing surface around the mortises is shaped in a 3/4-inch to 6-inch radius concave curve centered on the mortise opening. (115)

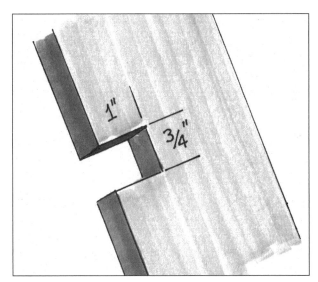

116. *Cut a notch into each handle central layer blank, which will become the mortise for the fulcrum beam tenon end.*

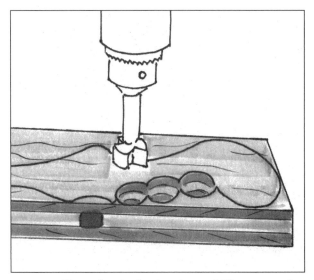

117. *Shape the pistol grip using a drill to create the finger indents. Ensure that the holes follow the slant angle of the grip.*

Using the above information, sketch an outline pattern of the grip arm on a 9 inch x 12 inch piece of paper or use the example arm pattern and enlarge it to the proper size for your hand. We will be using this pattern to build and shape the arms.

Making the arms

Plane three 5-1/2 inch x 27 inch boards so that their total thickness adds up to the arm thickness. The example arm is 1-1/8 inch thick, so each board is 3/8 inch thick. If you choose a different arm thickness, the center-board must be at least 1/4 inch thick, so adjust the outer two layers appropriately.

Cut six 3-1/2 inch x 13 inch pieces from the above boards to become the laminations for both arms. Retain the extra wood to make the sizing board, fulcrum beam, and batten.

Cut a notch in both arm center boards. It will become the mortise after the arm has been glued up. Locate the 3/4 inch wide by 1 inch deep notch 7-1/4 inches from the top end of the center board. Methods of cutting the notch can be with a dado blade, or with a band saw or handsaw and then chiseling the chip out. Regardless of the method, clamp both center boards together when cutting so they have identically located notches. **(116)**

Assemble, glue, and clamp the laminations into two identical arm blanks. Clear any glue squeeze-out from the mortise hole and allow the glue to set overnight.

Trace your grip arm pattern onto both arm blanks by aligning the pattern with the mortise on the arm blanks.

The opposing arm does not require a grip handle so you may reshape it as artistically as desired. The only requirement is that the distance between the mortises and the blade-mounting pins must be identical on both arms.

Start to shape the grip arm by drilling three holes to form the pistol-grip finger indents. Note that these holes will be drilled on a line slanted in relation to the bottom of the mortise. Since my fingers are fully 1 inch wide when gripping a handle, a 1 inch Forstner drill bit mounted in the drill press formed three holes side by side. Drill the outer two holes first, then drill the middle one. Use a 1 inch drill to form the upper and lower horn-to-handle curve prior to cutting the outline of the two arms. **(117, 118)**

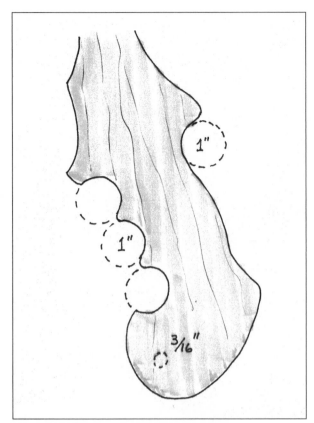

118.   Shape the upper horn with a drilled hole to form a smooth transition.

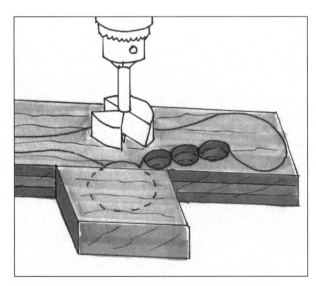

119.   When using a Forstner bit to form the radius of the fulcrum bearing surface, add a waste block to balance cutting forces and produce a square cut.

While the arm blanks are still square, cut the blade slot with a band saw to accurately square and center the slot. Cut it from the bottom of the arm blanks to a depth even with the bottom of the grip area, using the band saw fence as a guide. Note the orientation of the arm blanks because you want the fence reference to be on the same side of the saw on both blanks — which translates to having the arms blanks reversed.

The slot or blade may have to be shimmed to have the blade fit snugly in the slot. To shim the blade, apply thick tape to the ends where it slides into the arm slots. If you prefer, you may shim the slots by applying glue to one surface of a piece of veneer and sliding it into the slot. Next slip in the blade on the unglued side and clamp from both sides.

Locate the blade retaining pin at least 1 inch below the grip and 3/4 inch from the front edge of the arm. Using a 3/16 inch brad-point bit, drill the blade mounting holes squarely through the arm, stopping just prior to exiting out the rear side of the hole. Flip the arm over to finish the hole. Slide a 3/16 inch metal rod, slightly longer than the arm is thick, into the hole. To remove the rod, push it out with a 10d nail or another 3/16 inch rod. Remember that the location of the blade-mounting holes is critical, so you may wish to drill both blanks at once by using double-sided tape to mount them face-to-face before drilling.

Centered on the mortise hole, shape the fulcrum bearing surface of both arms to the selected radius. Shape it using a Forstner bit, a drum sander, or the rounded end of a stationary sander. I use a 1-3/8 inch Forstner bit with a scrap piece of wood clamped to the face of the arm to keep the bit cutting vertically. The more squarely you cut the bearing surface, the easier it is to fit the fulcrum arms. **(119)**

The grip arm blanks have now been perforated with the several holes and slots locating critical features, so it is time to saw out the final form. Using a band saw with a narrow blade, a coping saw, or scroll saw, cut out the arms following your drawn outline.

The fulcrum beam

Rough-saw the fulcrum beam-sizing board to 10 inches x 3/4 inch from scrap. With the arms lying on the bench top, install a blade using a mounting pin in one end. Install the sizing board into the mortise holes and adjust its length until you can just install the blade and other pin in the opposing arm with the arms vertical. With the same three boards used to make the arms, cut three fulcrum beam blanks longer than the beam-sizing board and about 2 inches wide.

With the beam-sizing board still installed, carefully trace the curve of the fulcrum bearing surface on one end of the outer boards. Using double-sided cellophane tape, mount the two outer layer boards together. Using a stationary sanding disk or a rasp and file, shape one end to match the bearing surface. **(120)**

Slide the shaped end against the grip arm. Mark the other end for shaping by tracing the curve onto the underside of the outer layers **(121)**. Cut to length, leaving enough extra to shape that end. Fit both outer

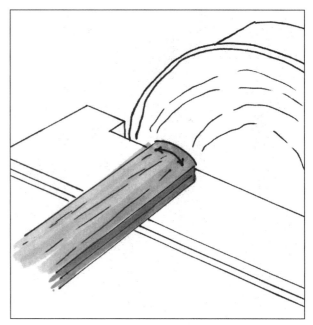

120.   *Shaping the ends of the fulcrum beam outer layers is easily accomplished using a stationary disk sander.*

121.   *Size the fulcrum beam outer layers by tracing the curve of the arm onto the underside of the fulcrum beam blank.*

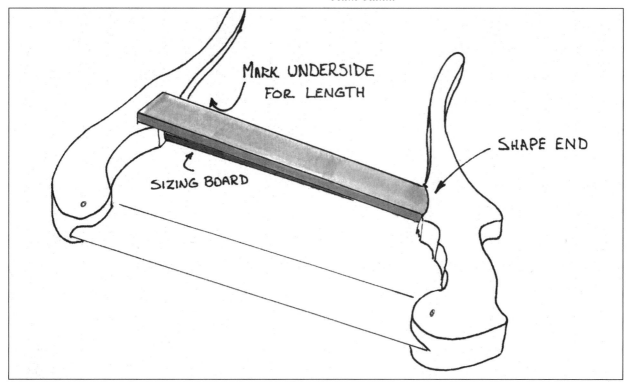

MARK UNDERSIDE FOR LENGTH

SHAPE END

SIZING BOARD

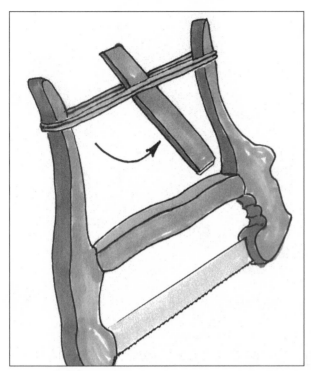

122.   *The tensioner batten twists the cord which tightens the arms. Slide the batten toward the fulcrum arm to keep it from unraveling.*

123.   *A square knot is an excellent knot to use for the tensioner cord.*

boards in place and check that they bear equally against the curves.

If you trimmed too much off of the ends, you can rebuild a small amount of the length by gluing veneer strips to the bearing surfaces of the arms. Apply glue to one side of the small veneer strips and place them between the bearing surface of the arm and the fulcrum. Lightly clamp the assembly togeth-

er so the fulcrum beam acts as a clamping caul for the veneer strip.

We now use the sizing board length and the outer layers of the fulcrum beam to create the center layer. Cut the center board to the beam sizing board length but leave it 2 inches wide. Use the outer layers of the fulcrum beam to pattern the end cuts on the center board. Mark 3/4 inch tenon ends using the sizing board as a pattern. Use a coping saw or band saw to cut the curved bearing surface into the center board, remembering to leave a 3/4 inch tenon on each end. Shape the bearing surface with a carving knife or chisel.

Ensure the fulcrum beam center board fits identically to the sizing board. Glue the two outer boards to the installed center board. Clamp the glued fulcrum assembly and remove it from the arms. Allow the glue to set overnight. Shape the beam as desired.

Assembling the frame

The tensioner requires cord that does not stretch. Upholstery cord, 1/8 inch woven cotton cord, and lawn mower pull-cord are great. Poly-fiber cord stretches too much and will lose tension quickly. Read the package before buying cord in a retail store. I have bought cord that says in large print "Cotton Cord" and in small print "and polyester fibers," which did not work well in this application.

Mount the fulcrum beam in the arms. There should be a small amount of play in the mortise-and-tenon joints to allow the frame to be tensioned.

To make a batten, the task is as simple as cutting a board about two inches longer than the upper arms of the frame. Scraps from the early cuts may inspire greatness and creativity can have its reign. **(122)**

Wrap the cord around the upper handles twice and tie it in a square knot. Your scouting days will come in handy here. Not a scout? Look at the square knot drawing and follow it exactly. **(123)**

To tension the cord, slide the batten between the cords and twist it around a few times. The cord will

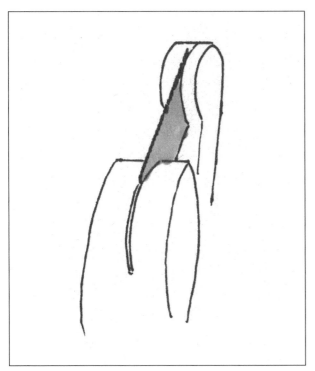

124.   Sight down the blade to ensure the frame is totally in alignment. Adjustment can be made by trimming the fulcrum arm interfaces.

fied by trimming the fulcrum bearing surface of the beam and arms. **(124)**

If the blade does not tension correctly, the tenons may be too tight or the fulcrum is too short. Disassemble the frame and lightly trim the tenons on the lower edge. Taking too much off will make the saw frame unstable.

Once all is in good shape, you can decide if you want to glue the tenon into the grip handle mortise. Do this only if the frame seems to wiggle too much while sawing.

Spread glue on both sides of the mortise and slide the tenon in. Tension the blade, set the frame at the correct angle, and allow the glue to dry. Please don't glue both tenons — though this would be a good way of giving you further practice in building bucksaws.

shorten due to the twisting and the blade will be pulled tight. How tight is tight? A tight cord is comfortable to twist a half-turn further. Over-tightening the blade will distort it. You can tension in increments of half-turns by sliding the batten back and forth through the cord.

The frame can now be finished and smoothed. For the grip portion of the arm, use a 3/8 inch round-over bit to curve the edges to a uniform feel with the least amount of work. Files and rasps allow much more comfort control with not much more effort

You will be looking down at a very handsome bucksaw about now. All that is left is to check that the blade is straight, and apply a finish.

Sight down the length of the blade to ensure it is straight. Determine what is misaligned. If the blade slots are parallel to the sides of the arms, the arms themselves may be skewed. This is likely to be recti-

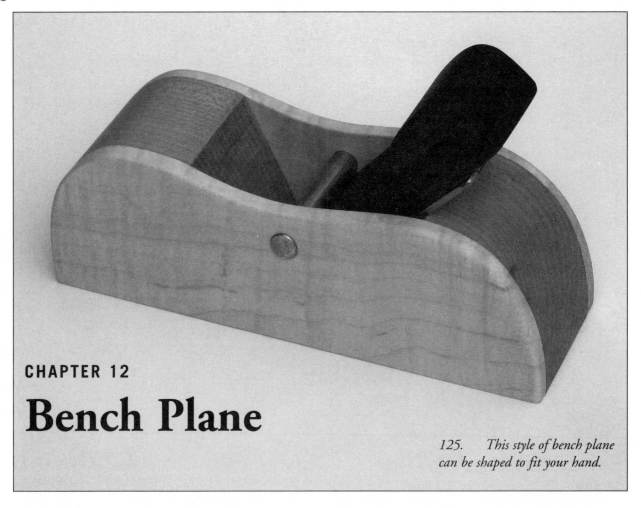

CHAPTER 12

Bench Plane

125. This style of bench plane can be shaped to fit your hand.

Bench planes are the workhorses of the plane family. They are the ones you pick up whenever you need to flatten the wood, straighten an edge, or clean up a joint surface. For a while, steel-bodied planes had all but replaced the wooden version, but lately wooden planes have seen a nostalgic revival with much credit going to James Krenov, who was the inspiration for building my first wooden plane.

The wooden plane described below has a plane iron without a chip-breaker held to the bedding block via a wedge that presses against it and against a metal cross pin. It is best at cutting very fine shavings versus removing large quantities of wood quickly. The short body size and narrow iron makes it ideal for one-handed work, often necessary in joinery.

Important wooden plane features

The following discussion applies to both planes described in this book as well as to most planes you will encounter.

A plane slides on its bottom surface, termed the sole, riding on the high spots and bridging the low spots of the wood. The blade or iron extends a couple of thousandths of an inch below the sole, slicing shavings off the high points while missing the low spots. A flat sole is necessary to produce a flat planed surface plus it improves the consistency of cut. The space between the cutting edge and the forward part of the sole is termed the throat clearance. A narrow throat clearance helps control the consistency of the cut. **(127)**

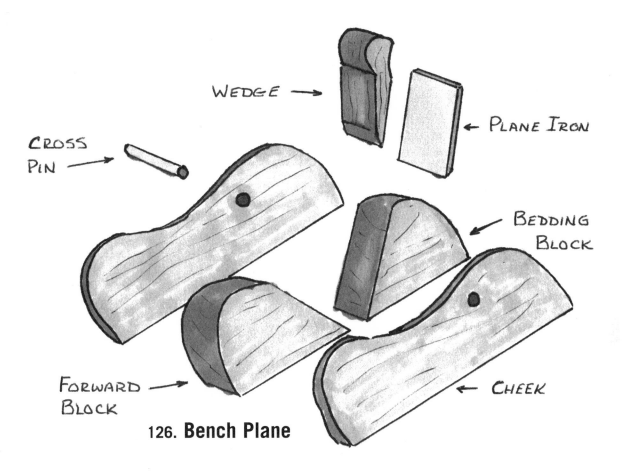

WEDGE

PLANE IRON

CROSS PIN

BEDDING BLOCK

FORWARD BLOCK

CHEEK

126. Bench Plane

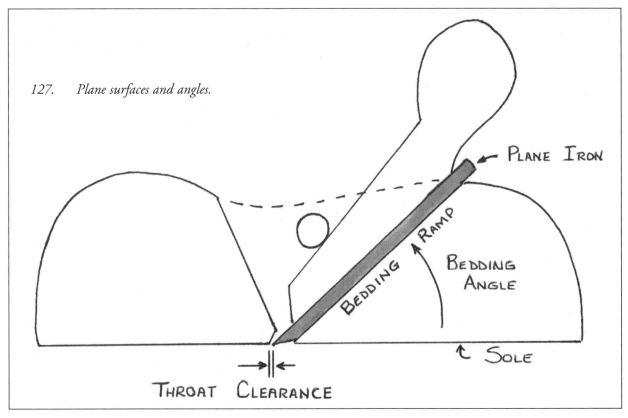

127.   Plane surfaces and angles.

PLANE IRON

BEDDING RAMP

BEDDING ANGLE

SOLE

THROAT CLEARANCE

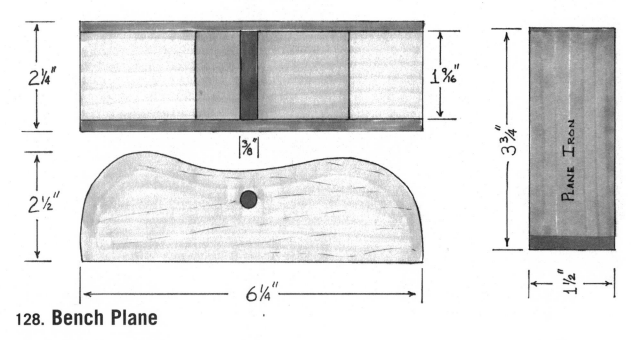

128. Bench Plane

Cut list	
Purpose	**Material**
Central section	10 inch x 3 inch x 1-1/2 inch
Cheeks	2 each 10 inch x 3 inch x 1/4 inch
Wedge	4 inch x 1-1/2 inch x 1 inch
Wedge pin	3/8-inch brass or steel rod
Plane iron	1-1/2 inch x 3 inch x 1/8 inch steel plate

The plane body carries the blade or cutting iron set at a fixed angle as measured from the sole, called the bedding angle. To allow the cutting edge to penetrate below the surface of the wood, a minimum clearance angle of 10° is necessary, which is measured from the sole to the lower surface of the iron's cutting edge.

Wooden planes depend on friction to hold the iron stable while cutting. As the bedding angle is reduced, the forces pushing the blade back overcome the wedge's ability to hold it stable. A 45° bedding angle is typical for a wooden plane. Metal planes with blade adjusters can bed at lower angles because they do not depend on friction alone to stabilize the blade.

The angle from the sole to the top edge of the iron is termed the cutting angle. If the bevel of the iron faces downward, the bedding angle is also the cutting angle. If the bevel is on the top surface of the iron, the bedding angle is the clearance angle. Low cutting and clearance angles will reduce the force required to shear the wood, making it possible to use this plane one-handed. **(129)**

The difference between the cutting and clearance angle is the iron's sharpening angle. Typical sharpening angles are between 25° and 30°. A shallower angle will reduce the strength of the edge. This plane has a downward-facing bevel on the iron, so it has a 30°edge and 45° bedding angle, producing a 45° cutting angle and 15° clearance angle.

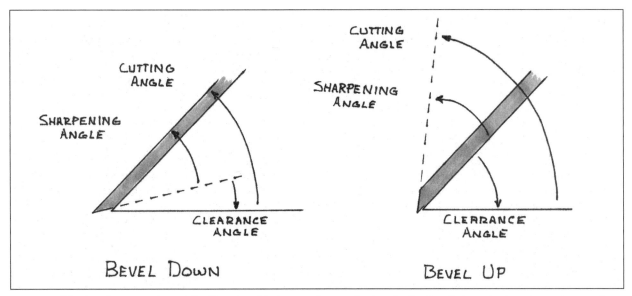

129. *The bevel orientation will affect the effective cutting angle drastically. Bevel down is the orientation used on planes described here.*

To determine the approximate angle an iron is sharpened, measure the thickness of the iron with calipers then measure the bevel length and the length of the back under the bevel. If the bevel length is twice the iron's thickness, the angle is 30°. It is 26° if the length of the back under the bevel is twice the thickness. **(130)**

The vertical sides, termed cheeks, on a plane must be exactly 90° to the sole only if it will be used on a shooting board, which we make in Chapter 17, page 120, or if the plane is used on its side, as is a shoulder plane (Chapter 13, page 93). Otherwise the cheeks can be shaped for comfort in the hand.

Many planes use a chip-breaker to keep the cleaving action of the iron from gouging the wood surface. It breaks the wood shavings immediately after cutting so they can't gain leverage to pull additional fibers off the surface. If you have purchased one of the referenced irons (Appendix A), it comes with a chip-breaker, which will add machining steps to the construction. Those will be addressed as we proceed through the project.

Since a chip-breaker complicates building a plane iron we will omit it but we do use another method of reducing tear-out. Significant pressure placed on the wood in front of the cutting edge, plus a very narrow throat clearance, will also break the shavings and reduce tear-out.

A last point is that the somewhat flexible wooden-bodied plane absorbs some of the inherent vibration created by planing. Reduced vibration helps smooth the planing motion and create a flat finished surface.

Which iron to choose

We are making a small bench plane to be used in one hand for trimming fine shavings off completed joinery. A narrow blade of moderate thickness and length is needed. Our plane will use a 1-1/2 inch x 3-3/4 inch blade.

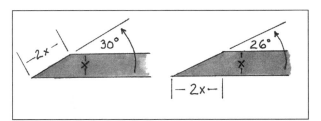

130. *Sharpening angle can be determined by a straightforward measurement.*

Building a bench plane

Procedure	Tool	Material
Cut iron	Hacksaw	Scrap circular saw blade
Square iron	File or belt sander	
Bevel cutting edge	File, disk sander, or grinder	
Sharpen iron	Sharpening stones	
Cut body blank pieces	Table saw or band saw	Maple or other hardwood
Smooth body pieces	Jointer, planer, or sandpaper	
Cut rough iron bed	Table saw or band saw	
Flatten iron bed	Block or bench plane or sandpaper	
Shape forward section	Band saw, file, and sandpaper	
Locate cross pin	Drill	3/8 inch rod
Assemble plane body	Clamps	Glue
Clear glue squeeze-out	Razor, scraper, chisel	
Flatten sole	Plane, sandpaper, jointer	
Adjust throat opening	Chisel	
Shape body	Band saw, chisels, scraper	
Apply finish		Oil and wax

If you work with mahogany, poplar, walnut, cherry, or soft maple, many tool-grade steels will produce a reasonable cutting edge that will stay sharp. If you work with hard maple, oak, or hickory, the hardest, toughest blade you can buy will be a good investment.

Scrap high-speed steel (HSS) circular saw blades are well-tempered tool steel of respectable hardness in the Rc50+ range. A carbide-tipped blade body is somewhat softer steel but acceptable none the less. Avoid low carbon steels since they will not hold a sharp cutting edge.

I've made plane irons out of old lawn mower blades given to me by a local repair shop. They are similar in hardness to the circular saw blade but much thicker. Another source could be an old chisel. Select one that has square sides and no taper to the body thickness.

These scrap steels are fine-grained, high-carbon varieties that will be serviceable as plane iron stock as long as you do not demand maximum edge retention. I prefer this source of metal because it can be shaped to my needs without my having to compromise on what is available in a catalog, plus it is cheap and readily available.

Buying an iron

Some will find it preferable to purchase an iron instead of making one. This is especially true if your choice woods are very hard, or if you demand ultimate performance. Currently there are several sources of top-quality plane irons, which are listed in the materials section (Appendix A) at the back of the book. These vendors specialize in making exceptional cutting irons that are about twice as thick and hard as standard irons. The instructions for building the plane body detailed below are fully applicable to purchased irons, with a couple of minor modifications to accommodate the chip-breaker.

When purchasing a plane iron note that some need the cutting edge to be shaped as well as sharpened.

Plane irons and metal

If you are relatively familiar with most of the domestic woods, you know that walnut and poplar are quite soft and oak and hard maple are hard. There are engineering tables to give values for the relative hardness but we tend to just depend on experience with the species of wood we are working. Just by looking at the board, we can frequently determine the species, and know its hardness.

Plane irons need to be hard and tough so they can stay sharp and resist nicks, plus the grain size in the metal must be small to allow creating a smooth and sharp surface at the cutting edge. Determining hardness in metal is not like our methods with wood because all steels look pretty much the same.

Hardness largely results from the percentage of carbon in the steel. High-carbon steels (greater than .5% carbon) can be identified by observing the sparks that fly off of the grinding wheel. You won't know exactly how much carbon but if the sparks fly fast and furious, it is high-carbon steel. If they are few or just single shooting embers you are handling low-carbon steel or some soft alloy. All quality tool steels are high-carbon steels with a fine-grained composition.

The Rockwell-C test measures hardness of metal in Rc values, where a higher value indicates harder metal, but hardness comes at the price of brittleness. A very hard blade tends to chip under stress at its sharpened cutting edge. Tempering the hard steel mitigates this nasty side effect by softening the steel to a point where it is hard enough but much less brittle, thus tougher.

A thicker iron will flex less under the stress of cutting, which will translate into less chatter. Standard irons installed in retail metal planes are about .08 inch (1/12 inch) thick. They perform well when cutting thin shavings but become unsatisfactory when taking deep cuts. The increased stress on the cutting edge flexes the blade and creates chatter. The standard chip-breaker stiffens the iron as well as reduces tear-out but a thicker blade still is a significant improvement. The wedge in the wooden plane works like the chip-breaker to keep the blade from flexing.

The amount of energy needed to cut, and the amount of stress that flexes the blade, are proportionate to the width of the blade and depth of cut. A narrow blade requires less force because it is cutting less wood. If used to smooth the top of a table, the plane blade could be wider to allow fewer passes to cover that large area, because when smoothing, the blade is set to cut extremely fine shavings.

When choosing an iron with a chip-breaker, the chip-breaker must at least be checked for a tight fit to the blade body, and most likely will need honing to produce that fit.

Now it is time to move from theory and background to actually starting the project. If you purchased a ready-made plane iron or a used iron it will still be instructive to read the following section since you will probably want to tune it up.

Making the plane iron

When making a plane, the iron dictates the width, height, and length of the plane body and the angle at which it can be bedded. Thus we will make or buy the iron first.

High-speed steel and carbide-tooth 10 inch blades have approximately .08 inch thick bodies. Smaller diameter blades are thinner, which may make them too flexible for this project. If you don't happen to have a junk 10 inch or larger circular saw blade, ask a friend.

Using a hacksaw, a file, a grinding stone and some clamps, we can make a plane iron in a couple of hours. It is an exercise (physically and figuratively) that will educate you in creating cutters of any shape.

Hacksaw technique

Hacksaws cut best when you allow the saw blade to do the work and the cut is at a low angle to the metal. Don't saw perpendicular to the steel. If you can't start the hacksaw on the edge of a piece of metal, it is because the blade is at too high an angle. The lower angle also increases your ability to track a line while sawing. Release the downward pressure on the backstroke of the cut. If you force the cut too much, you are likely to start chipping the hardened teeth off the blade making the balance of the job very uncomfortable. Plan on consuming two hacksaw blades to extract and square the plane iron: one to learn how to use the hacksaw, and one to finish the work.

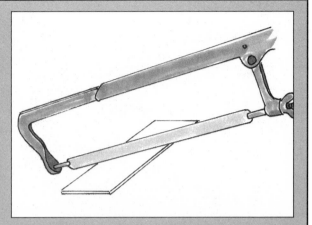

131.   *The proper hacksaw angle for cutting steel is very low. This reduces chatter and helps the saw track the cut line.*

Cut out the iron

Draw cutting lines on the circular saw blade as shown in the illustration. The finished dimensions of the iron are 1-1/2 inches x 3-3/4 inches. I've made a template out of 1/8 inch hardboard so I can trace the rectangle on the blade quickly. **(132)**

Clamp the saw blade to the bench with the first cut line overhanging the edge by at least 3/4 inch, and saw the iron out using the sequence shown. Cut along the sides first, then cut the iron off the blade, and last, square-cut the cutting edge. Reposition the clamped blade prior to each cut to reduce vibration.

Shape the plane iron

With the iron in relatively the right shape, we need to dress up three sides. The two long edges need to be made straight and parallel, and the cutting edge needs to be squared and beveled before sharpening. Most of this can be done with a file.

First, smooth off the edges of the iron on all four sides to de-burr the metal. Re-mark the iron blank to establish straight parallel edges. Use a 10-inch or longer mill file to straighten the edges of the iron while it is

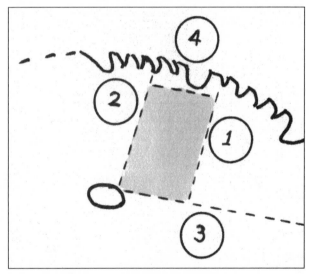

132.   *Follow this cut sequence to extract the plane iron out of a saw blade.*

mounted low in a metalworking vise. The file cuts in the direction away from the end tang or handle. Push only in that direction.

I often use my stationary belt sander instead of a file, but be careful to ensure the metal doesn't get too hot. Use light pressure when sanding and quench the metal often in a bowl of water to keep it cool.

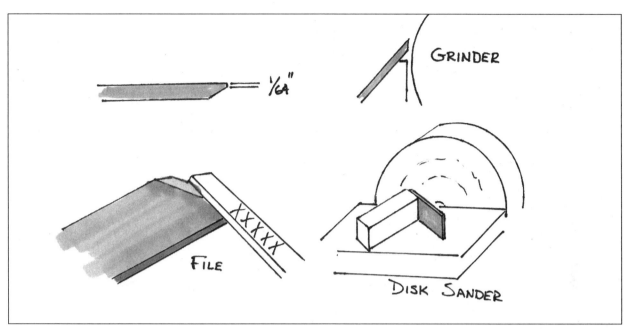

133.   *Bevel the iron to within 1/64 inch of the back then check that the cutting edge is square to the sides. Final honing will remove the last bit of bevel.*

Square and bevel the cutting edge

After straightening the edges, mark an accurate squared line to define the cutting edge and use a file, grinder, or stationary disk sander to remove metal to the line.

Using a file or grinder, start in the high corner and work to the line. Finish by filing along instead of across the cutting edge. **(133)**

Using a stationary disk sander, lay the blade on the support table and hold the blade square to the disk surface, lightly pressing the iron against the disk, and quench the steel frequently. Be very careful to keep your fingers clear of the spinning disk.

Once squared, we must bevel the edge. Using a file, mount the blade with its cutting edge up in a metal vise. File, at a 60° angle from vertical, across the edge until a 1/64 inch wide flat is left. To gauge the angle, the bevel should be twice as wide as the thickness of the iron. We will hone the sharp tip of the edge as described below because filing could leave it uneven.

Alternately, with a grinder or disk sander leave 1/64

inch of edge for honing because as the metal gets thinner toward the edge, it will overheat quickly and lose its hardness. If the metal turns blue or purple, it has overheated. The only option is to grind away even more or cut a 1/8 inch off the end and start again. Quench in water frequently. How often should you quench? Every two seconds. That is: 1, 2, quench; 3, 4, quench. You don't have to quench when using a file or a water-wetted wheel.

To use the stationary disk sander, get a 1-1/2 inch x 1-1/2 inch x (at least) 4 inch piece of wood that is square cut on one end. With the sander running, lay it flat on the sander table and push the end of the wood against the rotating disk. This creates a surface that is parallel to the disk face. Using the block of wood at a 30° angle to the disk, support the iron and lightly sand the bevel. Be careful to keep your fingers away from the moving disk or you may wind up with flat-top knuckles. Quench frequently.

For a grinder, set the tool rest at a 30° angle to the wheel and grind the entire edge with repeated sweeps across the stone. Quench frequently.

Hone the edge

Honing an edge is nothing more than making two flat surfaces meet at an angle. If both surfaces are smooth as well as flat, the edge will be even sharper. If the edge is so smooth that it looks like a mirror, the edge will be as sharp as possible. It is your choice how many and how fine stones you use. Some woodworkers insist on honing to a mirror finish, but my view is learn to hone your tools quickly and you will sharpen more frequently. The result will be you will have a sharp tool more often.

Once the bevel has been shaped, flatten the back of the iron on a medium sharpening stone (equivalent to 1000-grit water stone). Move the iron back and forth at one angle until scratch marks are visible across the entire surface within 2 inches of the cutting edge. Using a finer stone, move the iron at a different angle until all of the previous scratch marks are gone and new ones show in the new direction.

With the back flattened, flip the iron over and hone the bevel angle in the same manner. When sharp, a slight burr will form on the back surface of the edge. The burr is evidence that the beveled surface has intersected with the flat back. Flip the iron over once more and with the iron flat on its back, drag it once across the finest stone you are using. Done. Well, you may wish to strop the edge on a brown paper bag once or twice to totally remove the burr. Now – really done!

An excellent way to check if the edge is sharp is to look straight toward it with a bright light above you. Hold the blade at waist level and against a dark background such as the shadow under your workbench. If you can see a glint of light right on the edge, that is a flat spot. If just sharpened, it could be the wire edge. Strop the edge a couple of times on a brown paper bag and check again. If the glint moves to a different location or disappears, the edge is flawless. **(134)**

I use blue- and red-coded diamond stones by DMT, followed by buffing on some worn 600-grit wet/dry sandpaper laying on a piece of MDF. A

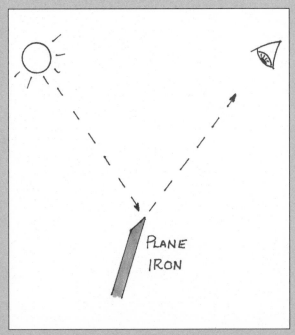

134.   *Check for a sharp edge by looking at the cutting edge. A glint of reflected light indicates a dull surface and more honing required.*

1000- and 4000-grit waterstone combination works just as well. Oilstones are another choice: start with a coarse grit, move to a finer grit, and finally hone on a hard Arkansas stone.

Regardless of which sharpening system you use, make sure the stone has a flat surface. With the diamond stones, as long as the surface is intact, it is flat. To flatten waterstones or oilstones, lay a fresh sheet of 220 sandpaper, grit side up, on a flat surface such as a piece of MDF or plate glass. Lay the stone face down and rub it over the sandpaper in a random motion. When the stone has taken a uniform coloration over its entire surface, it is flat.

One last thought: once you have accomplished the task of shaping and honing the iron, your hands will look several shades darker than when you started. To regain my normal skin color, I have found Boraxo or Lava soap to be a necessary part of my sharpening kit.

Build the plane body

With the iron complete and sharpened, we can build the plane body to fit around it. The body consists of a wedge, two identical outer cheek plates, and two central blocks. The bedding block holds the iron on the bedding ramp, and the forward block is called that for the lack of a better name.

To make the plane look as if it is made from one piece of wood, band-saw wide material into three sections, plane them flat, and glue them back together once the central blocks have been shaped. In the following text, we will treat the wood as individual pieces with grain oriented in the same direction.

Shape the central body block

The body of the plane is made from a dense hardwood such as maple, white oak, or beech. It's best to orient the grain so it is quartersawn at the sole.

Plane a 16 inch x 3 inch piece of wood to the width of the plane iron plus 1/16 inch (1-9/16 inch for this plane iron). Cut off a 12 inch section to form the central block of the plane. Reserve the 4 inch section to make the wedge.

With a table saw or band saw and miter jig, cut the central block in half at a 45° angle. Check that the saw blade is vertical. Orient the wood on its side to cut the bedding ramp. Feed the block slowly through the blade to reduce the risk of skewing the cut.

One of the pieces will be the bedding block. If cut well, the bedding ramp for the iron will be straight and flat and at right angles to the other surfaces. First check that it is at 90° to both sides of the block.

Use a steel ruler as a straight edge to check for flatness. Align the ruler diagonally across the iron bed on both diagonals and check for gaps between the ruler and the bed. Align the ruler along the length of the ramp on both edges and in the middle. Check directly across the ramp in several places. Flatten any gaps with a well-tuned block plane, or re-cut the bedding block.

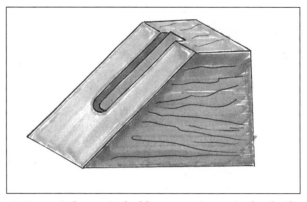

135.   A slot cut in bedding ramp is required only if using a blade with cap iron. Size the slot to be wider than the cap iron screw.

A less desirable alternative is to sand the ramp flat on a sheet of sandpaper attached with spray adhesive to a piece of 3/4-inch MDF. Take care to not rock the block or round off the thin end. A power jointer is unsafe for small pieces of wood. Do not use it for this task.

Irons with chip-breakers

If your iron has a chip-breaker, you'll need to rout a slot into the bedding ramp for the chip-breaker screw head **(135)**. Measure the screw head width and height. Use a router bit that is at least 1/16 inch larger than the screw head to cut a slot slightly deeper than the screw head height into the center of the ramp. The slot will start from the rear of the ramp and extend only far enough to allow the blade to be slid past the end of the ramp by about 3/8 inch. Mark where the slot is to terminate on both sides of the bedding block. Clamp a stop block to the router table fence to ensure the slot will terminate at the proper location.

Using a router mounted in a router table, set the fence to cut to the exact center of the width of the ramp. Raise the bit to the desired height and feed the bedding block, with the ramp on the table, into the bit. Start from the rear end of the block. Slide the iron onto the ramp and ensure there is enough room for the screw so the iron can be adjusted forward and back plus side-to-side by 1/16 inch.

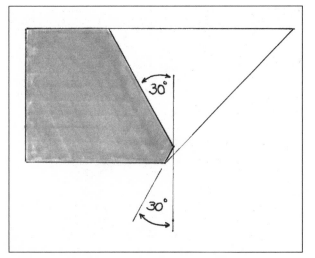

*136.   Shape the forward block with opposing 30°
cuts. The large cut allows chips to clear the plane body
while the small cut lengthens the life of the plane when
sole reflattening.*

The forward block

The remaining piece from the above cut is the forward
block. It is now cut to slope away from the iron so
there is a place for the shavings to eject and room to
insert a finger to help remove them. Every couple of
years, a wooden plane's sole must be re-flattened due
to wear from use. To increase the life of the plane body,
we will cut a counter-sloped bevel to minimize the
increase in throat clear-
ance during re-flattening.
When using an iron with
chip-breaker, this life-
extending bevel must be
omitted because it will
interfere with the chip-
breaker.

Miter the forward section
of the plane to a 30° angle
then slice 1/8 inch off the
tip at a 30° angle canted
in the other direction, as
shown in the drawing.
(136)

Cut the cheek plates

Cheek plates will be glued to each side of the central
block. Ensure that the grain of the cheek plates and
central block run in the same direction and orientation.

The cheeks are planed to 1/4 inch thick and sawn to
12 inches x 3 inches. The bottom edge of each cheek
is planed flat and square.

Drill the cross-pin hole

Drill a cross-pin hole in the cheeks 1-1/2 inches up
from the bottom and 6 inches from one end. I prefer
a 3/8 inch thick brass rod as a cross pin but steel is
great — less attractive but less expensive. To drill the
hole, place the two cheek plates on top of each other
with their bottom edges aligned exactly and secure
them together with double-sided tape. I generally drill
a marker hole with a small-diameter drill first and use
that hole to drill a 3/8 inch hole most of the way
through the cheeks. Turning the cheeks over, I complete the hole while avoiding the risk of tear-out.

Measure the total width of the plane body at the
cross-pin holes and cut the cross pin to that length.
De-burr and buff the ends of the cross pin. Slide it
into a cheek to ensure that it fits snugly.

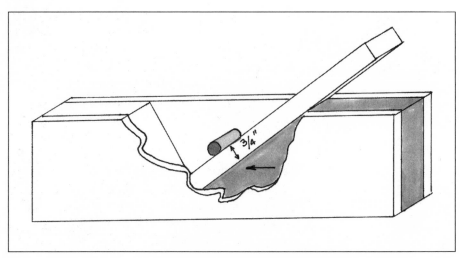

137.   Align the cross-pin holes using a thickness planed board as a gauge.

Align and assemble the plane

We will use a 3/4 inch x 1-1/4 inch board to align the cross pin in relation to the bedding ramp prior to assembly or sizing the wedge. **(137)**

Assemble the cheeks and central sections on a piece of waxed paper on a flat surface — like a table saw top, jointer bed, or a piece of 3/4 inch MDF. Insert the cross pin through the two holes in the cheeks. Place the 3/4 inch x 1-1/4 inch board on the bedding block ramp and slide the bedding block forward until the board touches the cross pin. Clamp the cheeks to the rear bedding block only, checking that the cheeks didn't shift by ensuring that the cross pin can be slid as easily as when it was inserted. Check that there are no gaps between the 3/4 inch board and the cross pin. Make alignment marks across the top of the cheeks and bedding block.

While still clamped, remove the 3/4 inch board and insert the plane iron flatly on the bedding ramp with the bevel edge down. Slide the forward block until it touches the edge of the iron. Remove the iron and tap the forward block toward the bedding block by an extra 1/32 inch. The goal is to have the entire width of the blade obstructed slightly by the forward block for later tuning of the throat clearance. Make an alignment mark across the cheek plates and forward block.

Now repeat the above operation with glue spread on both sides of the central blocks. Use the marks to realign the assembly and clamp the assembly using thick blocks of wood as clamping cauls to spread the pressure across the thin cheek plates. Make all the checks as above by reinserting the 3/4 inch board and then the plane iron to ensure that the assembly is correctly aligned. Remove the cross pin, clean off all glue squeeze-out, and let the glue set overnight.

Cut the rough wedge

Using wood the same width as the central block, saw a 1-1/2 inch thick, 4 inch long wedge blank.

Mark the 4 inch wedge blank with a vertical line 1

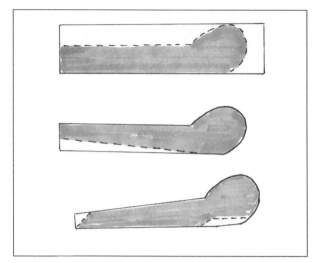

138.   *Shaping the wedge is done in several steps. The rear relief cut in the final step allows easier blade adjustment while the angled tip helps shavings eject unrestricted.*

inch from one end. This marks the enlarged head area. The total length of the wedge ramp will be approximately 3 inches. **(138)**

Set the fence of the band saw 13/16 inch from the blade. Orient the wedge block on edge with its ramp end toward the band saw blade. Cut up to the line marking the head area. Retract the block and move the fence out of the way. Cut along the vertical line, severing the waste from the wedge block.

Note: For irons with chip-breakers, set the band saw fence from the blade to 7/8 inch minus the combined thickness of the chip-breaker and iron.

Using a plane or sanding block, smooth and flatten the top surface of the wedge. Next form the large end of the wedge to a pleasing shape that will also assist in pulling it out. Next, sand or plane one side of the wedge until it fits between the cheeks without resistance.

Final-fit wedge

Refer to page 90 (Adjusting the Plane) to understand how to install and retract the wedge.

Place the plane iron onto the bedding ramp, slip the

cross pin into its holes, and slide the wedge forward. The wedge hits the cross pin but does not fit under it. The bottom surface of the wedge is now tapered to maintain a flat surface, using a hand plane or on a coarse belt sander, to allow the front of the wedge to just fit under the cross pin.

The rear end of the wedge should be no more than 1 inch past the rear end of the plane iron. Fine-tune the taper. If the front of the wedge hits the forward block, cut off the excess and shape the tip of the wedge as in (**138**). The tip of the wedge should position about 1/2 inch to 3/4 inch up from the cutting edge. If the wedge becomes too loose, glue a piece of veneer to the top of the wedge and size it again.

Retract the wedge and trim the bottom edge of the large end as in (**138**) so that it is easier to tap the iron. Don't trim past where the wedge meets the body.

Tuning the plane body

At this point we have a 12-inch long rough body of a bench plane. The first tuning of the plane is to flatten the sole. Install the iron and wedge so the iron is past the cross pin but nowhere near the sole. Tap the wedge into place until it is tight. Flatten the sole with a well-tuned bench plane or on sheet of sandpaper on a flat surface. If you choose rather to use a power jointer, do not install the iron because the iron could vibrate free and fall into the jointer knives.

Check for flatness as you did on the bedding ramp. Check for sole-to-side squareness if being used on a shooting board.

Adjust the throat clearance

The throat clearance desired for this plane is twice the thickness of a piece of copier paper or .008-inches. This will be the maximum shaving the blade can take without jamming.

Install the iron with its beveled edge down and slide it forward until it touches the forward block. Snug the wedge.

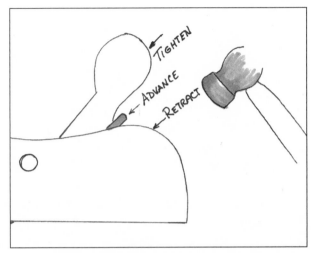

139.   *Using a hammer or mallet to adjust the blade is quickly mastered. Ensure the wedge is tight by frequently tapping it in while adjusting.*

At this point, the sole of the plane has been flattened and the iron has been installed correctly but it's unable to extend out to the sole. Hold the plane with the sole visible and look through the throat toward a bare light bulb. Note if the thin line of light visible is parallel to the edge of the iron blade. If not, square the forward block with the iron as detailed below.

Remove the iron and using a 3/4 inch chisel or a very thin fine-toothed file held at the angle of the bed, slice off only enough wood to square the forward block to the blade. Reinstall the iron. Check to see if the iron slides through the throat when it's flat on the bed. Check for parallel again. If the iron does not clear the forward block, use the light to determine where to trim. Progress in this manner until the iron just clears the forward block. Slide a folded piece of copier paper in the throat to check clearance. Trim until the iron and folded paper fit squarely but snugly through the throat.

Adjusting the plane

Lightly tap the wedge in tight while the plane is resting on a flat hardwood surface (**139**). The plane iron will advance slightly but the wooden surface will restrict its motion as the wedge is driven in. Adjust the blade until it is flush with the sole. Tapping on the rear of the plane

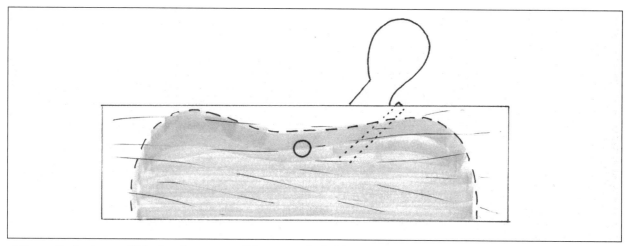

140   Body shape will be bandsawn out of the square body blank. The down-swept mid-body improves shaving ejection while the large rear curve provides a comfortable hand-hold.

body will retract the iron and the wedge slightly. Tap the wedge in lightly to retighten it. Repeat this until the blade is below the surface of the sole. Now tap the back of the plane iron to advance it slightly.

With the plane held upside down in your hand, sight down the sole from the front of the plane. Tap the rear of the iron until you just start to detect the edge of the blade. If the blade is tilted with respect to the sole, note which side of the iron is most exposed and tap on that side of the rear edge of the iron to straighten it. Retract the blade again and tap the wedge tight.

Clamp a scrap board on edge in a bench vise and attempt to plane the edge. If the blade is retracted, it will not cut. Tap the rear of the iron lightly and attempt to plane the edge. When you detect the slightest of shavings being taken, the blade is out far enough. Take a few more passes with the plane. Each time the shavings taken should increase as the plane flattens the edge and thus contacts it more often.

At first, adjusting the plane can be a tedious balancing act, but once you're practiced at the task it can be done in a minute or two, and once adjusted, it need not be readjusted often.

Once the shaving size is about right, take a long shaving from the edge of a board. If you detect any chatter, the wedge needs to be inspected to ensure that it is square to the cross pin and flat on the surface of the plane iron. If this is okay, next check that the iron bed is flat. Remove the cross pin for this check and use a small steel rule in the manner described on page 87.

Finally, check that the blade is being supported on the bedding ramp right down to the bevel. If it is unsupported, the blade will tend to chatter, leaving a poorly planed surface.

Ejecting the shavings

Shavings will start to fill the cavity of the plane. To get them out, tilt the plane over and run your finger into the cavity to dig them out. It is a quick and necessary motion when dealing with wooden planes.

If the blade is cutting too thick, the shavings will wedge in the throat of the plane. Retract the blade and readjust. If the throat doesn't seem to clear even after making finer shavings, they may be jamming against the leading edge of the wedge. Remove the wedge and look at the shavings. If they look like they were in a fight with an accordion, the front edge of the wedge must be reshaped to a smooth surface right down to the iron surface, or else you can cut the front edge of the wedge back 1/4 inch and reshape it.

Shape the body

We now have a functional plane though it is rather ugly and uncomfortable to hold. Shaping will improve this (**140**). With the plane body on its side and the wedge, cross-pin, and iron removed, use a

141, 142.   The plane described in this chapter is at left. I subsequently shortened the body to better fit my hand, as shown at right. That's the beauty of making your own planes — you can tailor them to suit yourself and your work.

band saw to form its general shape. Ensure that the upper edge of the body is at least 3/8 inch above the cross pin, to provide enough wood to reduce risk of splitting the cheeks. Contour the rear of the plane so that the end of the iron extends above the outline of the body to allow for easier adjustment. Next, round the edges of the upper body with a rasp or coarse sandpaper to make it more comfortable to hold. **(141, 142)**

The body of the plane is pushed with your hand and there is no reason why it should not be comfortable to push. Contour the rear of the plane to fit your hand, using a round rasp, spokeshave, and card scraper. Now is the time to make this plane your own.

Lightly round or chamfer the edges of the sole to reduce chipping.

Taking care of the details

When the plane is complete, apply either oil and wax, or just wax to the top of the body in order to allow the whole plane to breathe with seasonal moisture changes. If the top were sealed with a moisture-barrier finish, the sole would warp seasonally. I wax the soles of all my planes — metal and wooden — to reduce friction.

143. Like the bench plane, the shoulder plane can be tailored to fit your hand.

CHAPTER 13
Shoulder Plane

Shoulder planes are for cross-grain and end-grain finish work on joint surfaces. A significant feature is that the blade cuts the full width of the plane body, so it can cut right into the corner of the shoulder and cheek of a tenon while riding on its sole or on its side.

The wooden shoulder plane we will build excels in severing cross-grain fibers easily, but as an end-grain plane, the shavings must be extremely thin or the plane blade is apt to chatter and leave a gouged surface. There is no chip breaker because these orientations of cut do not present a risk of tearing the surface.

In wood, it is very difficult to create a rigid low-angle shoulder plane because of the cutout next to the blade, which reduces support for the cutting edge of the iron, and because of the lack of a mechanical adjuster. At 32° this plane has about as low an angle as is feasible.

Refer to page 78 in the bench plane chapter for a gen-eral discussion of wooden planes and their parts.

Start with the iron

As with the bench plane, the iron must exist before we can fully dimension the body. Note the shape of the iron in (**144, next page**). The wide head of the iron will define the body width, while the thinner tang will dictate the central block width. If you prefer to buy an iron, refer to Appendix A for sources.

Cut out the iron

Mark out the iron width with a 1-inch wide ruler, using the edges to help keep the lines parallel. Square the cutting edge to the sides by marking along the end of the ruler. Next mark the width of the tang, ensuring it is parallel to the iron sides or tapering toward the end. Mark the location of the shoulder cuts about 1 inch from the cutting edge.

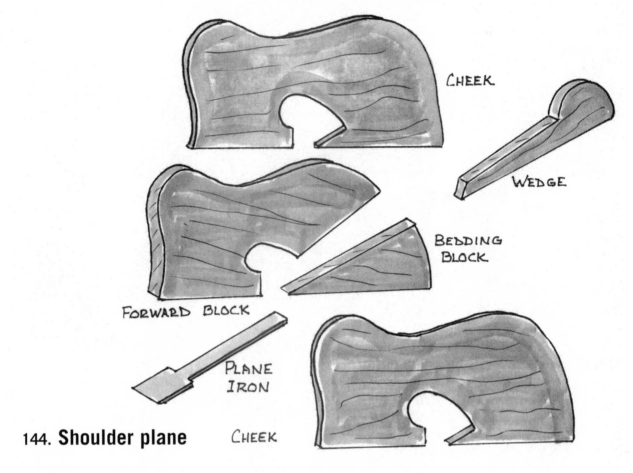

CHEEK

WEDGE

BEDDING BLOCK

FORWARD BLOCK

PLANE IRON

144. Shoulder plane

CHEEK

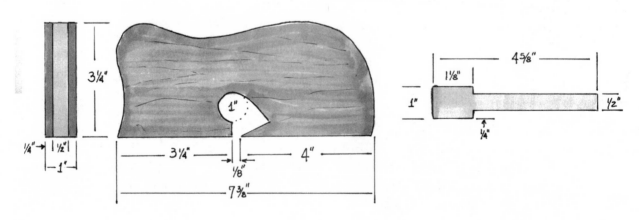

Cut list

Description	Material
Central section	10 inch x 3-1/2 inch x 1/2 inch
Cheeks	2 each 10 inch x 3-1/2 inch x 1/4 inch
Wedge	6 inch x 1/2 inch x 1-1/2 inch
Plane iron	1 inch x 4-5/8 inch x 1/8 inch steel plate

Building a shoulder plane

Procedure	Tool	Material
Cut iron	Hacksaw	Scrap circular saw blade
Square iron	File or belt sander	
Bevel cutting edge	File, disk sander, or grinder	
Sharpen iron	Sharpening stones	
Cut body blank pieces	Table saw or band saw	Maple or other hardwood
Smooth body pieces	Jointer, planer, or sandpaper	
Cut rough iron bed	Table saw or bandsaw	
Flatten iron bed	Block or bench plane or sandpaper	
Shape forward section	Band saw, file, and sandpaper	
Locate ejection hole	1 inch drill	
Shape wedge	Band saw, coping saw	Maple or other hardwood
Glue plane body	Clamps	Glue
Flatten sole	Plane, sandpaper, jointer	
Adjust throat opening	Chisel	
Shape body	Band saw, chisels, scraper	
Apply finish		Oil and wax

To cut out the blade, we will first cut the blank to full width and then remove the shoulders of the tang. **(145, 146)**

Refer to page 84 for instructions on the basics of cutting a blade out of a scrap circular saw blade. Always clamp the blade blank in a metal vise for sawing.

If your hacksawing skills are lacking, like mine, you may end up with one tang shoulder wider than the other. File the blade to symmetrically dimension the shoulders. This will be important when cutting out the cheeks. The desired head width is 1 inch and the tang at the head intersection is 1/2 inch, producing two shoulders of 1/4 inch each.

Clamp the newly cut iron into a vise and using a wide, single-cut mill file, file the iron's head edge straight. Flip it around in the vise and file the other edge parallel to the first, checking for a consistent width with calipers. File the tang tapering slightly toward the tail of the iron.

To bevel the iron cutting edge, refer to page 85.

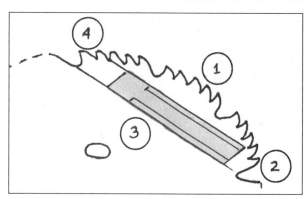

145.   *Cut iron out of a circular saw blade.*

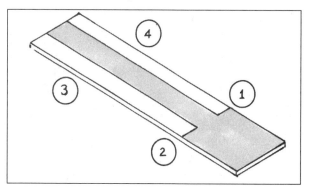

146.   *Hacksaw the blank to form tang and head.*

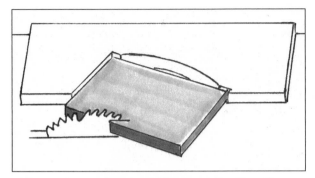

147.   A taper jig on a table saw or bandsaw for cutting the body blank. The curved relief cut in the jig helps fit the body blank to the jig.

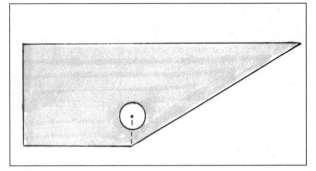

149.   Locate the drilling center for the shaving eject hole directly above the sole to taper cut transition.

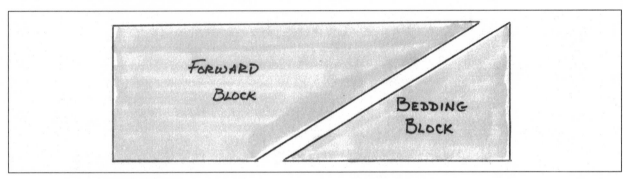

148.   The central block after the taper cut.

Cut the central block

The central body block starts out as a 12 inch long by 5-1/2 inch wide board that is 1/16 inch thicker than the width of the iron tang, resulting in a 9/16 inch thick board. We will cut it into three pieces: the wedge blank, the bedding block, and the forward block.

First, rip a 1-1/2 inch piece off of the board to be used as the wedge blank. Reserve it for later shaping. Next, saw the remaining board into two at the bedding angle. To saw it at a low angle, we can either cut free-hand with a band saw following a drawn line, or use a taper jig.

Using a taper jig as seen in **(147)** set to 32° on the table saw or band saw, cut the workpiece so that the smaller triangular piece, the bedding block, is 6 inches long at the sole. That will leave an irregular shaped board, the forward block, with about a 6 inch sole section. **(148)**

Form the cheeks

Measure the head-to-tang width difference on each side of the iron, and thickness a 24 inch x 4 inch board to those dimensions to become the cheeks of the plane body. Nominally they will be 1/4 inch thick. Plane or joint one edge flat and square to become the sole. Mark that edge and cross-cut the workpiece into two approximately 12 inch boards.

The shavings of a shoulder plane eject from the open sides of body. To create the opening, lay the forward block on a bench hook (which we make starting on page 117) with the sole against the fence. Mark a center 1-1/2 inches up on a perpendicular line from the sole/ramp corner. Drill a very small pilot hole to define the center. Align and tape the cheek boards together using double-sided cellophane tape. Again using the bench hook, align them under the forward block with the board ends even and the sole edges

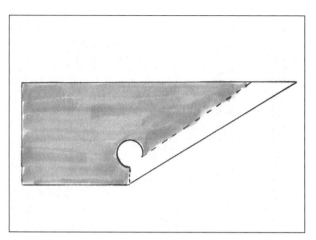

150. Cut a shallow wedge from the forward block making room for the iron wedge. Save the cut-off piece.

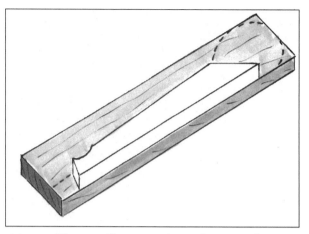

151. The cut-off piece can be used as a rough pattern for the iron wedge.

against the fence. Mark a center on the cheek using an awl or a small finish nail through the drilled hole. **(149)**

Drill a pilot hole through the taped cheeks, then use it to center a 1 inch Forstner bit and drill halfway through, flipping the workpieces over and finishing the hole from the other side to minimize tearout. Drill the 1 inch forward block hole.

Form the forward block

The forward block's angled surface is parallel to the iron ramp. We must provide room for a wedge and define a wedge taper. The wedge will angle from 1/2 inch to 3/4 inch over a 6 inch ramp. Draw a line defining that taper which starts in the hole, 1/2 inch from the sloped edge, and ends 3/4 inch from that edge. Cut to this line with a band saw or handsaw. Save the scrap to help lay out the wedge. **(150)**

Fit the iron and wedge

At this point the bedding block ramp can be flattened and squared with a well-tuned hand plane, or on a piece of sandpaper on a flat surface. Refer to page 87 for information on checking for true flat. It is crucial that the iron be supported along its entire length on the ramp, so it will not flex or slide out of place when in use.

Using wood cut earlier from the central block, fashion a wedge blank 8 inches long and 1-1/2 inches wide. Use the scrap cut from the forward block to approximate the wedge angle and mark it slightly over-size. Using a small plane or sanding block, flatten the upper ramp surface of wedge. Hold off on shaping the forward edge and relieving the rear edge. **(151)**

Assemble the plane

We now have two cheek boards and a forward block with a 1 inch hole in them, a bedding block, a rough-shaped wedge, and an iron. It is now time to assemble the body. We will glue the central body to only one cheek so we may do some further fitting before losing access to the interior.

Place one cheek board on waxed paper on a bench hook with its bottom edge against the fence. Glue and clamp only the forward block to it while aligning the holes. Apply glue to one side of the bedding block. Place the bedding block in its approximate location. Lay the iron on its side against the bedding block as intended when in use, and slide the bedding block and iron forward until the iron just touches the forward block. Clamp the bedding block in place and let the glue set. **(152, next page)**

Clear out any glue squeeze-out. Trial-fit the wedge and correct its taper so it is flush against both the for-

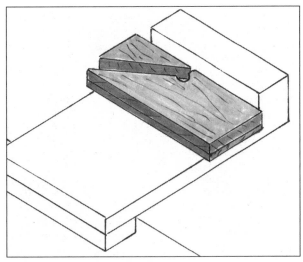

152.   Setup for gluing the body on a flat surface with a fence with which to align the sole.

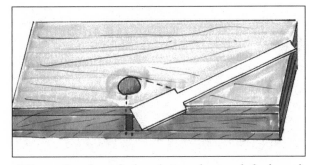

153.   Cut through the sole into the eject hole through the throat opening. Determine the length of ramp needing to be exposed to allow for the blade.

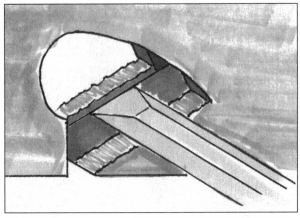

154.   Pare the rough saw cut on the cheeks level with the bedding ramp. Trim carefully, trying for a flat surface across the ramp.

ward block and plane iron. Cut and shape the front edge of the wedge (refer to **138**, page 89) so it extends approximately halfway over the wide area of the iron.

Again using the bench hook, apply glue to the forward and bedding blocks and lay the other cheek on top, aligning it with the 1 inch hole. Using a 3/4 inch board as a clamping caul, clamp everything in place and allow to dry overnight.

Cutting the iron opening

We next need to expand the shavings ejecting hole to allow the iron to bed to the ramp. Once the glue has fully set, draw a line on the cheek indicating the line of the bedding ramp. Using the plane iron as a guide, mark a point on the line 1/8-inch past where the head ends. Draw a line from the upper edge of the hole to this point. Draw a line perpendicular to the sole from the forward block edge of the throat opening to the hole. **(153)**

Using a band saw or coping saw, cut slightly above the ramp line up to the intersection of lines. Retract the blade and cut along the vertical line from the sole up to the hole. Finally, remove the waste by continuing the cut from the top of the hole back down to the ramp. There should now be an opening straight across the sole about 1/8-inch wide. This is the throat opening for the iron.

On a shoulder plane the iron is inserted from the sole, pushing the tang onto the bedding ramp. Attempt to fit the iron and wedge again. You will note the iron does not lie flush against the ramp. Remove the iron and work from both sides of the ramp, making fine chisel cuts until the cheeks are flush with the ramp. **(154)**

I set the plane on its side on a bench hook and work vertically with a 1/2 inch chisel, cutting from the ramp toward the lower cheek. Do not cut into the ramp itself nor cut the cheek areas lower than the ramp.

Once the iron lies flat on the ramp and cheeks, check

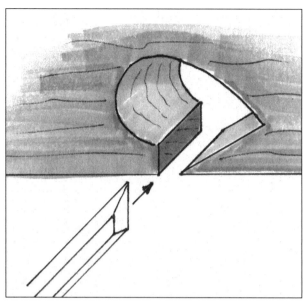

155.   *Trim throat until the blade just clears the forward edge of the throat. A tight throat will minimize chip-out when planing.*

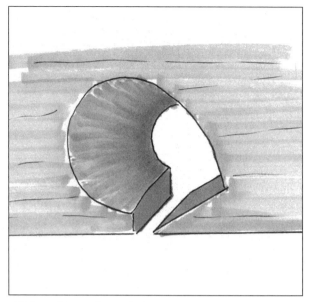

156.   *Tapered eject hole.*

to see if it can slide forward past the sole. If it cannot, use a chisel to trim the lower edge of the forward block from both sides to achieve a 1/64-inch throat clearance in front of the iron. **(155)**

Final-fit the iron

Fit the iron and wedge and adjust until the wedge tip is halfway over the widened head of the iron. If it is loose when fully inserted, glue a strip of veneer to the top of the wedge and fit it again by trimming the bottom edge.

With the wedge installed and the iron installed but retracted as far as it can go, flatten the bottom of the plane with a well-tuned handplane or by using sandpaper on a true flat surface. Check that the sole is square to the sides.

Ensure that the body width is very close to the blade width. In joinery, the shoulder plane is to be used to clean up and square the shoulders of tenons and other right-angled areas, which means the blade must be able to extend to the edge on either side of the body.

Check that the blade can be squared to the sole by sighting down the sole from the front of the plane. Adjusting involves tapping the rear end of the tang to the right or left. If there is not enough side play to the tang, it will have to be filed to a greater taper.

Ejecting the shavings

The hole for ejecting shavings may be left the way it is but if it the edges of the hole are tapered wider toward one side, the shavings will eject toward that side. This is especially useful when planing shoulders with the plane on its side.

If you are left-handed, the taper should be to the right side of the plane. For right-handed users, it would be the left. This taper can be cut using a bench chisel or a low-sweep carving gouge. Do not trim the bedding ramp, only the edges of the hole above the iron. **(156)**

Shaping the body

Next, draw a line on the side of the plane indicating where the body must be shaped so that 1/2 inch of the

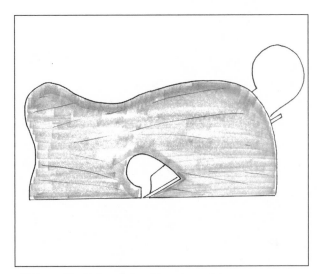

157. *Traditional shoulder plane shape.*

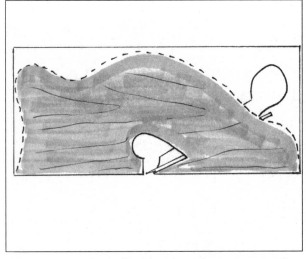

158. *Humpback shoulder plane shape improves the rigidity of the body.*

tang would be exposed. Contour the rear of the plane with a band saw to allow room for your hand to push the plane forward. See outlines below, and the finished planes at the end of this section for some ideas of contour shapes.

The thinnest point in the body affects the rigidity of the plane. That point is above the shavings hole. A humpback design, though not as elegant as the traditional shape, is stronger. **(157)**

The plane can be used with one or two hands. The forward horn assists by providing a grip point. Shape the rear to give the other hand a comfortable spot away from the tang of the iron. Rounding over the edges of the upper body will make pushing and holding the plane more comfortable. **(158)**

Adjusting the plane

The shoulder plane, like most wedge-design wooden planes, is adjusted with a mallet or hammer. Tapping the tang of the iron moves the blade forward. Tapping the rear of the wooden body makes the iron retract and loosens the wedge. Tapping the wedge tighter moves the iron very little. Tapping the edge of the tang aligns the blade squarely to the sole. See **139,**

page 90 to help understand these adjustments.

Experiment until you can cut very fine shavings across the entire iron width. If the plane chatters as it cuts, the shavings are too thick or else the iron is poorly supported.

Finishing of any wooden plane is best with linseed oil and wax, or just wax. The plane needs to react to the environment uniformly throughout its body or it will warp. Since the sole must be finished with nothing but wax, the upper body must have a breathable finish as well.

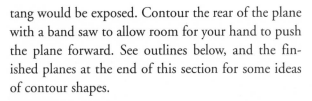

CHAPTER 14

Saw Sharpening

159.   Saw cutting wood with the two sharpening profiles produces different cutting effects.

Whether sharpening a saw for the first time or as regular maintenance, the procedure is practically identical. Look down the length of your saw's toothed edge from the front of the saw. You'll see most of what you need to know. The suite of checks is:

Is the blade straight?

Is the tooth line level?

Are the teeth evenly set?

Are the teeth sharp?

This chapter will guide you through the process of sharpening saws with rip or crosscut teeth. **(159)**

Build a sharpening vise

Normal bench and metal vises are poorly suited to holding a saw during sharpening, thus building a special vise is in order. The vise consists of two wood arms hinged together at the bottom, with wide boards attached perpendicularly at the other end to create the jaws. **(160)**

Measure the length of the saws you are interested in sharpening. These will determine the size of the jaws

of your sharpening vise. If the saws vary greatly in length, you may want to build several vises. We will be building a vise to sharpen our 6 inch backsaw and 12 inch bucksaw.

To create the jaws, cut two boards to 9 inches x 2-1/4 inches, and cut a 30° angle off each end starting 3

160.   Sharpening vise.

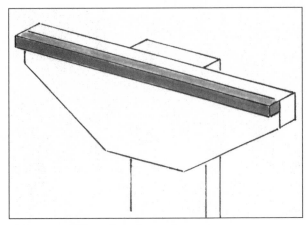

161.   *Jaw boards with jaw face strips.*

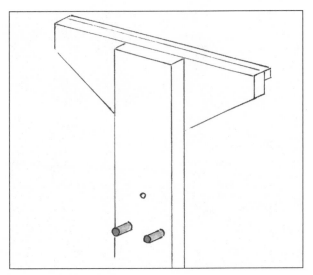

162.   *Slip stop pegs.*

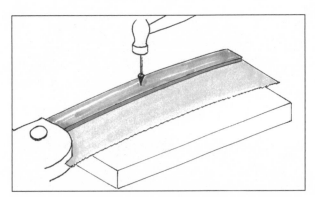

163.   *Straighten a sideways bowed backsaw blade by tapping on the blade back not the blade itself. This is a gentle operation that if done aggressively, could ruin a saw.*

inches from the end. The small blade on the backsaw restricts its insertion in the vise, so a cutout to allow clearance for the handle will improve the vise's usefulness. Cut as needed for your particular saws.

Cut two 2-1/2 inch x 3/4 inch arm boards to 24 inches long. Cut 2 inch pieces off each board and glue them to the end of each board. With three screws each, attach the jaw boards to the other end of the arm boards on the same side as the small piece.

Mount a hinge on the small blocks, with the knuckle toward the end, to attach the two arms.

Backsaws require jaw faces added to allow for the wider blade-back. Cut two thin strips off a 1/2 inch pine board to be used as jaw faces. Glue the strips to the upper edges of the jaws. If needed, bevel them so they close squarely. **(161)**

If you would like the vise to work as a stand-alone tool, install a screw and wing nut through the arms about three inches below the jaws to tighten them. When positioning the clamping screw, take into account where the fulcrum beam of your bucksaw is located. You want the saw frame to be fully assembled and tensioned when working on the blade. The vise can be permanently screwed to your sharpening station, or it can be portable with screw holes to allow it to attach to a sawhorse when needed. Otherwise, the sharpening vise can be held in a bench vise. You may wish to drill two holes in the arms to accept removable dowels that will keep the saw vise from slipping through the wood vise jaws. **(162)**

Straighten the blade

To straighten the blade the degree of bend needs to be considered. If the cutting edge has a sharp kink, it will have to be hammered straight by tapping the blade edge and checking for straightness. Lay the saw blade flat on a hardwood surface and hammer lightly at the offending location.

If the blade has a gradual bow to one side, correct it by lightly hammering the blade back instead of the

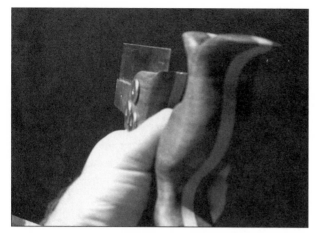

164. Sighting down the row of teeth may help determine if the saw needs preliminary leveling.

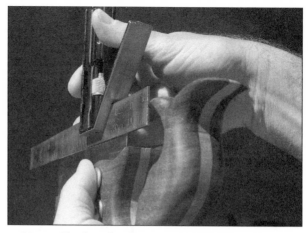

165. Checking level using a straightedge is more accurate but is difficult to see unless you view the saw and straightedge at an acute angle.

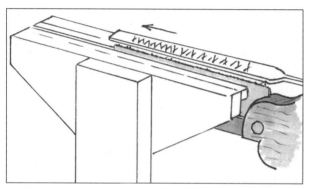

166. Leveling the saw teeth with a file. Wear protective gloves so leveling the teeth is all you do.

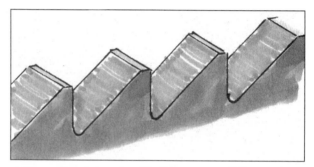

167. Leveled teeth will all have a small flat at the point. When the point is once again restored, the teeth will be sharp and level.

blade itself. Lay the blade with the bow up and tap midway along the back. Check frequently. **(163)**

Kinked bucksaw and bowsaw blades should be replaced, though a bow will typically be eliminated when the blade is tensioned.

Level the teeth

The row of teeth must all be at the same level or the blade will seem to bounce along while sawing or retracting from a cut. One way to check for level is to sight down the tooth edge from the handle while holding the saw upside down. **(164)**

When checking a bucksaw or bowsaw, do it while the blade is mounted and tensioned in the saw frame.

Putting a straightedge along the teeth is a very good check as well. View the saw and straightedge at an angle and you will more easily detect edge irregularity. **(165)**

To level all the teeth, clamp the saw, teeth up, in a vise. Because a backsaw has a thick back, clamping will require holding two long batten sticks next to the tooth edge of the saw while clamping so that they retain the saw edge. An alternative is to build the sharpening vise discussed earlier in this chapter. **(166)**

Run a long, fine, single-cut file lengthwise across the top of the teeth from the rear of the saw toward the front. Repeat until you see a flat spot on top of all the teeth, indicating a leveled saw. **(167)**

Set the teeth

When a saw cuts, the teeth sever the wood with their sharp points and edges, creating what is called a kerf. The loose wood fibers ride in the gullets between the

168.   *Setting teeth on a saw is nothing more than bending them over. The important detail is that each tooth must be set identically for a saw to work optimally.*

169.   *A saw set tool makes accurate tooth-setting simple.*

170.   *Mark alternate teeth with a marker so you don't lose track of which tooth is next to be set.*

teeth until the blade clears the piece of wood. The force of cutting distorts the wood fibers as the teeth slice through, but they spring back minutely after the teeth pass. As the saw progresses down in the cut, those fibers drag on the saw blade, making it difficult to move the saw.

The solution is to bend the teeth so they are alternately set to either side. This widens the kerf and provides the clearance needed to saw without experiencing drag.

Sight down each side of the saw and notice if any of the teeth protrude beyond the others. If so, these teeth will create a ragged surface by tearing at the wood beyond the other teeth, and they will leave scratches in the surface instead of cleanly severed wood fibers. **(168)**

Mark the protruding teeth, lay the saw flat on a piece of hardwood, and use an oilstone as a hone. Run the stone lightly from the rear to the front over the sides of the teeth until all the teeth appear to have similar sets. Do this evenly on both sides of the blade.

If the saw blade seems to bind when in use and you have already checked and straightened it, the saw will need resetting.

Tools called saw sets are designed specifically for this task and have a dial marked with settings for different teeth per inch (TPI). The readings are for cross-cut saws. Rip saw sets are smaller so use a setting of 16 TPI for the 12-TPI or 13-TPI backsaw we made. **(169)**

Before starting to use the saw set, it is advisable to mark every other tooth with a permanent marker. Turn the saw around and, noting which teeth were marked on the other side, mark every other tooth again. Every tooth has a mark, half on one side and half on the other. **(170)**

Adjust the saw set's dial to the desired setting. Slide the saw blade into the loop of the saw set, align a marked tooth with the punch point, and squeeze the handle. Repeat for all the teeth marked on that side. Turn the saw around and do the alternately marked

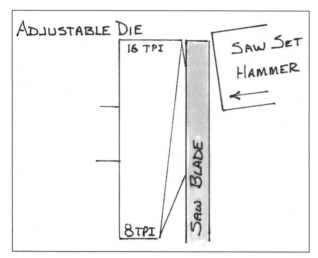

171.   Setting the teeth with a saw set. The handle pushes the saw set hammer against the adjustable die. When a tooth of a blade is between them, it gets bent to a precise angle.

172   Setting the teeth.

teeth. Sight down the edge of the blade and see if there are any teeth that seem to stick out. Try to understand why they do and correct your procedure. The aberrant tooth set will be corrected when finished sharpening. **(171, 172)**

Sharpen the teeth

A sharp chisel cuts wood cleanly with less fiber tearout. A sharp plane leaves a smooth surface. A sharp saw is no different and essential to making well fitting joints. It seems that few woodworkers ever attempt sharpening of a saw. I suspect this is because they are unaware of how it is done.

To sharpen a saw, we will use a 4 inch X slim or 5 inch XX slim taper triangular file, the right size for saws with 12 tpi or more. This is the same file used to make the blade for the backsaw. The triangular file has three surfaces making 60° angles to each other, which determines the geometry of the sharpened teeth.

I prefer my joinery saw to be sharpened for rip sawing. When making joints, I cut a lot of end-grain and only a little cross-grain. This also minimizes my time at the sharpening bench.

	Rip cut	Cross cut
Starting a cut	no	yes
Cutting long grain	yes	no
Cutting end grain	yes	no
Cross cutting	no	yes
Ease of sharpening	yes	no

When deciding which way to sharpen the saw, consider the orientation of the wood you are likely to be cutting. If you have two similar backsaws, you might sharpen one as cross-cut and one as rip. Actually, some craftsmen have sharpened saws with both styles of sharpening on one saw. Let's list the pros and cons of each. (table above)

Rip saws use a gouging action to remove wood by digging down into the fibers with the straight edged points of the teeth. The sides of the teeth do cut but are minor wood removing surfaces.

Cross-cut saws have angled sharp edges to efficiently slice across the wood fibers. They present a pointed edge to the wood. This is not an aggressive cutting surface.

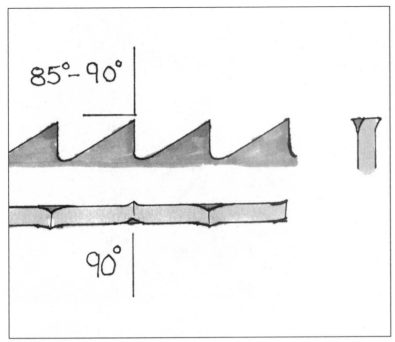

173.   *Rip saw sharpening angles act like multiple chisels. 90° is a more aggressive cutting angle than 85°.*

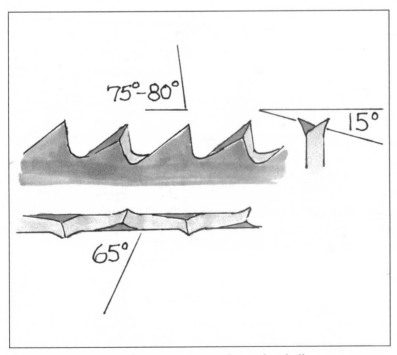

174.   *Cross-cut tooth geometry is complex and a challenge to master. The tips of the cross-cut saw slice through the wood fibers.*

If this is the first time you are sharpening the backsaw, you will note that the tops of most of the teeth are flat. This is more or less the condition of any saw that has just been leveled. The difference is that when resharpening a saw, the teeth have already been set. Thus, on a newly made saw, we will need to set the teeth, level the teeth, and finally sharpen them.

Sharpening the rip saw

It is tempting to sharpen the whole saw by filing from one side, but the major disadvantage is that you will create burrs on only one side of the teeth. Old timers insist you file every other tooth and then turn the saw around to file the alternate teeth, but they don't agree on which tooth is sharpened from which side. **(173)**

Install your triangular file's tang into a handle, otherwise you risk running the tang into your hand. Hold the file so that the front edge of each tooth will be filed with a vertical surface of the file. Hold the handle in one hand and the tip of the file in the other. Keep the file level and square to the blade. Take only forward strokes to keep from prematurely dulling the file. Don't push too hard or you may change the set of the teeth. Let the file cut slowly and smoothly.

Stroke the tooth so that the file applies pressure to the front of the tooth as well as to the sloped back of the previous tooth. Proceed down the row of teeth making incremental progress, versus trying to totally sharpen one tooth before moving on. Repeat until you no longer see the flat spot on the top of the tooth, which means it is fully sharpened. Repeat on all the teeth. When done, run an oilstone lightly down each side of the blade from back to front to knock off the burrs. You now own a sharp rip saw.

The true proof is to get some wood and saw off a small piece. Did the saw cut quickly? Was the forward stroke smooth? Does the cut surface seem smooth? If any of the answers are no, read this section over again.

Sharpening for cross-cut

The cross-cut sharpening technique is more complicated than rip sharpening because the teeth have a more complex shape. It is still rather simple once you understand the geometry of the tooth, so let's investigate that first.

Unlike the rip-saw tooth, the cross-cut tooth is filed to a pyramid shape. The beveled surface is the inside edge of the tooth. If the tooth is leaning away, the bevel is on the near side. Study (**174**) to visualize these concepts. To create this shape of tooth, clamp the saw in a vise and find the first tooth that is bent away from you. You are looking at its inside edge.

To sharpen the inside surface into a triangle, set the file in the gullet in front of the tooth at a 65° angle so that the file handle is toward the saw handle. Tilt the file so the surface facing the front of the tooth is tilted about 75° to 80° toward the tooth. Then lower the file handle by an inch so the file stroke is upward about 15°. Stroke only in the forward direction, applying even pressure to both the front of the tooth and the back of the tooth in front of it. Make several strokes before moving on to the next tooth bent away from you, and repeat down the length of the saw.

Now do what the old timers say: turn the saw around. Again you are looking at the inside surface of the teeth that are bent away from you. You should notice that those teeth have a shiny surface cut into them. That was made by the strokes you just did. We will do what we already did on the other side of the saw, except it will be at the reverse angle. Find the first tooth bent

175. New saw handle.

A new handle

Along with sharpening your saws, how about giving them new handles? The instructions on page 63 can apply to any tool with a D-style handle. The original handle in the photo was a production item meant to fit anyone from a 7-year-old kid to a 600-pound gorilla — far too big for me. Tailoring a handle requires applying the handle-sizing instructions to the original mounting outline and screw layout.

Its new handle made my panel saw a favorite part of my everyday tool kit. As a bonus, I can tell right away that this is my rip saw — I re-handled my crosscut saw in cherry.

away from you. Set the file in the gullet in front of the tooth at a 65° angle so that the file handle is toward the saw handle. Tilt the file surface facing the front of the tooth to 75° to 80° toward the tooth and drop the file handle abut one inch. You know what to do next.

When you are done filing, check to see if there are any flat spots on the tops of the teeth. If there are, once again file those teeth until the flat spot just disappears. Try to file all the teeth each time, to maintain even spacing.

Lightly wipe the sides of the saw teeth with a flat-folded piece of 220-grit sandpaper running from the rear of the blade forward. As with the rip saw, take a test cut and determine if the saw cuts satisfactorily.

176.   Shooting board, page 120.

177. Bench hook, page 117.

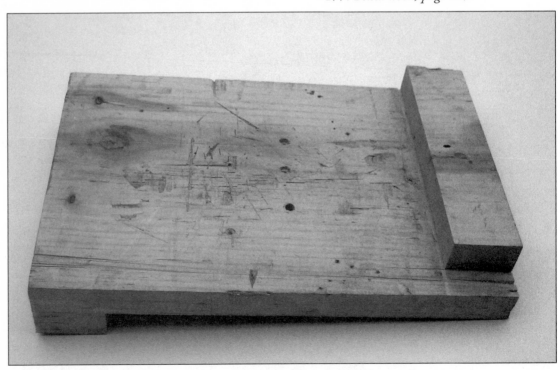

Holding tools

178.   Cam clamp, page 110.

How often have you wished for just a couple more clamps or some other way of holding all those pieces steady for a few minutes? While we cut apart or glue together our wood pieces, holding on to them is a main theme in woodworking. Holding tools are lowly but extremely important members in the craftsman's tool family.

While first learning to build guitars, I was introduced to the wooden cam clamp. This is the traditional clamp of the luthier. So I bought four of them. Then I bought another four of them. Soon my clamp budget ballooned and I resorted to rubber bands and tape. It didn't take me long to learn to make these essential tools.

Reducing the cost of acquiring clamps can make a big difference in which projects are affordable and which are out of range. The cam clamp can be made out of

small cut-offs laying around the shop, plus some readily available and inexpensive metal or even wood for the bars.

The bench hook and shooting board are almost unknown to the average woodworker. This is a pity since even in a power-tool shop, these simple tools can speed work and preserve your work surfaces. They can be made for general use or purpose-made for a single use, since the bench hook can be made of almost any wood species including the most highly evolved, that is, plywood.

Though there are many more holding tools we could build, these few are all that are needed to accomplish joinery.

179. You can make cam clamps in a wide range of sizes.

CHAPTER 15
Cam Clamp

Some say you can't have too many clamps. A shop-made cam clamp is a low-cost solution to an otherwise expensive statement. The configuration described here is useful in a variety of clamping situations, plus I have found many other applications, such as jigs, for the cam-clamping head alone.

Cam clamps consist of a cam head, a stationary head, and a bar extending between them. The clamp can exert up to 400 pounds of pressure in the size discussed here.

Selecting a bar

The steel bar we will use is 1/4 inch thick, 1 inch wide, and 12 inches long, resulting in a clamp opening of 8 inches. The throat depth can be between 4 inches and 10 inches, depending on your needs. I like the 5 inch depth for all but very special situations.

For larger clamp openings, it is important to increase the width and thickness of the bar to minimize the

amount it bends. A 20 inch jaw opening using a 1/4 inch by 1 inch bar is as large as I would go. As the clamps get larger, the weight increases substantially until the tool becomes unwieldy.

A wooden bar is an excellent alternative for making a really lightweight clamp with the sacrifice of reduced clamping pressure and durability. A strong and dense wood like hickory or beech would be good bar material.

Making the clamp heads

Our clamp heads will be 7 inches long, 1-3/4 inch high, and 3/4 inch thick, made of a hardwood like ash, white oak, hickory, or maple. One head will be stationary at the end of the bar while the cam head will slide freely on the bar.

Described below are two methods of head construction, either solid wood or laminated.

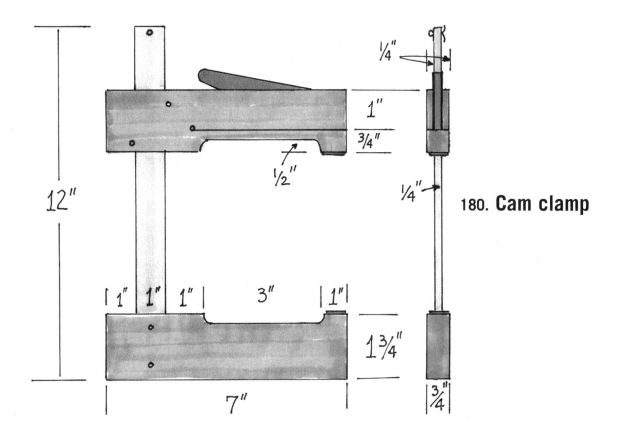

180. **Cam clamp**

Making a cam clamp

Procedure	Tools	Materials
Cut bar to size	Hacksaw	1" x 1/4" x 12" metal bar
(1) Shape solid cam head	Plunge router, mortising jig	1" x 1-3/4" x 3/4"
	Hollow chisel mortiser	
	Hand mortising or tenoning jig	
(2) Laminated cam head	Band saw	3 each 7" x 1-3/4" x 1/4" hardwood
Cut cam slot	Table saw, dado blade	
Cut bar mortise	Table saw, dado blade	
Form jaw relief	1-inch drill, band saw	
Cut jaw slot	Band saw	
Form cam	Band saw, rasp, disk sander	
Install cam	1/16 inch drill, hammer	
Attach head to bar		
Install stress pins		
Attach anti-mar pad		

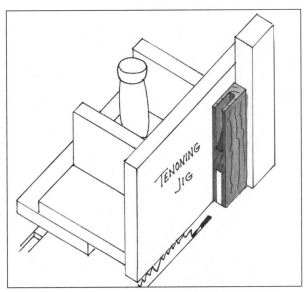

181.   Creating the bar mortise using a tenoning jig and dado blades. Multiple passes with a regular blade will do the same job – just slower.

Solid wood clamp heads

To make the heads from solid wood, we will machine a bar mortise and a cam slot using the tools of your choice.

Cutting the bar mortise

Cut two 7 inch x 1-3/4 inch x 3/4 inch pieces of wood as the two head blanks.

We will position a 1 inch x 1/4 inch bar mortise 1 inch from the end of each head. Your choices for making the mortise are a plunge router and mortising jig, a hollow chisel mortiser, hand mortising, or a tenoning jig.

To use the tenoning jig to cut the bar mortise on the table saw, we cut a slot through the end of the head and then glue in a filler piece to enclose the bar mortise. Because it is a deep slot, we will make multiple cuts with a regular blade instead of using a dado cutter.

Clamp the head blank vertically in the tenoning jig. Set the jig to cut just off the center of the thickness of the head. Raise the blade to a height of 2 inches and pass the head blank through the blade, then turn it

around and make a second pass to widen the slot. Check the width against the clamp bar you are using. Move the jig around one-half the needed width increase, and repeat the two cuts. You can always make extra cuts to make the mortise wider, and we want the mortise to be a close fit to the bar so it may be better to make small incremental cuts. **(181)**

Plane a 1-3/4 inch wide board to 1/4 inch thickness. Slide the piece of wood into the slot to capture the bar. Mark and cut it to the required length. Apply glue to both faces and slide it into place. Capture the bar snugly on the stationary head but leave 1/16 inch clearance on the cam head. Clamp and remove the bar. After the glue dries, cut the filler piece flush with the end of the heads. **(184)**

If using any of the other methods, make the mortise hole exactly the width of the bar on one head and 1/16 inch wider on the other, to allow the cam head to slide freely along the bar. Mark the heads so you will know which is the cam head and which is the stationary head.

Cutting the cam slot

We will next make the cam slot using a dado cutter or multiple passes with a small-diameter saw blade. Dado sets of 6-inch or 8-inch diameter work best for 7-inch to 10-inch clamp head lengths. A 10-inch dado can be used on 10-inch and longer heads. **(182)**

Using a 1/4 inch wide dado, set the table saw fence so the dado cut is dead center on the cam head thickness. Clamp a long thin stick to the fence extending toward the blade, between the blade and the fence. Position it to restrict travel so the crest of the blade enters no further than 1 inch into the head. Raise the blade to 1 inch and cut the cam slot in the cam head only.

Laminated clamp heads

Making three-layer laminated clamp heads differs from solid heads in the way we make the bar mortise and cam slot, because they can be pre-formed in the central lamination section.

Cut seven pieces of wood to 7 inches x 1-3/4 inch x 1/4 inch. The 1/4 inch dimension was selected to match the bar thickness. The woods may be of different species but they should all be hardwood with similar grain orientation. One of the central pieces will now have the cam slot and bar mortise features cut into it, while the other central piece will have only the bar mortise cut. The seventh piece will become the cam.

To allow for a cam to be installed, draw a line 1 inch from an edge (this will become the top edge) extending about 1 inch in from one end. Next draw a 30° line from the drawn line to the center top edge.

Two inches from the other end of the jaw, draw a line across the width of the workpiece. Do the same on the central section of the stationary cam head. With a table saw and miter gauge set at 90°, cut across each blank at the 2 inch mark. Retain both pieces you have cut off. **(183)**

With a band saw or handsaw, cut along the diagonal line. Retract the blade and cut the line starting from the end toward the diagonal cut. Discard the waste.

Apply glue to the three-piece sandwich of the cam head, positioning the central section so the cam slot cut is aligned on one end. Clamp the assembly lightly over the cam slot area and slide in the metal bar. Next, slide the cutoff end toward the bar leaving 1/16 inch clearance on one side. Tighten a second clamp over the end piece and remove the bar, which should slip out of the mortise with little resistance, and let the glue set overnight. **(184)**

Build up the stationary head as you just did the cam head but don't leave any clearance in the bar hole. Retract the bar and allow the glue to set overnight.

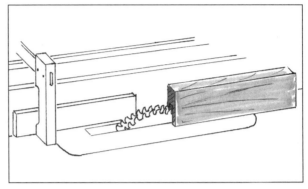

182.   Cutting the cam slot on a table saw requires setting a stop to limit the cut.

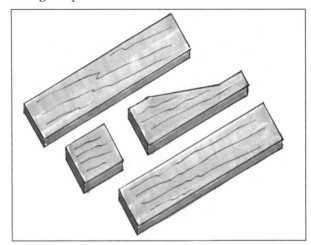

183.   Layout of the parts for a laminated cam head. The outer two layers require little milling while the interior layer contains all the features.

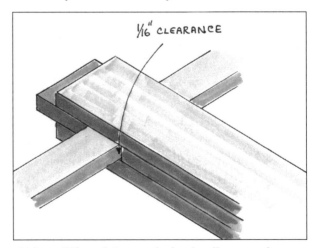

184.   When gluing up the heads, allow some bar clearance on the cam head and none at all on the stationary head.

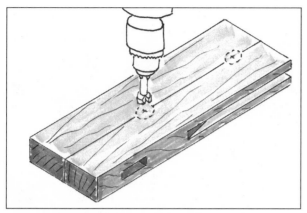

185. *Relieving the jaws starts with drilling two holes while the two heads are clamped jaw to jaw. Center the hole right on the interface between the jaws.*

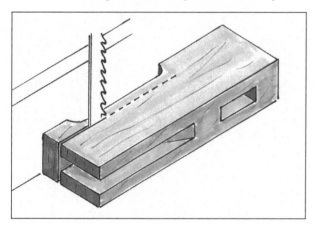

186. *Cut the jaw slot on a bandsaw by aligning the bottom of the cam slot with the blade. Stop the cut an inch or so away from the bar mortise.*

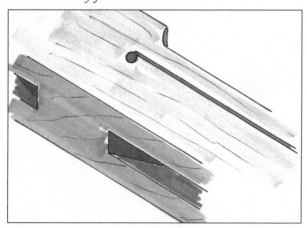

187. *Drill a slot relief hole to reduce risk of splitting the jaw when in use. The hole is offset from the slot.*

For either solid wood or laminated head

Regardless of which means you chose to make the heads, the following procedures apply.

Relieving the jaws

Clamp the heads together lengthwise along their lower edges and locate points 1 inch and 4 inches from the jaw end. With a 1-inch drill, make a hole at each point centered on the joint between the two boards, resulting in a half-circle being cut into each board. **(185)**

Set the fence of a band saw 1/2 inch from the outside of the blade and remove the scrap between the holes on both heads. This established a recess for clamping over minor obstructions, and increases flexibility of the jaw.

Cutting the jaw slot

The jaw of the cam head must to be able to open and close to apply pressure to the clamped object. Give it a little flex by sawing a slot along the length of the relieved area just below the cam slot. Set the band saw fence to have the blade align with the flat bottom of the cam slot when the head is lying on its side. The slot is cut to within 1 inch of the bar mortise. The jaw below the line should be 1/4 inch thick at its narrowest over the relieved area. **(186)**

We terminate the slot by drilling a 3/16-inch hole at the end and just above the jaw slot. This distributes the splitting forces so the head does not split when in use. **(187)**

Shaping the cam

Shape the cam out of a 1/4 inch x 1 inch x 5 inch piece of wood, or the piece left from lamination process, creating a round end and tapered end. Use a compass to mark a 1/2 inch radius circle at one end of the cam and trim accurately to the line with a band

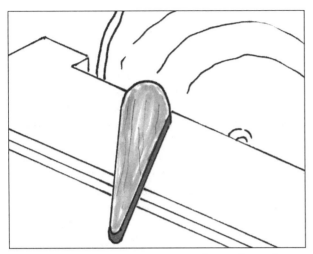

188.   *Shape the cam into a smooth circular end on a stationary sanding disk.*

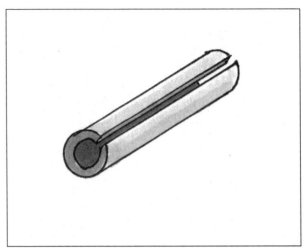

189.   *Slotted spring pin.*

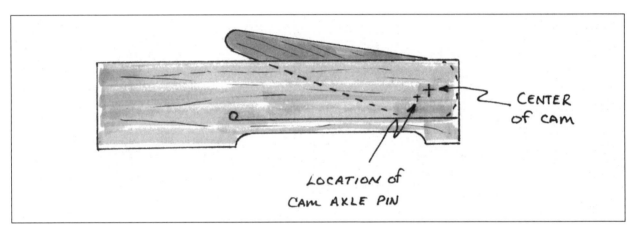

190.   *The camming action is produced by locating the axle offset from the center of the cam end.*

saw, scroll saw, or disk sander. Taper the cam handle to the other end. Sand the cut cam. **(188)**

Installing the cam

A cam is an eccentric circle, meaning the center of the circular end of the cam is not the center of rotation. If the cam was made with a 1-inch diameter rounded end, the center of the rounded end is 1/2 inch from the edge. To make it operate with a camming action, we will place the center of rotation 1/8 inch below and 1/8 inch further away from the end of the cam. **(190)**

On the side of the cam head where the cam is to be installed, mark 5/8 inch in from the end and 3/8 inch up from the jaw slot. This is the center of rotation of the cam and the axle pin location. Insert the cam into the slot with its handle resting on the slope within the slot and the circular end just even with the end of the head. Drill a 1/16 inch hole through both head and cam at the cam axle pin location.

Laying the cam head on a bench hook, hammer a 3/4 inch long, 3/32 inch slotted spring pin into the hole (refer to Appendix A for sources of slotted spring pins). Ensure the cam rotates freely. If the pin is too long, sand the end off after it is installed. **(189)**

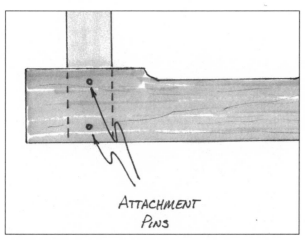

191.   Attach the stationary head with two slotted spring pins. Drill the holes large enough so the pins will fit in them only when compressed.

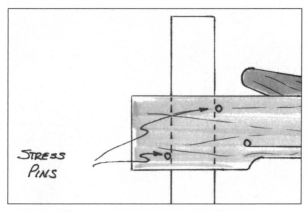

192.   The stress pins on cam head reduce wood compression and thus lengthen tool life. The pins must be positioned just beyond the edges of the bar mortise.

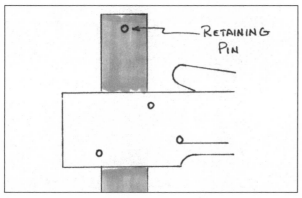

193.   The retaining pin — or a loop of wire — keeps the moving cam head from falling off the bar.

Attach the heads to the bar

The bar is the last thing to be fit to the heads. One head slides on the bar while the other is stationary. If the bar has rough edges, they will actually increase holding power so don't bother buffing them smooth.

To attach the stationary head, drill two 3/32-inch holes in the head centered on the bar mortise 1/2 inch from the edges. Slide the end of the bar into the mortise even with the edge of the head. Now use the two holes to drill two centers into the bar. Remove the bar and complete drilling the holes. Reinstall the bar, align the holes and hammer in two spring pins to secure it to the head. **(191)**

Slide the bar into the mortise of the cam head. It should fit with a little clearance. With the bar inserted, drill two 1/16 inch holes for the spring pins as depicted in **(192)**. The holes are located so they just miss entering the bar mortise, thus not decreasing the opening width. These pins will reduce the long-term compression of the wood around the bar, thus lengthening the useful life of the clamp.

With the clamp assembled, drill one more hole at the end of the bar to install a retaining pin so the free cam clamp head does not slide off. Insert a cotter pin or spring pin in the hole. **(193)**

Finishing touches

My cam clamps have cork squares glued onto the face of the heads so they will not mar the work being clamped. Leather or even softwood can be used in place of cork. I saw off sections of wine bottle corks and glue them on. The only other source of cork I know of requires me to buy large sheets when I only need small squares. **(194)**

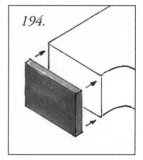

194.

Finish the clamp if you wish, or leave it as raw wood like I do.

195. *A bench hook holds the work, helps guide the saw, and protects the bench surface.*

CHAPTER 16

Bench Hook

The concept of the bench hook is probably as old as the workbench on which it is used. Actually it could be older because it serves as a means of holding a workpiece and could well be used anywhere there is an edge (e.g. stair tread, top of a stump). The lowly bench hook is little used in a modern shop equipped with all form of power tools but when it comes to hand work, it still shines in simplicity of design and sheer usefulness.

Building the hook – 1 2 3

A bench hook is made as a board of the length and width you require for the projects you typically build, or for a particular project you are about to do. The bench hook given here is a useful size for general woodworking.

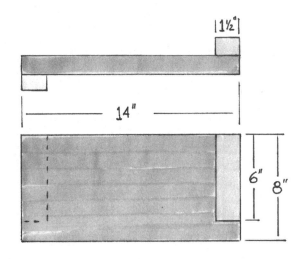

196. Bench Hook

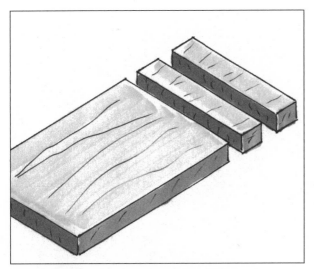

197.   *The three pieces of a bench hook can be cross-cut from any scrap board. The length and width are arbitrary. The fence pieces must be at least 1 inch wide.*

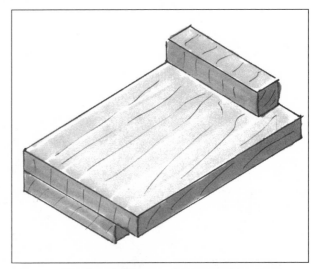

198.   *The fence is shortened on one side to act as a cut-off shelf that saves the surface of the bench below. Notice how the bench hook is reversible by just flipping it over.*

Start with a smooth, flat board about 3 inches longer than your desired bench hook. For our 14 inch x 8 inch x 3/4 inch bench hook, we will need to start with a 17 inch x 8 inch board. Square the ends using a miter gauge or cutoff sled on the table saw. Then saw two 1-1/2 inch pieces from the end of the board. The two pieces will be then shortened from 8 inches to 6 inches with the use of the miter gauge and table saw. **(197)**

If you are right-handed, glue and clamp one of the shortened pieces to the board, aligned with the left edge and end. Lefties need to align the fence to the right edge. After the glue sets, flip the assembly over, glue and clamp the other cut off to the bottom side at the opposite end, again aligning the board to the left edge. Reviewing your work, you will note that the bench hook looks the same when seen from either side. Both surfaces can be used. **(198)**

Three board sections face-glued together and there it is. Nothing could be simpler. But let's take a close look at some details that will make the hook into a durable, flexible tool for making joints as well as for general woodworking.

I can't recall the source of the statement but it went something like, "A workbench is meant to be worked on, not in." The gist of the thought is to preserve the workbench by avoiding drilling, cutting, or chopping into its surface. This, and holding things in place, are the primary functions of the bench hook. Let's take them one at a time.

Drilling with a hand-held power drill or with a bit brace may require that the bit penetrate through the entire workpiece, emerging on the bottom surface. To keep the outfeed side of the drill hole from splintering, it is necessary to support the wood surface with a backing board known as a sacrificial board. The bench hook is just that type of board. After it has been extensively perforated, the surface will need to be renewed, or a new hook made. If the bench hook is made of scrap wood, building a new one is a very practical strategy.

When crosscutting a workpiece with a handsaw, the bench hook is the easiest way to hold it. Just place the workpiece up against the fence using your free hand. The fence on the bottom of the bench hook will hold the bench hook at the edge of the bench using the same force you are already applying to hold the workpiece up against the fence. Align the cut so that the saw misses the fence, or else saw directly into the fence to reduce tearout. You can treat the bench hook as expendable.

I use a bench hook when I am chopping out tails and pins for dovetail joints. I will make a hook long enough to fit my workpiece, and use its fence to hold the work. The bench hook fence is a convenient stop for holding the wood when paring horizontally, and I can chop vertically with full support behind the wood being worked. When cutting tails, vertical paring can be done knowing the piece is fully supported from below and if the chisel slips, no harm is done.

If the above operations were conducted on the surface of my expensive European-style cabinetmaker's bench, it would not be long before the bench went into my scrap bin waiting to heat the house.

The art in tool-making

Tool as a word leaves an impression of a utilitarian and even grungy item. Recently there have been several wonderful books written with lovely pictures of tools that are as much artwork as work item. Oh how these books dispel those misimpressions.

Contrasting woods, figured wood, shiny brass and careful finishing can make any tool within this book elegant as well as functional. It is for you to bring out the real art in tool-making by adding the touches that display your own sense of design. Try inlay, carving, beading, or any other embellishment you desire to add.

Take risks. These are small projects that can be rebuilt if the first effort falls short of your mental image. Challenge yourself to add those elegant touches that would be too risky on a project that has already taken countless hours. Stretch yourself and attempt those intimidating bellflower or mariner's star inlays, or inlayed stringing. Work for the joy of discovery and soon you will need to be building more tools to accomplish ever-more ambitious artistry.

199. *The shooting board helps plane the end of the wood square.*

CHAPTER 17

Shooting Boards (90° & 45°)

The shooting board is a variation on the bench hook with the added features of being accurately aligned and having a shelf or ledge on which a plane can ride. The idea is to create a true and straight reference edge that is exactly perpendicular to the fence, so that when a workpiece is held against the fence, a plane laid on its side may be used to true up the end of the workpiece.

Back when it was common to rip a board lengthwise or to cross-cut to length using a hand saw, the shooting board was the indispensable tool that would actually square and straighten ends and edges.

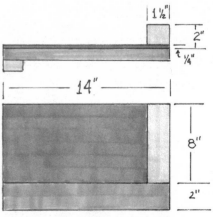

200. **Shooting Board**

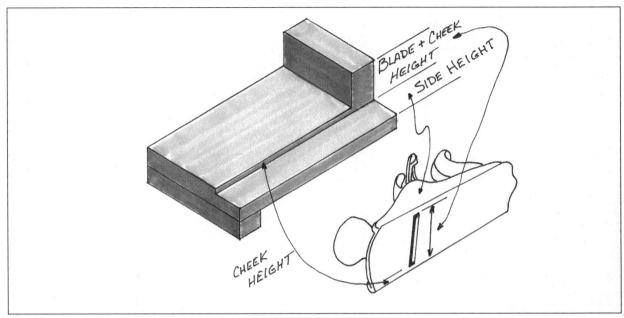

201. *Fitting the board to a specific plane by fully supporting the plane body and ensuring that the upper deck is higher than the plane deck by the cheek width of the plane plus at least 1/16 inch.*

Some preliminary measurements

A shooting board is intended to be used with a miter plane. The miter plane is a rare tool to own, so most people use a bench plane or a wooden plane for shooting board work. Whichever plane you choose from your arsenal of tools, make the shooting board to fit that exact plane and no other.

My tool of choice is the #4 bench plane. The sides of the plane have been squared to the sole, which is critical to the use of the shooting board. To start the shooting board, we must make a couple of measurements on the plane, but first we will discuss squaring the plane.

Squaring a plane body

You can square the sides of a wooden plane using a jointer, hand plane, or with judicious use of the stationary sander. A metal plane is most practical to square on a stationary sander. Allow the plane body to cool between sanding passes since excess heat can warp the metal. Lay the metal plane on a metal sur-

face after each pass on the stationary sander to accelerate its cooling. Check for square often.

Measure the cheek of the plane sole from the edge of the blade opening to the edge of the plane and add 1/16 inch. This dimension defines minimum upper deck height in relation to the plane deck — the ledge where the plane rides. Next, measure the width of the sole of the plane from the edge to the far edge of the iron, to find the minimum height of the fence from the plane deck. Measure the height of the side of the plane for the minimum width of the plane deck. **(201)**

My plane is 2-3/8 inches wide and has a cheek width of 1/8 inch. When I add the 1/16 inch it results in a 3/16 inch minimum height difference between the two decks. The fence wood will have to be at least 2-1/2 inches thick when measured from the plane deck.

The main body of the shooting board will be a 14 inch x 8 inch x 3/4 inch board planed to a smooth, flat surface. Softwoods such as white pine or cedar or

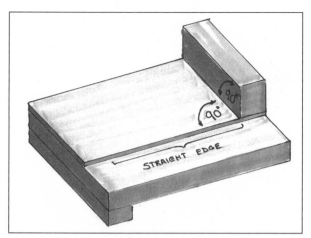

202.   The critical surfaces on a shooting board ensure accurate results when in use. Take time to double check everything before doing the final glue-up.

hemlock will work nicely as long as they are well dried. If you are not sure or if it was just purchased from a lumber yard, let the board sit in the living area of your home for a month before using it. If the wood is not dried, it's sure to warp when you cut into it. A warped shooting board is worse than no shooting board. **(202)**

Alternately, make the shooting board out of plywood but be selective since there may be a twist to the sheet. High-quality 9-ply birch plywood is a very stable product, as is medium density fiberboard (MDF).

If you have a router table with a fence, you can make the plane deck by cutting a 3/16 inch rabbet of a width equal to the height of your plane. Before routing, ensure that the edge of the board that rides against the fence is truly straight.

If using plywood, use a piece of 1/4 inch plywood to build up the upper deck. Before gluing it to the plywood base, true up one edge on the table saw and recess that edge enough to accommodate your plane lying on its side. If you are left-handed, the plane deck will be on the left.

As in the bench hook, I prefer the fence to be a crosscut off a wide board so that its grain direction matches that of the main body of the shooting board. Select

a straight-grained board with no defects such as knots or checks. If need be, face-glue two or more boards together to attain the correct height.

Set an accurate square against the upper deck edge adjacent to the plane deck. Place the fence stock up against the edge at the rear of the board. Apply glue to the bottom side of the fence, set it in place, and clamp one corner of the fence to the board. Now square the fence to the upper deck edge and apply a second clamp to the far end of the fence. Ensure the fence is in proper alignment and apply a third clamp to the middle of the fence. Allow the assembly to set overnight.

Alternately, you can drill several clearance holes vertically through the fence just large enough for a long screw with a flat head. This can then be used to attach the fence to the upper deck. With this method, if you have any error in the fence placement, it is correctable.

Variations on the shooting board

You could choose to make these tools at various useful angles. We will look at another very useful configuration, the 45° shooting board.

As seen from **(203)** this configuration of shooting board is meant to be used ambidextrously. The 45° fence can be made from several layers of plywood, or two thick boards.

To make the fence, cut a board or lamination at 90°. Accurately align the cut board at 45° to the guide edge using a combination square held against the guide edge and the fence. If using solid wood, attach the fence with screws to allow a small amount of seasonal motion since the wood grain angles won't match.

The hook design used on the previous shooting board will not work in this configuration because force is applied against the fences in two directions. By adding a second hook on the other end of the underside, you resolve this issue. Yes, the board will be tilted slightly upward when in use. The other solution is to clamp the shooting board between bench dogs.

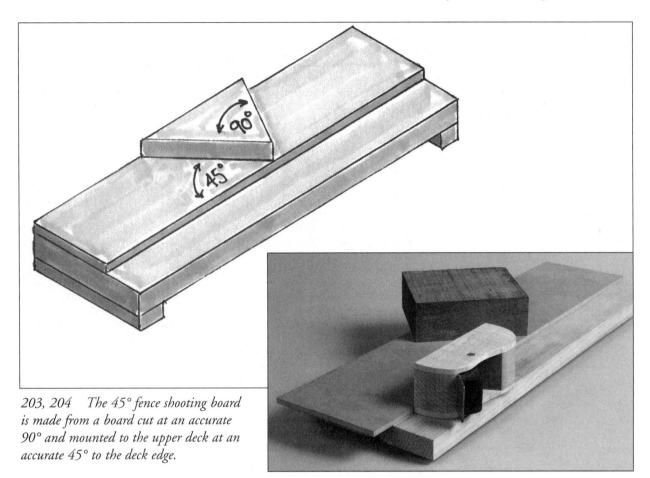

203, 204   The 45° fence shooting board is made from a board cut at an accurate 90° and mounted to the upper deck at an accurate 45° to the deck edge.

One further issue with this tool is the plane that you match to the shooting board must be squared on both sides. On the 90° fence shooting board, the plane was used on one side only.

Using the shooting board

Place the shooting board on a sturdy table or workbench with the hook hanging off the edge. Set your plane down on its side on the plane deck with the sole against the guide edge.

Place the workpiece to be squared against the fence with its end just overhanging the guide edge. Ensure that you do not rock the plane when cutting. It should be stable on the plane deck, with its sole in a true vertical orientation. Hold or clamp the workpiece against the fence and make repeated cuts until the plane is no longer cutting.

What has happened is that the cheek of the plane's sole is now bearing against the guide edge and the blade is no longer advancing on the workpiece. No matter how many more times you swipe the plane it can no longer cut the workpiece. In a way, this is template-cutting in an early form.

205.   *Shaped mallet, page 126 (top).*   206.   *Slip-handle mallet, page 132 (below).*

207. Turned mallets, page 130.

Striking Tools

Though we won't talk about making chisels, we can describe making mallets that strike chisels. Some chisels are not designed to be hit, so do be aware of what you are whacking. Bench chisels, which are used to cut joints, are most definitely in the whackable category.

Mallets come in various sizes depending on how much force you want to apply. Very compact, lightweight mallets are used by carvers to save their hands. Heavier mallets tend to be used for joint-cutting, though when making your own you can experiment with different weights to determine what is right for you.

Mallets come in different shapes as well. We will describe three styles: the shaped mallet, the turned mallet, and the slip-handle mallet. The shaped mallet is the simplest and can be made with mainly hand tools. If you have access to a lathe and know how to use it, the turned mallet is a simple example of spindle turning. Both of these mallets are made from one piece of wood.

The slip-handle (or carpenter's) mallet is a bigger, heavier tool. It is traditionally built out of one piece of wood that is through-mortised for the handle. One way to avoid the mortising effort is to make the mallet head a lamination, as was done with previous tools. We will use the lamination method.

Using mallets

Most of the weight is in the mallet head. When swung, the inertia of the head is what provides the impact force. For light work, use a lightweight mallet. For work that requires large impact force, build a heavier mallet.

When hitting a chisel handle with any mallet, a squarely placed blow will deliver the maximum force and control. The speed and weight of the mallet head at impact determines the force, higher speed equals higher force but less control. If you really flail the poor chisel handle, you lose control of the angle of impact. A glancing blow to a chisel can send the sharp end into places unintended, while the mallet head crashes onto your holding hand. It is a fact that wood is harder than skin.

Besides the risks noted, forcing a hit with arm strength will do harm to your body. After a long carving session shaping an arched-top guitar out of hard maple, I woke up the next morning with a new sensation in my elbow. Tendonitis is what I have to show for learning this lesson.

208. Its shaped head makes this mallet very versatile.

CHAPTER 18
Shaped Mallet

The shaped mallet has one flat and one conical striking surface, so it can be used in both heavy chopping and delicate carving.

Start out with a 3 inch x 3 inch x 9 inch piece of wood that is dense, heavy, and free of visible checks or cracks. Hard maple is an excellent choice of domestic wood, as are hickory, beech, and white oak. A master craftsman I know used lignum vitae to make a beautiful, small, and surprisingly heavy mallet.

The design detailed here is about 12 ounces when made of hard maple. Make one and use it for light joinery work or for carving. Make a heavier, larger version if you need a more powerful striking force.

Marking the blank orientation

Orient the blank so the crest of the conical face will have some edge (radial or quarter-sawn) grain exposed, because edge-grain has greater compression strength and the curved face is for more powerful striking. Mark an F on the flat-face surface. (209)

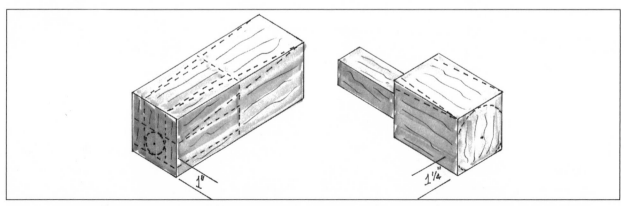

209. Mark the mallet blank by first locating the center of the handle and the large face. Trace lines along the sides to provide cutting references during rough-out.

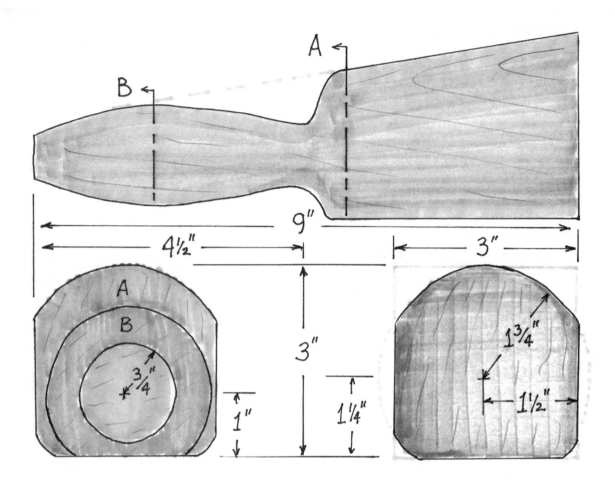

210. **Shaped mallet**

Building a shaped mallet		
Procedure	**Tools**	**Material**
Cut mallet blank	Band saw, table saw, handsaw	Hard maple or similar dense wood
Trace layout lines	Pencil	
Cut rough shape	Band saw, bowsaw	
Shape handle	Spokeshave, rasp, plane	
Shape cylindrical head	Spokeshave, rasp, plane	
Sand and finish	Sandpaper, scraper	Oil and wax

211.   Shape the conical face while holding the mallet between bench dogs.

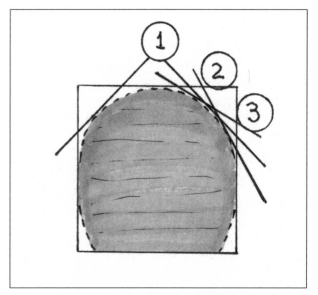

212.   Creating a smooth curve with a flat blade tool requires repeated material removal at varying angles. Start the sequence at 45° then take off the newly formed corners.

To mark the handle location, draw a circle on one end of the blank centered 1-1/8 inch from the flat face surface. A big hand will need a 1-1/2 inch diameter (3/4 inch radius) circle, while a small hand will do with a 1 inch (1/2 inch radius) circle. You can tune the handle later, so err on the large side.

Mark a line around the blank halfway down its length to define the division between the head and handle. Draw roughing-out lines from the edges of the handle circle around to the sides of the blank to the mid-point line. Draw two more roughing-out lines from each edge of the circle up and over the blank to the mid-point line.

On the opposite end, mark an oblong semicircle with a radius of 1-3/4 inches centered 1-1/4 inches up from the flat-face surface. As you can see from the illustration (**210,** page 127), the shape is not circular but flattens out on the side surfaces until half an inch from the flat face, where it curves in.

While you are marking the blank, draw four tapering lines from the corners of the mallet head end toward the handle end. Notice that the taper converges on the outer diameter of the handle.

Shaping the handle

The handle is offset from center of the mallet to allow it to be in a balanced position for use with either the flat or conical surface.

By shaping the handle first, we provide the clearance to smoothly shape the conical face. Rough-shape the handle area by removing a large amount of wood quickly using the band saw. On all four sides, cut the length of the handle lines. Remove the rough waste by cutting the mid-lines until you reach the handle cuts.

Choose a spokeshave, rasp, file, Surform, or Microplane to form the handle. Mount the wood blank by the head end, handle up, in a vise, or clamp it to the edge of a bench so the handle half is suspended and able to be worked from any angle. Shape it to have a barrel-shaped bulge in the middle. Don't concern yourself with getting a perfectly smooth surface yet, since you will do final-fitting later.

Shaping the conical face

Remove waste wood from the head portion of the

213.   An alternative is to hold the plane and move the mallet across the blade. Wear heavy protective gloves when using this method.

mallet by band sawing to the lines representing the conical head outline as noted in **(209)**.

If you are fortunate enough to have a workbench that has a vise and bench dogs, shaping the conical face will be rather quick.

Place the partially shaped mallet with the flat face up between two bench dogs extended high enough to tightly capture it. Using a bench plane, round off the edges of the flat face surface up to the circular reference lines. **(211)**

When satisfied that these small areas are complete, orient the mallet flat-face down and capture it lengthwise between two bench dogs. Use your bench plane to cut a 45° edge (1 in Fig. 212) off both corners of the conical face angling toward the handle end. Cut until you meet the circle marked on the large end and the front tip of the plane touches the butt of the handle. Next, shave off the points between those flats (2 and 3) and progressively cut between flats until the surface is trimmed to a smooth cone. **(212)**

The alternative to the above, if your bench does not

have bench dogs, is to clamp a plane upside down in a wooden vise with its sole flush with the top of the vise. If you clamp the plane too tightly or too high up in the vise, you are liable to crack the cast housing, so exercise caution. **(213)**

Move the wood lengthwise across the plane. Trim to the scribed lines as in the process described above, except you will be moving the wood instead of the tool. This requires wearing two heavy leather or Kevlar gloves for hand protection. This style of cutting can be done with a Surform or Microplane as well.

Shape the head-to-handle transition

The end of the mallet head and beginning of the handle is still a raw band saw cut. This surface can be sanded and smoothed or shaped to a more gradual transition. Regardless of which shape, ease the edges by rounding them to make them more durable.

Final steps

It is time to really fit the tool to your hand. The flat and conical faces are the primary striking surfaces, so make sure the handle feels comfortable in those positions. Take time to hold it at every angle you would likely work.

A barrel shape enhances comfort, as does a smooth surface. Once you have eliminated any deformity with a rasp or spokeshave, use a card scraper or 150-grit sandpaper to smooth the handle.

A smooth curvature of the conical face will improve the predictability of the mallet strikes. Sight down the mallet face from various angles and fair the curves with a spokeshave and card scraper. Complete shaping by rounding-over all the edges.

Finish the mallet with a protective coating of your choice. Remember that the head of the tool is going to be striking tool handles, so a hard, brittle finish will quickly deteriorate. My preference is to use an oil finish followed by paste wax.

214. *Mallet shapes and designs (mallets courtesy of Dan Power – Lexington Arts and Crafts Society).*

CHAPTER 19
Turned Mallet

The turned mallet is for those who have a lathe and knowledge to use it. Refer to a book on basic turning techniques if you are unfamiliar with the following procedures. We will cover the shape options and their advantages, and the general procedures.

A barrel-shaped handle tends to be comfortable. Turning this shape on a lathe is simple in comparison to shaping it with hand tools. Creating a smoothly tapered surface, and complex shapes, with decorative detail, are simple tasks in lathe work. They just all have to be round.

The center mallet shown here is a lamination of hard maple over a mahogany core, while the mallet on the left is turned from dense rosewood and is actually heavier than the large one. The shapes available via lathe work are infinite so I will offer just a couple of suggestions for functional mallets.

Form a barrel-shaped handle with the minimum diameter equal to one-half the maximum diameter. Maximum handle diameter should be less than the length of your hand, measured from your wrist to the tip of your middle finger, divided by 5. Minimum handle length is 1/4 inch longer than the width of your hand. Your hand will quickly fatigue using an overly large or small handle.

Design the head with a smoothly transitioning face so the impacts will be predictable even if your striking accuracy is off. Rippling or beaded surfaces are extreme examples of the wrong surface.

A larger diameter and heavier head increases striking

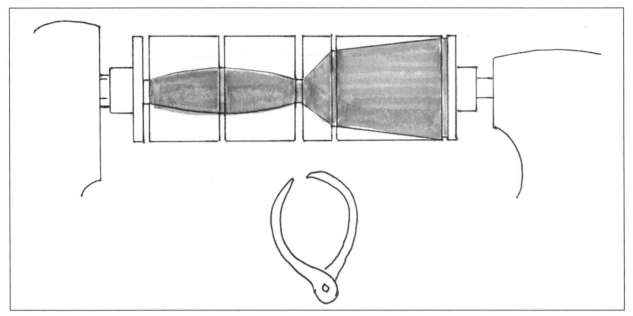

215.   To turn a mallet start by using the parting tool to create diameter references at known points. Use a caliper to check the references.

force without a substantial increase in physical exertion. For more control, make a short mallet. If you want a heavy mallet that is easy to control, create a short, large-diameter head on a short handle.

Turning a mallet

To turn a mallet, select a 3 inch x 3 inch x 9 inch piece of hardwood such as beech, hard maple, hickory, or white oak, where the growth rings make a shallow arc across the end of the turning blank.

Find the center on each end and mount the blank between the lathe centers. Tighten the sliding tailstock and crank the centers together until the wood has been captured securely. Start turning on the lathe's slowest speed. With a large roughing gouge, and a tool rest set near the center height, round the turning blank its entire length.

Next, reposition the tool rest closer to the wood and increase the lathe speed, but if the lathe vibrates, you are turning way too fast. Safety is the main concern, don't work past your knowledge level.

With a parting tool, I next cut a groove to the diameter desired on each end of the head and use a gouge to work a smooth straight or curved line between these two references. To size the reference groove diameters, use a bowed-arm caliper. **(215)**

When the shape has been defined, smooth the surfaces with a skew chisel. On concave surfaces, smooth with a round-nose scraper. A small gouge can be used to shape small details.

Frequently stop the lathe and check the feel of the grip as you approach the perfect shape and size. Finish with oil and wax, because this tool will get much surface abuse.

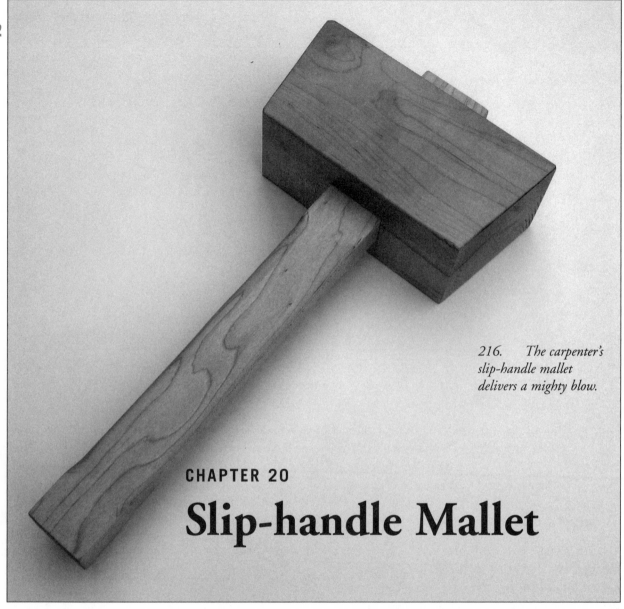

216. *The carpenter's slip-handle mallet delivers a mighty blow.*

CHAPTER 20

Slip-handle Mallet

The slip-handle, or carpenter's, mallet is the tradition heavyweight used for joinery and driving large-blade chisels. The long handle and large head combine to deliver maximum force. The mallet handle comes apart for compact storage in your toolbox.

Cut the wood

Start with a 36 inch x 3 inch x 1 inch piece of dense, straight-grained hardwood such as hard maple or white oak, ensuring there are no end checks or knots and that the surface is clear of visible defects. Cut 12 inches off the end and reserve this piece for the handle.

Cut the remaining board into three equal-length pieces for the mallet head. Using the table saw and miter gauge set to an angle of 5°, cross-cut one of the shortened boards into two roughly equal halves.

Build the head

We will next glue up part of the head so we may fit the handle exactly.

Using a bench hook covered with a piece of waxed paper, lay one of the longer head boards against the fence. Apply glue to one surface of the two angled

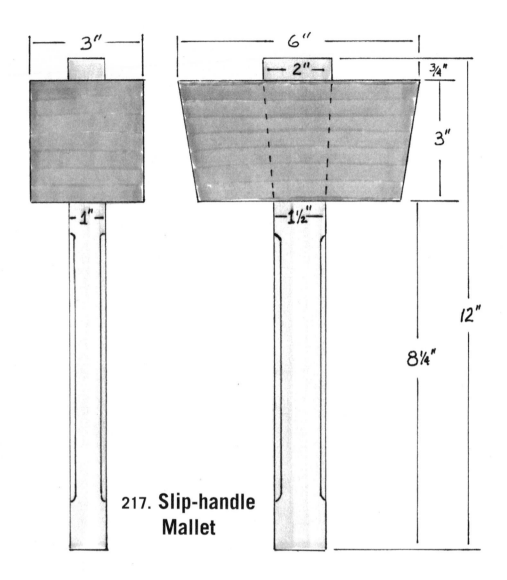

217. Slip-handle Mallet

Making the slip-handle mallet

Procedure	Tools	Materials
Cut mallet blank	Table saw or handsaw	Hardwood
Cut handle and head sections	Table saw or handsaw	
Glue up partial head	Clamps, bench hook	Glue
Cut and fit handle and taper	Band saw or handsaw	
Complete head assembly	Clamps, bench hook	Glue
Shape handle	Spokeshave, rasp, or router	
Apply optional handle pads	Clamps	Glue
Final sand and finish	Sandpaper	Oil and wax

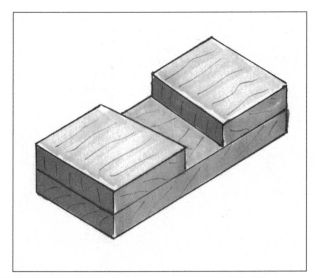

218. *Once the interior angle cut is made, the blocks can be positioned and glued to one outer face.*

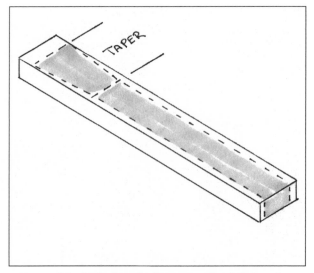

219. *Mark the handle for cutting by defining the taper and grip sections of the handle first. Mark the taper to approximate the actual taper measurements of the partially completed head.*

pieces and position them on the longer head piece 1-1/2 inches apart at the narrow opening of the V they form. Without glue, lay the other piece of the head on top of these three and clamp them all together. **(218)**

Make the handle

Allow the glue to set, then measure the width of the widest point of the V-opening. Rip the reserved handle blank to 1/16 inch wider than that width.

Mark two lines across the handle blank at 3/4 inch and 3-3/4 inch from one end to define where the handle will taper within the mallet head. Measure the smaller opening in the mallet head, which will define the width of the handle, and center that measurement on the handle blank. Draw parallel lines the length of the handle to define the handle width. Next draw tapering lines between the edge of the handle at the 3/4-inch line and the lines defining the handle width at the 3-3/4 inch mark. **(219)**

Use your band saw to cut along those lines and remove the waste. Place the shaped handle into the

head. With a plane or sanding block, correct the taper for a perfect fit with at least 1/2 inch of the handle protruding beyond the head.

With the handle removed, glue on the last piece to complete the head. Check that no glue squeeze-out is in the mortise. When the glue has dried, test-fit the handle in the mortise and sand or scrape the lower handle so it easily slips through the mortise. The only area of the handle that has to be really snug is the tapered section.

Shape the handle

The traditional slip-handle can be removed from the head for more compact storage. The handle can be made more comfortable by rounding the edges to give the hand a better grip, but leave the end squared so it informs the hand of slippage.

With a pencil, mark 1 inch in from the head and handle ends. Using a spokeshave, rasp, or 3/8 inch round-over bit in a router, shape the handle so its edges are fully rounded over between the marks, with smooth transitions to the square sections. **(220)**

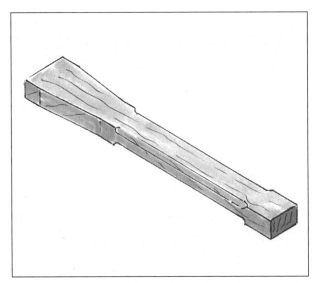

220. The shape of the traditional handle is created by just rounding over the grip area edges.

221. Optional pads on the handle add complexity but provide a more pleasant grip shape. Round over the edges to fit your hand.

Optional handle pads

An optional detail that can improve the feel of the handle is to add side pads. The purpose of the pads is to expand the handle dimensions for those with large hands, providing a more comfortable grip. They can be of the same or of contrasting wood. Install and fit the handle to the head before attaching the pads, because it cannot be installed or removed afterwards.

Cut two handle pads around 3 inches long and 3/16 inch thick. Cut the pads to the same width as the handle and about as long as your palm width. Glue the two pieces of wood to either side of the handle. **(221)**

With a spokeshave or other shaping tool, round the corners off the pads and taper them into the handle.

Cut the striking surface of the head

Because your arm swings the mallet in an arc, angled faces square up the impact force to the struck tool. To determine the angle, lay a straight edge across the head extending from the outer corner of the head to the outer corner of the handle end and mark a cut line. Make the cut with a handsaw or band saw. **(222)**

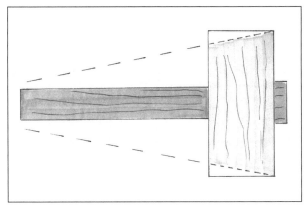

222. The face angle is set to the arc of the mallet swing creating a square impact surface on the chisel handle.

If the head glue-joints fracture and the user doesn't know it, the result may be seen flying across the room, or worse, toward someone in the room. This risk is extremely low if gluing and clamping were done correctly but there is a feature that will eliminate even that small risk.

Drill two 3/8 inch angled holes through the sides of the mallet head. The holes will be drilled at opposing angles and a 3/8 inch dowel will be glued in place to

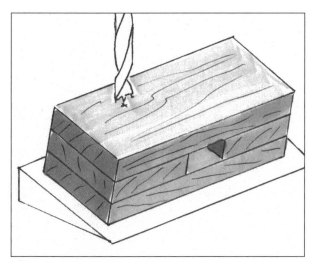

223.   Drilling angled head retainers is a highly recommended safety feature. The opposing angled dowels will keep the head from flying apart if any glue joints fail.

secure the head against flying apart in action. **(223)**

Place the head on its side and select a location mid-way between the mallet face and the handle. Preferably using a drill press with the table tilted slightly, place a sacrificial backing board under the head. Drill a hole through the head, retracting the bit frequently to clear the wood chips. When close to emerging from the opposite side, clear the bit of chips and slowly drill through, trying to allow the bit to cut the last of the hole versus pushing the wood out.

Turn the head over and do exactly the same thing. You have made symmetrical holes canted at an angle to each other. Cut off two 5 inch sections of 3/8 inch wood dowel and attempt to slide them into the holes. They likely are too tight and will have to be hand-sanded to reduce their diameters slightly. Once the dowels slide into the holes with only a little resistance, apply glue into the holes and hammer the dowels through. The moisture in the glue will cause the dowels to expand and glue tightly. Cut the ends flush, and sand.

Chisels and hammers

Striking tools made of steel can be dangerous when hitting other tools made of steel due to the risk of one steel shattering the other. Hardened tool steel is brittle and if not correctly tempered, it shatters when over-stressed. This is the cause of chips at the cutting edge of a chisel or plane.

A safer bet is to have hardwood strike steel or vise-versa. Some chisels have metal rings around the struck end of the handle to keep the handle from mushrooming under repeated blows. Make sure the wooden handle extends beyond the metal ring so the first thing struck is the end-grain of the handle. Besides improving the control of the blow, the wood mushrooming actually improves the seating and holding of the ring.

Plastic handled chisels can be stuck with either metal or wooden mallets but the wooden mallet will impart a less severe shock to the handle and extend its useful life.

Finally, the small striking face of a hammer is far more likely to miss the chisel end than the broad face of a mallet. Mallets may not last as long as hammers, but your fingers sure will appreciate the difference.

Final head shaping

Flatten the sawn end-grain of the faces with coarse sandpaper. Progress to finer grit paper until you have smooth faces. Round off all the edges of the mallet head with either 1/8 inch radius round-over bit in a router, a spokeshave, or a sanding block. Rounding the edges will reduce splintering from misplaced blows. Smooth-sand, and finish with oil and wax.

CHAPTER 21

Joint Basics

To those just starting out making joints with hand tools, the path to success looks long and arduous. My goal is to dispel that fear and offer a simple approach to making the mortise and tenon and the dovetail, the workhorse joints in most furniture and interior woodwork.

You have built some of your tools and you know each feature of them, now you will learn how to use them. If you complement those tools with sharp chisels (refer to page 00 for proper sharpening technique), it is going to be an easy transition from router-cut to hand-cut joints.

Well-fitted joints

There is a fundamental truth to all joinery: Well-fitted joints are good joints. A joint is too loose if it has visible gaps and the members are capable of moving in all directions when dry-assembled, and too tight if a mallet is required to put the joint together.

A perfectly fitting joint will require exact alignment and some muscle power to slide together. It will not need the help of a mallet to snug it the final smidgeon. There will be few visible gaps between the wood members. When assembled, you will wonder if it is necessary to add glue. The joint will have to be lightly tapped with a mallet to get it apart.

Will you make that well-fitting joint the first time you cut one? Not likely. That is a very important point. A couple of practice joints using low-cost woods are all you need to get past beginner's problems. When you

cut joints that are strictly for practice, you have the luxury of making a mistake and learning from it. I like to use two boards of around 20 inches in length. I cut a joint and its mate, assemble them, then cut the pair off and start again with the two shortened boards.

Please don't start making hand-cut joinery by making a curly maple blanket chest with exposed dovetails on all four corners, and a mortised-and-tenoned frame top with rosewood panels. You will learn to fear each cut even if the project were to come out looking good.

When you see "expert" woodworkers demonstrate joint-making, notice what kinds of wood they use. Mahogany and poplar are typical. I have heard them called "hero wood" because you can make joints with a fair amount of error, and still look like a hero to your audience. This is because these woods are soft and will allow limited compression when being pushed together.

The projects in the following chapters should be made with poplar and/or mahogany. Both woods are generally straight-grained and fairly soft. Poplar is one of the least expensive furniture-grade woods available, while mahogany can get expensive. With the exception of white pine, the construction-grade pines are too variable in wood density to make good joints — unless you are nailing them together.

The following section is for those who enjoy knowing the "why" behind anything they do. If that is not your inclination, skip to the "how-to" in the following chapter.

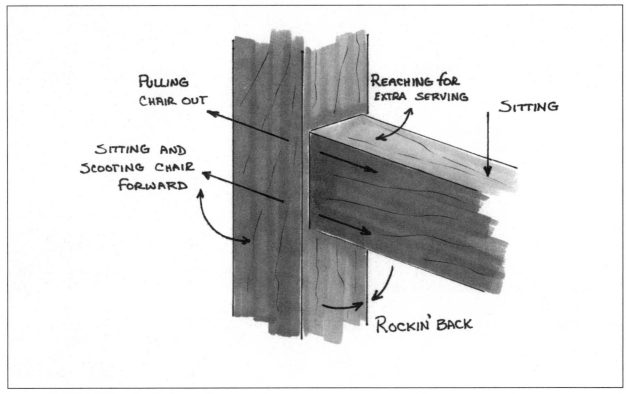

224   Stresses on a chair back leg joint.

A detailed analysis of joints

The joints used in furniture-grade woodworking are intended to make a strong, permanent connection with the least amount of labor, utilizing nothing more than wood and glue.

The three characteristics that define a joint are mechanical stability, the additional holding power when glued, and the joint's ability to survive the natural cycle of seasonal expansion and contraction. Before we discuss these points, let's look at the forces that attempt to destroy our hard work.

Stress forces

There are three forces acting on a joint: compression, tension, and shear.

Compression force is when two surfaces are being pushed together. If the compression force overcomes the strength of the wood, it will be crushed.

Tension force acts to pull things apart. The dovetail is the best example of a joint that addresses this concern by transferring any tension on the joint into compression between the mating bevels of pins and tails.

Shear is a sliding force that acts to move one piece against another. If the shear force is greater than the wood or glue strength, you get breakage. This is best visualized as a piece of molding or carving that has been chipped off a piece of furniture.

If we think of a dining chair, it experiences all these forces when we slide it out from under the table then sit on it, slide it back in again, and wiggle around while talking with friends or reaching for more meat loaf. **(224)**

The leg joints are being pulled apart by the dragging motion of the legs on the floor. Shear and compression forces are at work when our weight loads the joints in the vertical direction for as long as we are seated. When we start to move, the forces turn into twisting, which is a combination of all the forces at once. Just think of the stresses when large Uncle Charlie starts rockin' back in his chair.

Mechanical aspects of joinery

The mechanical configuration of a joint can provide enough strength and rigidity to hold the assembly stable even without glue. This characteristic places the mortise and tenon at the pinnacle of joinery. The tenon resists heavy loads, plus it and the shoulders stabilize the joint against twisting, while the addition of a locking pin or wedge prevents the tenon from being pulled out of the mortise.

Similarly, adding a pin at right angles to the beveled surfaces of a dovetail joint creates a very permanent joint. The tails and pins resist tension forces that try to pull the joint apart in one direction, the pin resists tension in the other direction, while the shoulders resist compression and twisting.

Glue

Glue creates adhesion between the wood surfaces in the form of polymer links and hydrogen bonds, which are most effective when the surfaces are smooth and flat with a thin film of glue in between.

A joint should slide together having just enough space for a thin layer of glue without leaving large gaps or compressing the wood. If the joint surfaces fit so tightly as to squeeze the glue out of the interfaces, a dry joint will result.

Glue works to form a strong bond by spreading the holding force over a large area while a nail depends on the strength of steel acting at a single point. Though glue is weaker than steel, its distributed holding force creates a superior total bond.

The discontinuous film of a poorly glued interface acts like a series of nails holding the wood together at discrete points. Glue is not as strong as steel and the concentrated stresses at those points force them to do

disproportionately greater work, resulting in early glue failure. Always check to ensure glue is spread thinly on both surfaces before you slide a joint together.

An excellent joint is formed when two boards are glued edge to edge, as when making a wide panel. Long-grain surfaces, as these edges are termed, take advantage of the strength of continuous fibers and smooth, void-free surfaces.

In comparison, end-grain glue joints are considered unreliable. The difference in gluing quality is because it cannot take advantage of the strength of the continuous fibers of long-grain wood plus the end-grain is porous and inhibits a strong and continuous glue film from developing.

Some glue is known to be gap-filling. These glues have the capability of adding structure to the joint by filling the voids left by poorly fit surfaces. Overall they do improve joint strength, but only in compression. When forces are twisting or pulling the joint apart, the thick glue doesn't add equivalent strength.

Wood

Wood resists breakage best in the direction of the grain. Cut 1/2 inch off the end of a wide board and try to break it. It snaps fairly easily. Now cut a 1/2 inch wide strip off the edge of that same board and trim it to the same length and try to break it. You may not be able to, because long grain is typically between ten and twenty times stronger than cross grain. Similarly, a board resists compression five to ten times better along the grain than across it, which explains why the grain runs up and down in furniture legs.

Wood is elastic so it can be bent to a degree and still return to its original shape. When we dent a surface with a hammer blow the wood will not return to shape because it has been overstressed due to compression. One goal of joinery is to minimize this destructive overloading. Adding surface- to-surface area is a primary way of reducing compression stress by spreading the force across a larger area. Another approach is to select woods that are inherently stronger. Maple, oak, and hickory are legendary for their strength.

A final limitation to joinery is that wood is not dimensionally stable over long periods of time. Short of sealing a piece of wood in a thick epoxy casing or putting it in a climate-controlled environment, moisture exchange with the atmosphere will cause it to change dimension on a seasonal basis. This would not be a problem were it not that wood expands and contracts at different rates along its three different axis of grain direction. If the joints have not taken this movement into consideration, differential motion literally tears the joints apart.

Wood preparation

Though it is possible to make joints in rough-shaped wood such as that which comes directly from the sawmill, in fine joinery, it is essential that the wood pieces are trued and squared. Besides, rough-sawn wood is a bear to polish.

With power tools

To true a board means to make the faces, edges, and ends flat and square to each other. In the contemporary shop, this means using the jointer, planer, and table saw as a system of tools. First the workpiece is cut to rough length. Next one wide face is run across the jointer until it is smooth and absolutely flat. The workpiece is then turned on its side with the flat face against the jointer fence and an edge is made square and straight.

The board is placed flat face down on the table saw with the jointed edge toward the fence and ripped to make the other edge parallel. The planer is used next to make the opposite wide surface flat and parallel to the first trued surface. The final operation is to cut the workpiece to length using the miter gauge on the table saw, which also squares the ends.

By hand

To do the same job by hand, the craftsperson cuts the workpiece to approximate length with a cross-cut saw and slightly over width with a rip saw. Next a plane is used to flatten one of the wide surfaces. Once flattened, the workpiece is held in a bench vise on edge and one edge is straightened and squared to the flat face.

The workpiece is marked for width using a panel-marking gauge, which has a longer beam and wider fence than the marking gauges we made earlier in this book. It is then clamped in the bench vise so a plane can be used to trim the workpiece to the width and square that edge to the flat surface.

To indicate the desired thickness, a mark is scribed on all the edges with a marking gauge, using the wide flattened surface as a reference for the gauge fence. The workpiece is laid on the bench and hand-planed to thickness using the edge markings as guides. Finally the workpiece is placed on the shooting board and the ends are planed square.

Thank goodness for those inventive souls who came before us, but it is wonderfully instructive to actually size a board this way, just do it with mahogany or poplar instead of hard curly maple.

Let's proceed to cutting joints using the tools we made.

225. *Defining tenon terms.*

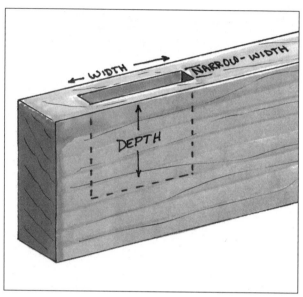

226. *Defining mortise terms.*

CHAPTER 22

Cutting the Mortise and Tenon

The mortise and tenon is considered a framing joint. It is typically seen joining two boards end-to-end at right angles, as in picture frames, frame-and-panel assemblies, and foundation structures for case construction.

This joint consists of a rectangular cross-section tenon extending from the end of a slightly larger board, which fits into an identically sized hole, called the mortise, in the face or side of the mating board. Its strength comes from the long grain of the tenon, the tenon shoulders against the face of the mortised board, and the tenon sides against the mortise walls. **(225, 226)**

A tenon depends on the strength of long grain so it is always cut at the end of a board. Tenon shoulders are created by reducing the size of the tenon with respect to the overall board. Squarely cut shoulders totally hide the joint while adding stability. Long grain provides optimum surfaces for gluing and they are plentiful in a tenon, since it is all long grain.

Mortises can be made in the end, edge, or face of a board though most frequently in the edge or face. Being a hole in the wood, the mortise interrupts the strong long grain and weakens the board. By sizing the mortise to be one-third to one-half the thickness of the board, we leave enough of the long grain intact to provide the strength required. The tenon glues to the long grain of the entire side wall surface of the mortise, providing an excellent glue bond.

Blind mortise-and-tenon

We will use the classic blind or closed mortise-and-tenon to make the face frame for an imaginary cabinet or case piece. The case measures 20 inches high by 15 inches wide and has one large opening, and we wish to build a frame to surround the opening. (**227**)

Determining the length of the frame pieces

Using the exact dimensions of the cabinet we can build a face frame that is flush all around the cabinet when installed. We first check that the wood of the sides, top, and bottom of the cabinet is oriented with the long grain circling around the case. This is necessary so that the seasonal movement of the face-frame wood will be in harmony with the wood of the case. (**228**)

The frame boards are 2-1/2 inches wide and 3/4 inch thick. We will follow the accepted design practice of making the vertical sides of the frame, called stiles, the full height of the cabinet. The horizontal top and bottom rail lengths will be calculated.

The two stile's widths add up to 5 inches. This means the rails will extend 10 inches between the stiles plus 3 inches to account for two 1-1/2-inch tenons.

Cutting and squaring the frame pieces

With this knowledge, using the bucksaw, we cut the two stiles to 20 inches in length and the two rails to 13 inches, leaving a 1/32 inch extra for squaring. We want the ends to be truly square so we can refer to them when marking the shoulder cuts. Since we cut the boards by hand, we will square them up on the shooting board.

Cam-clamp both rails together and place them on the shooting board so the ends overhang the plane deck by around 1/64 inch (**229**). Hold the boards tight to the fence and run the plane, lying on its side, past the board ends repeatedly until it stops cutting. Turn the boards end-to-end and repeat. The boards

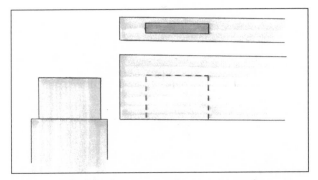

227.   The blind mortise and tenon joints do not project completely through the mortised board. Making the tenon slightly shorter than the mortise ensures a good fit.

228.   Mortise-and-tenon face frame.

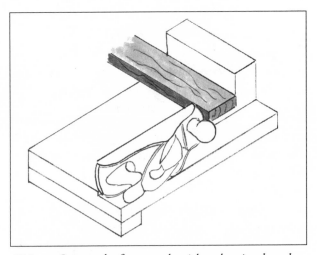

229.   Square the frame ends with a shooting board and plane. Hold the board firmly against the fence and take light shavings until the blade no longer cuts. Check the ends with a square and repeat if necessary.

are now square and exactly the same length. Repeat with the stiles.

Establishing reference surfaces

It is important to establish what is termed a reference face and reference edge prior to doing any marking-out for joinery. The fence of our gauge and the base of our square will rest on reference surfaces when scribing lines. This gives us a constant source of ground zero so minor thickness or width errors in our milling will not affect our efforts to mark with accuracy.

Reference surfaces must first be flat and at exactly 90° to each other. We must also determine what face and edge is most critical to our upcoming assembly. When making a flush frame-and-panel, we care about flushness only where we can see it so the exposed or good surface needs to be the reference. When mounting a top to a case piece we want the bottom surface of the top assembly to mate exactly with the top edge of the case, thus the reference surface is the bottom of the assembly.

When making a face frame as we are doing, the reference surface can be determined by how it will be assembled and attached. If the frame is going to be glued flat to the front of the cabinet, we may choose to declare the back surface as the reference so we have no gaps at the interface. If the frame is going to be rabbeted before being attached to the frame, we will require the reference to be the exposed surface so we can use that as a reference for our tool fence.

Whichever the determination, marking gauges maintain relative accuracy versus precision measurements, and the consistent use of the reference surfaces is critical to maintain relative accuracy.

Marking the frame pieces for the joints

At this point we need to decide which surface of each board will be exposed as the good face, which in this situation will also be the reference face. Make a light

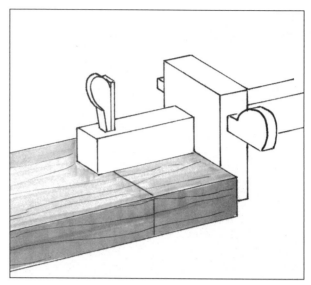

230.   Mark the tenon shoulder line using a cutting gauge against the tenon board end. This mark is actually the first cut on the tenon shoulder.

pencil mark on that surface of the board to indicate it as the reference surface. Check the edges of the board and square one edge to the reference surface using your bench plane or a jointer. Mark it as the reference edge.

With square ends on the rails, we can use our cutting gauge to score the shoulder location. Set the gauge with a steel rule so the point of the cutter is 1-1/2 inches away from the fence. Secure the beam with the wedge. (**230**)

Lay the rail on the bench hook so the end of the rail is past the fence. Holding the gauge in one hand, firmly hold the fence of the gauge to the end of the board, and with moderate pressure, slice a line all the way around the rail ends to mark the cut for the tenon shoulders. Because we used a cutting gauge, we actually have started the tenon shoulder cut, as we will see soon, and at the end of the job this cut will be the only visible part of the joint.

Locate the mortising gauge and a 1/4 inch chisel. Place the chisel against the fixed pin of the gauge. Move the sliding beam until it touches the other edge

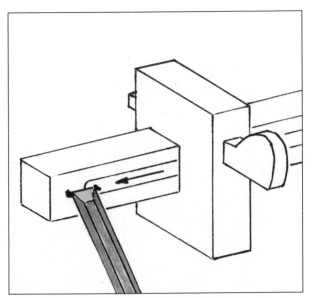

231.   Set the mortising gauge with the chisel being used by sliding the pins snug against the chisel sides.

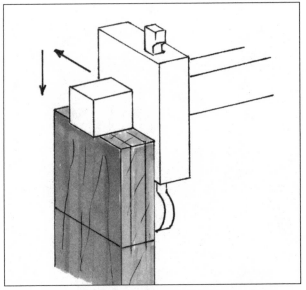

232.   Mark the tenon thickness using the mortising gauge slid along the reference surface. Set the fence so the pins mark a mortise somewhat centered on the board.

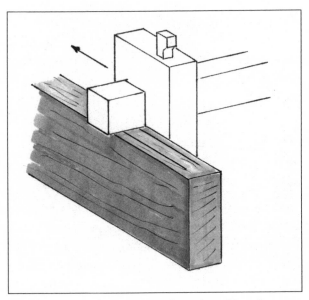

233.   Mark the mortise without disturbing the gauge setting – being sure to slide the fence against the reference surface.

of the chisel. Not disturbing that setting, slide the entire beam so that the fixed point is 1/2 inch from the fence. Tighten the wedge or screw to secure the beam and slider. (**231**)

Holding the fence firmly against the reference surface, scribe the dual lines that define the tenon, starting at the shoulder line on one edge, up over the end, and down the other side until you reach the shoulder line again. (**232**)

We next turn to the stiles to mark the mortise edges using the mortising gauge as it is currently set. The goal in marking is to cut the mortise on exactly the same lines as the tenon. Locate the reference surface of the stile, place the mortise fence against it, and scribe the two lines in the approximate area of the mortise. (**233**)

The width of the mortise is generally marked using a combination square, a second mortise gauge, or a dual-beam marking gauge. We will use the dual-beam

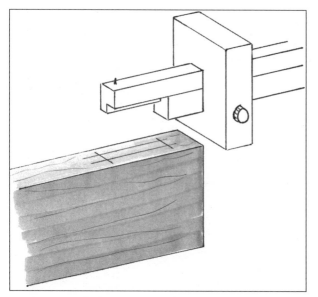

234.   *Mark the mortise width using a dual-beam marking gauge. Each beam is set to mark one of the ends.*

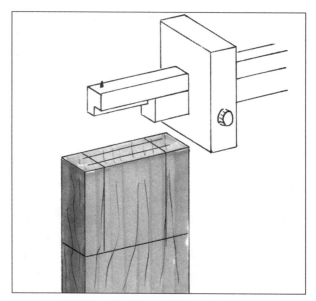

235.   *Marking the tenon width using the same settings of the dual-beam marking gauge. Reference the gauge fence to the outer edge of the board.*

gauge. The rule is to have the mortise at least two times its own thickness away from the end of the board, to leave enough wood to resist cracking the mortise ends when the finished furnishings are in use. So we set our dual-beam gauge to 1/2 inch and 2 inches and mark the ends of the mortise. (**234**)

Using the dual-beam gauge, mark the width of the tenon on the ends of the rails. Extend the new lines down the faces of the board to the shoulder line. (**235**)

This gives us 1/2 inch shoulders covering both ends and 1/4 inch shoulders covering both sides of the mortise, plus a 1-1/2 inch tenon. If the lines are at all hard to see, lightly rub chalk over them so they will stand out.

We have one more marking operation before starting to cut wood. Using a lettering scheme, mate all of the ends into pairs by writing the letters A through D on mating rail and stile ends. Don't mark in areas that are to be cut away. (**236**)

236.   *Marking a letter on the paired joint pair will mate the joints for the rest of the project.*

237.   *Using the scribed lines to guide where the chisel cuts are made for cutting the mortise. Start the repetitive chisel cuts from 1/8 inch away from one end.*

238.   *Clear the chips out of the mortise with the chisel held at a glancing angle. Keep your hand behind the chisel tip so a slip won't wind up as a trip to the hospital.*

Cutting the mortise

We cut the mortise first because if we make any errors that change the size of the hole, it is much easier to fit the tenon to the mortise than the other way around.

Clamp a fully marked stile to the fence of the bench hook with the marked edge up and the stile extending toward the right. Place the 1/4 inch chisel across the width of the mortise, with the bevel toward your left, and align it to the edges of the scribed lines of the walls. Starting about 1/8 inch away from the right end of the mortise, firmly tap the handle of the chisel with a light mallet. This will produce a stop cut between the two scribed lines, meaning that it stops the tendency for the wood to split by severing the long fibers. Move the chisel about 1/8 inch to the left and tap again, repeating this until you are about 1/8 inch away from the other end of the mortise. By now some of the chips you have made probably have popped out. (**237**)

Hold your chisel at a low angle and slice the remaining pieces out of the mortise area. Repeat this full cutting procedure one more time. (**238**)

Chop or drill

We have established a clearly defined area within the mortise layout lines. We could keep chopping chips out until we reach a depth of 1-1/2 inches, or we could use a drill to remove substantial amounts of wood before sizing the mortise with a chisel.

I advocate chopping, but many others believe that is the slow method. Since I get good results, I don't mind taking a little more time. To be fair, I will describe both. First the chopped version.

Chopping method

The mortising chisel was designed specifically for this activity. The 1/4 inch size is a massive piece of metal that is thicker than it is wide. I find a regular tapered bench chisel is just as good. Both types of chisels need to be held perpendicular to the surface to make a square mortise cut. The mortising chisel also has to be held parallel to the mortise walls or it will widen the mortise with its massive body.

A bench chisel has a thin edge so if you hold it angled to the mortise sides, it actually presents a narrower

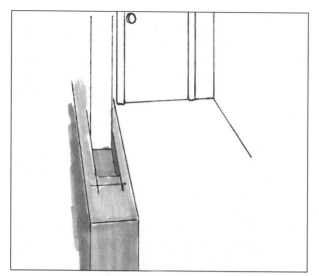

239.   As the cut deepens, aligning the chisel vertically to a visual reference to keep the walls of the mortise square.

240.   Shearing the walls with the chisel edges is a way to guarantee parallel walls.

body to the cut. This is not a problem because we will use the chisel to slice the sides parallel and to width, as you will see.

We have made two passes with the chisel, to excavate a shallow mortise. Now we must take greater care in aligning the chisel vertically so our mortise is not skewed to one side.

Rotate the bench hook to the end of the bench so the stile is pointing away from you. Find a vertical feature in the background, such as a door jamb or corner of two walls. Align your chisel visually with these features and proceed as before, taking out small chips back and forth across the length of the mortise but leaving 1/8 inch uncut on each end. Attach a piece of masking tape to the chisel 1-1/2 inches from the tip to allow you to gauge your progress. (**239**)

As you get deeper into the hole, you will find it easiest to clear the chips by turning the stile upside down and shaking them out. Since the workpiece is attached to a bench hook and not to the bench, this is not a real problem.

Once you are down at the desired depth, level the bottom by using the chisel like a scraper by placing its

beveled edge down and wedging it against the uncut 1/8 inch ends. With the bottom level, take multiple paring cuts to square the ends of the mortise to the marked lines. We will next ensure the walls are straight and the proper distance apart.

This is where a mortising chisel is the best tool but a good bench chisel also works just fine. Place your chisel bevel down, angled the length of the mortise, and lever the chisel up to vertical. The chisel's two long edges are being used to shear wood from the walls of the mortise. Since the chisel is precisely 1/4 inch wide, the two walls are parallel and the proper distance apart. Repeat this with the chisel angled in the opposite direction. (**240**)

Drilling method

Again we have defined the shallow mortise. This time we will use the drilling method.

Use a brad-tipped drill bit that is 1/4 inch in diameter or slightly less. Install a depth stop on the shank of the drill, or wrap a piece of masking tape around the bit 1-1/2 inches from the end. Drill numerous holes vertically within the mortise cavity to remove the majority of the wood, using the indent that was chopped out as your guide.

With a hand-held electric drill, I find that I make more vertical bores if I visually align the drill bit with a door opening or corner of a wall in the distance. Align the wood and bit as shown in (**239**). Extract the bit from the hole frequently to clear the chips. (**241**)

Using a bit brace, you will install an auger bit. I improve vertical boring by placing my chin on the top knob, and look down at the bit while turning the crank. The auger bit clears chips out of the hole effectively so there is no need to retract the bit until the hole reaches full depth.

You will be left with a series of holes, possibly with bridges of wood between them. With your chisel at about a 45° angle, pare the bridges down. Avoid trying to cut the bridges out by holding the chisel vertically against the sides of the mortise. This puts tremendous strain on the wood and may split the walls before the bridge succumbs. (**242**)

With the wood removed from across the hole, it is time to square the mortise walls. Refer to (**240**) for the method of shearing the walls.

Checking the mortise

Once you have cut the mortise, use the joinery check gauge (page 40) to see how vertical the walls are. Place the tool with its notch down and slide the rod deep into the mortise. With the tool base resting on the workpiece, shift the tool so that it is touching the sides of the mortise and look for gaps between the rod and the walls. If there are any, use your chisel to pare the wall more vertical. Check frequently. (**243**)

The final check is to flip the joinery check gauge over so the notch is up, and push the rod down until it hits the bottom of the mortise. The length of exposed rod should be at least 1-1/2 inches. If it isn't, use the drill or chisel to excavate more wood.

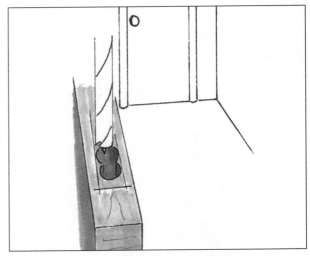

241.   Drilling out large amounts of waste with a hand held electric drill requires holding it exactly vertical. Use a visual reference.

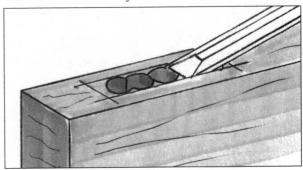

242.   Use a chisel at a low angle to pare wood bridges in the grain direction. Take repeated slices versus trying to chop the bridges out risking splitting the wood.

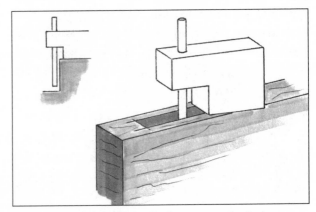

243.   Use the joinery check gauge to check the squareness of the mortise walls to the edge surface.

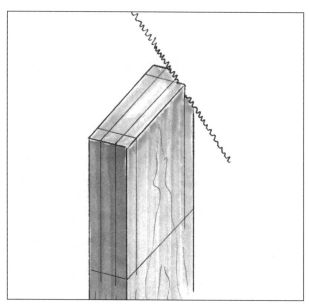

244.   Start the tenon cut with the saw tilted at around a 45° angle to the edge and saw following both the vertical and horizontal lines to keep the saw squared.

Cutting the tenon

Matching the A–A pair of ends, align the rail so that it is at right angles to and flush with the end of the stile. Expose the mortise and check whether the ends of the mortise hole align with the marks on the tenon ends. Correct if needed.

When cutting the tenon, the objective is to cut to the line on the waste side. On the mortise we cut to the inside of all our lines to form a hole. Since we used the same setting of the marking gauges, the marked lines on the tenon are exactly coincident with the mortise. On the tenon the waste side is the outside of all lines.

Clamp the rail vertically in a bench vise with its wide face toward you and extended 6 inches above the top of the vise. Place the saw to the waste side of a line. Start the saw cutting at a 45° angle to the top and face of the workpiece. In this way you will be cutting two lines at one time — the line at the end of the board and the line up the face of the board. Try to stay exactly to the outside of both lines. This will cause the saw to be naturally vertical. (**244**)

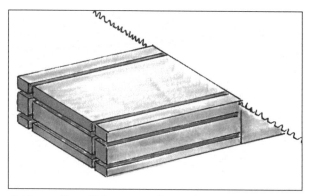

245.   Cut off the waste after making all four cheek cuts. Saw shy of the shoulder line and trim to the line with a chisel later.

Your grip on the saw should start out firm, with your index finger pointing along the side of the handle and toward the cut. The objective is to make the first 1/2 inch of the cut exactly vertical. After that, you can loosen your grip on the saw handle and allow the saw to track itself within the deepening kerf. As the cut gets deeper, level the saw out to horizontal, stopping the cut just before the shoulder line.

When cutting the long, broad cheek of the tenons, the procedure is the same though slower, since there is more wood to saw through.

To remove the outer waste of the tenon, place the workpiece against the fence of the bench hook and saw about 1/16 inch to the waste side of the shoulder line all the way around. (**245**)

Try-fit the tenon into the mating mortise. If it is too big, pare it down to size. If it is too loose, smooth the tenon surface and glue on a layer of veneer. After building the surface up, you can pare it back to size.

The shoulder plane, it is the preferred tool for paring across the tenon. Clamp the rail to a bench hook and do not take off too much wood. (**246,** next page)

The joinery check tool is used with the notch up to gauge if the tenon is parallel to the wide surfaces of the workpiece. Slide the rod down to meet the surface of the tenon and move the tool over the tenon surface to see if there are high or low areas.

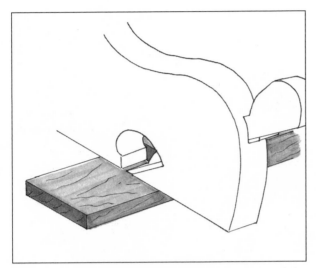

246.   *Use the shoulder plane to trim the cheeks if the tenon is too thick to fit the mortise.*

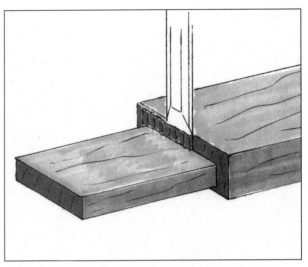

247.   *Cut the shoulder line with a chisel by setting the blade in the scribe line and paring vertically.*

To pare the tenon with a chisel, hold the tool in both hands, giving maximum control to the cut, while the rail is clamped to the bench hook. Slice very thin shavings from the face of the tenon using the back of the chisel as a guide.

When the tenon fits into the mortise with only a small amount of resistance, pare the tenon shoulders to the line. Place the rail on the bench hook and the chisel in the previously scribed shoulder line, stand with your head above the chisel and, with both hands, apply steadily increasing pressure as you pare. Clean any debris out of the shoulder-to-tenon corners and you are done. (**247**)

Assembling the frame

Assembling the frame is just a matter of applying glue to all the mortise surfaces with a flat thin stick, and sliding the tenon in place. Clamp and square the frame by checking its opposing diagonals with the case-squaring stick, page 42.

Before the glue sets, extend the case-squaring stick to fit exactly across the diagonal of the clamped frame. Move it to the opposing diagonal and check that it too fits exactly. If not, rack the frame to close the gap about halfway, and check again.

Good practice that was! There is more to come. If we hold off applying glue, we can use the already built frame to add a mid-rail through mortise-and-tenon joint. Otherwise, we will have to use the half-lap or open mortise.

Through mortise-and-tenon

The blind or closed mortise has a tenon that extends part way through the stile while the through mortise is cut completely through the stile and the tenon length is the full width of the stile. (**248**)

The through mortise is made by marking the mortise

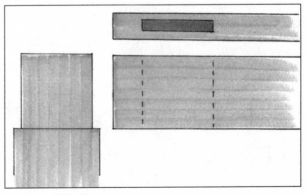

248.   *The through mortise.*

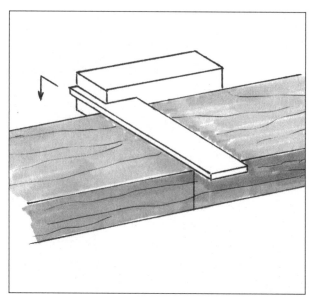

249.   *Mark the mid-rail shoulders by setting the square base on a reference edge and marking across the board face. Next, set the square base on the reference surface and continue the line down each edge.*

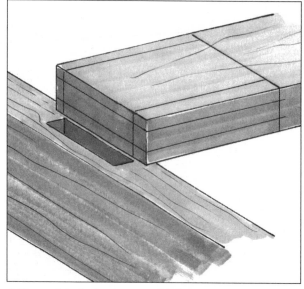

250.   *Mark the tenon width from the actual finished mortise. The shoulders and tenon thickness have been marked already.*

location on both edges of the stile, then cutting toward the center of the board from both edges.

Our mid-rail will be 2-1/2 inches wide, 3/4 inch thick, and 15 inches long. Using the mortise gauge setting of the previous face frame, we start by marking the mortise location on both edges of the stiles, working from our reference surfaces. Measure from the top of the stile to the top edge of the mid-rail and mark that point on the reference face. Let's position the mid-rail to be 8 inches from the frame top edge. Mark a point 1/2 inch from this line to define the edge of the mortise, and trace the line around to the other edge.

To mark a line from one edge of the board to the other, place the point of your pencil on the mark and using one of our wooden squares (page 46), slide the square up to the pencil point with the square base on the reference edge. Now scribe the line across the reference surface. Place the square against the reference face and mark down each edge. (**249**)

There should now be a line that goes around three sides of the workpiece. Do this for the other stile. Use the mortising gauge to scribe the locations of the mortise walls on both edges of the stiles with the fence against the reference surface. Mark another line 1-1/2 inches further down the stile to define the width of the tenon. We will mark the tenon only after we cut the through mortise, since we did not use a gauge setting for those marks.

Start your cut as previously detailed, but this time you will create the shallow mortises on both edges. Once the shallow mortises have been cut, either chop or drill into the board about half way from each edge. Working equally from both openings will compensate for minor errors.

Align the mid-rail edge against the first location mark we made on the stile, and mark the tenon width from the actual mortise width. We can use the mortising gauge to mark the thickness of the tenon — assuming we cut the mortise accurately. Fit the tenon like before except the tenon will be 2-1/2 inches long. Apart from this minor difference, the tenon work is identical. (**250**)

251.   The wedged tenon requires cutting two kerfs near the edges of the tenon which will be spread apart by wedges to create a dovetail effect.

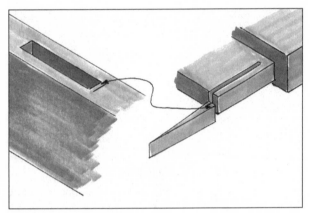

252.   Use the wedge to determine the bevel of the mortise ends by first marking the width of the kerf on the wedge wide end. Place the wide end next to the mortise end and mark the bevel at the outer edge of the wedge.

Adding wedges

A tenon may be wedged to improve its holding power or even to eliminate the use of glue. To do this, we need to determine how large our wedge shall be, how many wedges to use, and where they should be located.

The tenon wedge must be the same width as the thickness of the tenon. The taper should be on the order of 10:1. The simplest way to cut a wedge is with your handsaw. Take a scrap of wood and cut a shallow angled wedge off of one corner. Split the wedge in two

with a handsaw or knife if there is enough total width. (**251**)

The number of wedges is always one or two. This is because the wedge must be located close to the ends of the tenons so that pressure of the wedge bends the tenon wood slightly outward. To prepare the tenon for accepting a wedge, saw a kerf into the tenon about 1/4 inch from each end of the tenon and the length of the tenon almost to the shoulder.

Some craftsmen will now slide the tenon into the mortise, drive in the wedges, and declare success. I'm not one of those folks. The reason is that what has effectively happened is, we have crushed the wood fibers of the tenon and wedge, and created a tight friction-fit to the ends of the mortise. Over the course of several seasonal expansion/contraction cycles, the wedge and tenon fibers will continue to compress until the friction-fit has loosened.

We will bevel the end-walls of the through mortise to accommodate the thickness of the wedge. The goal of the wedge is to act like a dovetail in creating interference between the two wood surfaces. This will keep the joint from ever coming apart.

Use the thickness of the wedge to mark the amount of extension needed to the mortise opening. Clamp the stile onto a bench hook and use a 1/4 inch chisel to cut from the line down into the mortise ends about 1/16 inch. Estimate the angle needed to pare into that cut. Checking frequently, pare a straight end-wall bevel ending at least 1/4 inch inside the smaller opening. (**252**)

The final task in assembly is inserting the tenon and gluing and tapping the wedges into place. If you wish to use glue on the tenon, that will add even more strength to the finished joint.

The job is complete when the tenon end and wedges have been planed flush with the edge of the stile using your block plane.

253.   The half-lap.

CHAPTER 23

Half-lap Joint

If a face frame (such as the example above) needed a mid-rail due to the case having a shelf, we might elect to use a half-lap joint to allow modification of the already glued frame. The joint is easy to cut but not quite as strong as the through mortise-and-tenon because we have just one glue surface and not as much resistance to twisting forces. In a face frame, twist is not a significant concern.

Another name for the half-lap joint is the open mortise. The joint has a tenon cut flush with one face and half the thickness of the board. The mortise is cut to half the thickness of the stile so when mated, it looks like a regular mortise-and-tenon joint from one side.

With the frame removed from the case, start layout by locating the joint on the frame stiles. Let's locate this rail 12 inches from the top of the frame. Mark the distance from the top of the frame to the top of the mid-rail on the back side of the stiles. The mortise will be cut to the full width of the rail. Using the mid-rail as a gauge, align it with the location marks and mark the width of the rail on the stile. Extend these marks around from one edge to the other.

Measure across the frame at the mid-rail location to determine the full length of the mid-rail board. Cut the board to length and square the ends with a shooting board and plane.

Place the fence of the cutting gauge against one edge of the stile at the mid-rail location and set the point by extending the beam until the point is just to the other edge. Mark the tenon shoulder lines on the good face of the mid-rail, using the cutting gauge. (**254**)

We next set the gauge for the mid-point thickness of the frame. Check that the new mid-rail is exactly the

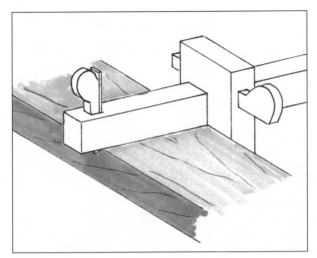

254.   Finding the length of the tenon using a marking gauge to set the exact width of the stile.

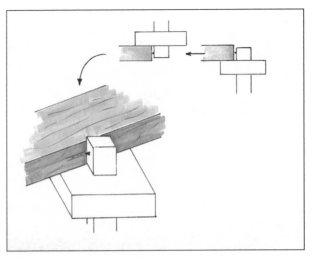

255.   Finding the half-thickness of a board is done by repeated guesses. First approximate a mid-point setting on the marking gauge. Mark the edge from both wide surfaces then find the midpoint between the two marks to reset the gauge.

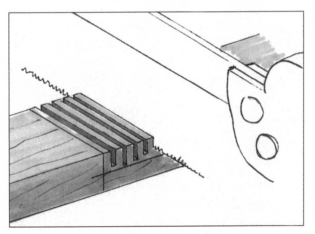

256.   Make repeated cuts within the open mortise area shy of the mid-thickness line then chip out the waste quickly.

Mark that center all the way around the ends of the mid-rail and on both edges between the locating marks on the stiles.

Finding the half-thickness of a board is valuable when wishing for symmetry, but there is another way to gauge the half-lap joint depth cuts. Rest the marking gauge fence on the reference surface of the stile and scribe a line with the gauge set to approximately half-thickness. Mark the rail in exactly the same way by using the reference surface of the rail. In this case, the mating surfaces are not exactly at the half-thickness point but the marks are exactly where they need to be to guide your saw and chisel cuts. Be sure to scribe the line lightly. If you were to make a deep scribe, the bevel of the gauge knife would offset the line and cause error.

Cut the open mortise

Knowing the location of the mortises, the width of the tenons, and the half-thickness of the frame pieces, we can start sawing. Start with the open mortises. (**256**)

same thickness as the face frame. Using the cutting gauge, estimate the center of the thickness of the mid-rail and scratch a small line into the edge near the end. Without changing the gauge setting, place the fence on the opposite surface and scratch another line right next to the first. Now readjust the beam to the half-thickness by moving the gauge point about half the distance between the two lines. To readjust the gauge, lightly tap the end of the beam on your workbench without releasing pressure of the wedge. (**255**)

Saw a kerf to just shy of the marked half-thickness of the stile. Make the cut 1/16 inch to the waste side of one of the marks for the mortise. Move over 1/4 inch and make another cut. Do this every 1/4 inch until you are at the other shoulder.

Wedge a chisel end into the kerfs at the center of the cut, and twist. The short-grained pieces will chip out. Don't worry about getting down to the bottom of the cut, we are next going to clean up the mortise and make it flat.

Use the shoulder plane to quickly clean the mortise. Orient the plane across the board and start by taking off all the jagged wood. Once down to the bottom of the kerf marks, aim for trimming to the originally marked half-thickness lines. Cut from both edges of the board to keep the mortise bottom flat. (**257**)

Otherwise, with a 3/4-inch chisel held at a low angle you can pare down to the half-thickness line using the back of the chisel as a reference to make a flat surface.

Cut the lap tenon

Since we made the mortise the full width of the rail, we can now cut the tenon across the width of the end grain. Cut on the good face (waste) side of the half-thickness line, as on page 149.

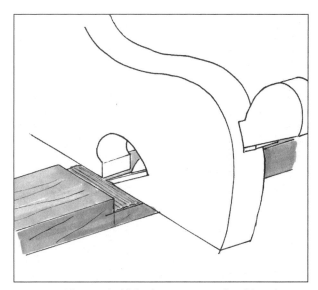

257.   Trim to half thickness using a shoulder plane or pare from each edge with a chisel.

This time, to remove the waste we will chisel a start and saw to the line. Place the corner of the chisel on the waste side of the shoulder line. Slice across the board with the chisel at a slight angle, shearing a continuous bead of wood from the shoulder. Now place the mid-rail on the bench hook, set the backsaw blade into the chisel slice, and saw the rest of the shoulder. (**258**)

Fit the tenon into the mortise by paring the mid-rail tenon face and edges if needed.

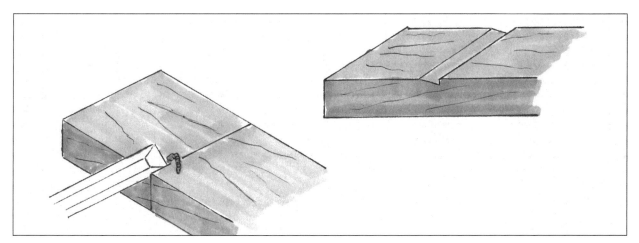

258.   After the shoulder lines are scribed with a marking knife, slicing the shoulder the waste side with a chisel held at a slight angle will produce a trough that will guide a careful saw cut at the shoulder line.

259.   *Tenon comparisons highlight how much wood is removed for a single wide tenon. Twin tenons are not that hard to cut and result in much greater strength.*

CHAPTER 24

Twin Tenon

If making a ladder or a cross bar under the drawer of an end table, the twin tenon would be the correct joint to use.

Picture two intersecting boards of the same width joined to form a T. If a single through tenon were to be used, the mortise hole would severely reduce the strength of the bisected board by cutting the board virtually in half along much of its width. There would be only two thin strips on the outer edges of the board with continuous long grain. (**259**)

If we instead cut two or more mortise holes into the bisected board leaving considerable amounts of wood between them, we will still have a strong board. Cutting mating multiple tenons on the end of the intersecting board produces long-grain tenons that are inherently strong, and when widely placed, that will withstand twisting forces.

Marking a twin tenon requires the use of a mortising gauge and a square when the mortise is located near enough to the edge of the board to allow use of the gauge. We will treat this situation since the wide board example adds complications that do not address learning to use joinery tools.

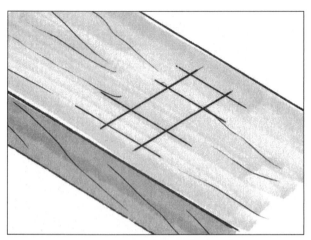

260.   *Multiple mortises can be layed out by using the mortising gauge referenced from both edges. The cross-grain lines are scribed across both mortises.*

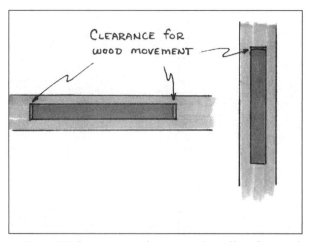

261.   *Wide tenons need mortises that allow for wood movement. Leave a gap at one or both ends of the mortise.*

The layout of this joint is similar to the blind or through mortise and tenon. Marking a through mortise again requires extending a line around the board edge and onto the opposite face so we can cut from both faces toward the middle. In our example we will use two tenons spaced equally from both edges with intersecting boards of the same width. This allows us to set the mortising gauge pins and fence once for all the markings.

When cutting a mortise within the marks just made, there may be a temptation to chisel parallel to the grain. Resist the urge and chisel only across the grain as we did earlier so we continue to cut across long grain fibers. This will be making closely spaced stop cuts in succession that will allow us to create the chips needed to excavate the mortise. After substantially competing the mortise, we can pare the side walls with the chisel in either orientation.

Twin tenons tend to be small thus the mortises are as well. Cutting them out with a chisel, as we did with the previous examples may be difficult. This is when a drill really does make sense as a time-saving tool. Select a drill bit that is noticeably smaller than the narrower of the two mortise dimensions. Chip out two layers of chips as we did on page 146 and then use the undersized drill to remove wood quickly to about half thickness of the workpiece. Flip it over and finish the task.

The result will be a small rectangular recess with a round hole in the middle. Begin paring with a narrow chisel until close to the straight outline marks. Return to using the wider chisel to make the final paring cuts to straighten the walls alternately from both faces.

The tenons are then checked against the mortises to ensure that the markings defining them are still valid. Make the outer cuts as if making one wide tenon, then make the inner cuts to define the gap between tenons. Pare to the shoulders as on a normal tenon. (**260**)

Wide tenons

For simplicity of explanation, the above scenarios left out a couple of important details that need further discussion.

A tenon over 2 inches wide must consider wood movement as a significant factor. When the grain direction of the the tenon and mortise pieces are at right angles to each other, the wood motion due to humidity changes will cause them to move differentially. The wider the cross-grain interface, the more serious the consequences. (**261**)

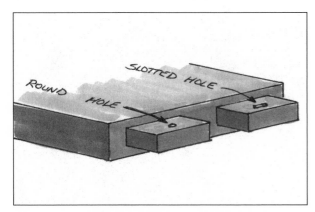

262.   *Pin both tenons with one drilled for the pin size and one slotted to allow movement.*

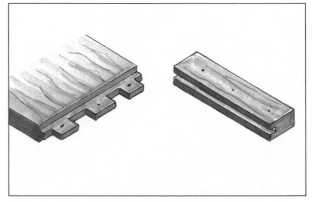

263.   *Pinned breadboards use slots in the outer tenons so natural wood movement will not be impeded by the pins. Very wide boards require wider slots to allow for more movement.*

To allow for seasonal motion within the mortise, the tenon width should be kept 3% shorter than the mortise width. In real terms, that means a 6 inch wide mortise should have a 5-13/16 inch width tenon if the joint is built in the dry season or in an air-conditioned area. If this space is not allowed for, there is a real risk that the mortise near the end of the board will crack once the tenon expands.

This same fact predicts that the glue integrity within that joint will degrade over time due to this same differential motion. A partial improvement is to use glue that allows a small amount of creep. White and yellow wood glues remain somewhat plastic and do allow some creep, while hide glue and urea-formaldehyde glue are known for their rigidity and will fail over time.

To make a really wide mortise-and-tenon, for example on a headboard attaching to a bed frame vertical, we need to treat this more like a breadboard end. One of the tenons will be made as usual and glued in while the other will be allowed to float in its over-wide mortise, thus allowing for seasonal wood motion. (**262**)

The floating tenon should be pinned to hold it in the mortise. Since we still have to allow for motion, cut a width-wise slot in the tenon to enable the pin to slide.

Breadboard tenons

A special case in mortise and tenon joinery is the breadboard end. This joint is common on country furniture and panels for drafting boards as well as actual breadboards. It is a marvelously engineered joint with characteristics worth discussing.

Wide panels or boards have a tendency to warp over time as they dry to the ambient moisture conditions of their surroundings. We use kiln-dried lumber to minimize this in-use drying but in the earlier centuries, when air-dried wood was standard, table tops warped regularly.

A logical solution is to put a brace across the ends of the table but that caused significant risk of splitting of the tabletop. Some genius figured that allowing slippage would solve the problem and thus the breadboard end was invented. (**263**)

The essence of the joint is a dual-depth tenon with matching mortise, secured by pins. The shorter of the two lengths runs the full width of the tabletop end. The longer portion of the compound tenon juts further into the breadboard end-board to improve the retention of the pins.

If the deeper tenon was to be made the entire width of the tabletop, the resulting mortised board would be

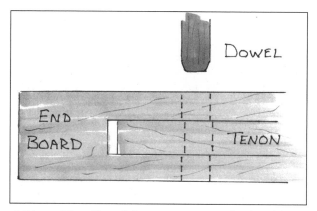

264.   The offset of the pin compresses the dowel but does not actually move the end board. Keeping the offset to a minimum will capture the joint tightly without stressing the wood around the dowel.

weaken severely. Instead, a shallow tenon edge is made continuous to keep the table flat. The deeper tenons protect the pin slot from breaking out due to short-grain stress caused by cutting the slot.

The three tenons in the illustration are all located away from the edges of the table so the end board has most of its structure intact. Three 1/16 inch diameter holes are drilled through the end board to intersect the three long tenons at about mid-length and width. The end board is removed and the three holes are re-drilled to enlarge them to 1/4 inch.

The three pilot holes through the tenons are now re-drilled to 1/4 inch as well except they are offset away from the tenon ends by about 1/64 inch. Two holes are now elongated by bracketed holes drilled on either side of the outer tenon holes. A complimentary amount of extra width is needed in the mortise to allow the tenon to move within. A small file is used to make the elongated hole smooth and uniform, and the end boards are reinstalled on the tabletop. **(264)**

Finally 1/4 inch dowels are tapered at their ends to get past the slight off-set of the holes, and driven in. Trim the dowels flush to the surface and the joint is complete.

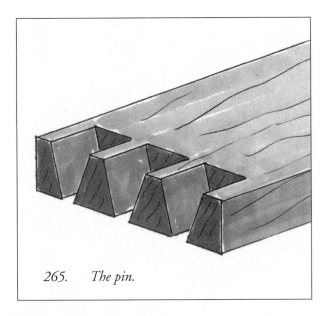

265.   The pin.

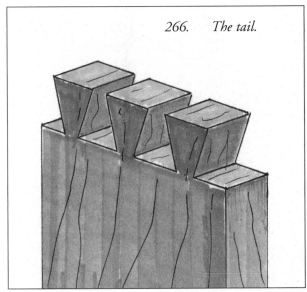

266.   The tail.

CHAPTER 25

The Dovetail

The dovetail is considered a casework or box joint. It provides great strength when joining boards end to end, as would be needed for the four sides of a box. Two types of dovetail joints are common in case construction, the through dovetail and the half-blind dovetail. These are the ones we will describe. This section builds on the knowledge gained when cutting the mortise-and-tenon joint, so please read about that joint before proceeding.

The dovetail is intimidating because of all those angled cuts and the precision required when having the joint exposed to view. The key to success is sharp chisels, a reliable method of marking, and a thin-blade saw with at least 12 teeth per inch and minimal set. Before making the joint, we need to discuss its parts and the marking process.

The pin

The pin in a dovetail joint is analogous to the tenon. It extends from the end of the workpiece with all of its sides showing long grain. To create pins, we essentially cut small mortises in between them (**265**). The beveled sides of the pins secure the joint in two of the three axes of motion. The beveled sides have no interlocking capability in line with the pins, which means the pins can be pulled out of the joint. For this reason, the pins are always cut into the drawer front versus the sides, so the beveled sides resist the pull of the drawer being opened.

The fashion in hand-cut joinery is to make ultra-thin pins and very wide tails. I'll admit that these look nice but there comes a point when the pin just doesn't have enough wood strength to do its job. If you are going to stay with the current fashion, my suggestion is to

267.   Whether starting with pins or tails first, marks made in dovetailing look like these.

increase the number of pins until the sum of all their widths adds up to around one-fourth the width of the wood. I would set a 1/4 inch as the practical minimum width at the narrow end.

The Tail

The tail of a dovetail joint is analogous to the mortise. The fact that both members of this joint provide long-grain structure indicates its strength. The pin, however, is a stronger structure when compared to a tail with matching wide and narrow dimensions.

The tail is made of long and short grain. The long grain is uninterrupted from the narrow base to the end of the tail but the beveled edges of the tail are all short grain. The more radical the bevel angle, the weaker the wood. Stay between 7° and 14° as a good compromise. (**266**)

Ensure that the boards being used for dovetail joints have clear, straight grain at the ends. A knot or a strongly diagonal grain increases the difficulty of cutting and also weakens the joint.

Through dovetail

The through dovetail has the joint members exposed on both faces. On either surface you can see parts of the tails and the pins. This means you see the long grain of one board and the end grain of the other. The change in grain orientation makes the exposed end-

grain appear darker than the long grain, creating a pleasing detail.

So where do you start? Tails first or pins first. Both are right answers, so I will list the benefits of each. (**267**)

Tails first

When laying out the tails first, I find that I can visualize the completed joint more readily. The tail-first option also allows me to speed up the work by stacking several boards face to face in the vise, and cutting them all at once. This makes it easy to have matching joints on multiple corners, plus I am able to square the saw-cut more easily over the wider combined boards.

Further support for cutting tails first has to do with the mechanics of sawing. While it is straightforward to make saw cuts straight down the grain of the wood while cutting the edges of pins, it is not so easy to start a tail saw cut and then follow a line when sawing into the grain at an angle. By making the difficult cuts first, we can more easily attain what matters in the dovetailing: matching the pin-to-tail spacing and angles.

Pins first

When designing with narrow pins it is easier to fit a marking tool into the wider tail mortise if you have chosen to make the pins first. I believe marking a tail from a pin is easier and thus more accurate than marking a pin from a tail. We will see how those

Joint marking basics

One would think something as simple as marking a line should not deserve much attention, but the way the line is marked has everything to do with the way the joint is cut. We will expand the following thoughts when we mark our cut edges on the mating workpiece.

When marking out a joint, you have the choice of using a pencil, knife, or point. Each has its advantages. The pencil is great for marking tight-grained, light-colored wood such as beech, maple, or poplar. I prefer the .5 mm mechanical pencil over a regular wooden pencil because the line width is consistent and fine.

The marking knife is excellent for all woods but it is hard to see the line on open-grained or mottled woods such as oak and hickory, or dark woods such as walnut or rosewood. Using white chalk over the knife-cut on dark woods and a charcoal stick on light woods makes the lines stand out. Just be sure you can wipe it off when you are through. Mineral spirits should do the trick.

When using the wooden squares we built, the knife will occasionally trim off some of the edge of the square instead of just following it. Bad for your square and for marking accuracy. I would choose a metal square in that situation.

The point, such as an awl, is a good choice if you find the knife starts following a grain line instead of the square edge. Use the point lightly at first, then retrace the line several times. Dust with either charcoal or chalk.

Any of the markers above can be mounted to a marking gauge as we saw earlier in this book. The knife equivalent is the chisel-pointed cutting gauge, and the point is the pin-pointed marking gauge. The pencil was not designed into any of the gauges but could easily have been by drilling the appropriate-size hole in the beam.

marking methods differ as we demonstrate both.

Marking the dovetail is done very differently from marking the mortise and tenon. The dovetail is first marked, using a dovetail gauge and square, on one joint member and then sawn. The cut joint is then used as a template for tracing the joint edges onto the mating piece of wood.

The mortise and tenon is marked using the reference surfaces of the wood and marking gauges. The mortising gauge and the dual-beam marking gauge are used to mark the thickness and width of both the mortise and the tenon. Each joint member can be cut independently since they are not dependent on a tracing as in the dovetail.

Layout of the pins

Whether we start dovetail layout with the tails or pins first is mainly personal preference. For this example, we will start with pins first.

Let's say we are building a box that is 1 foot square and 4 inches tall, and we are going to dovetail all four sides together with the grain running around the box in a horizontal orientation. The first thing to do is determine spacing and order.

It is traditional to have a half-pin on each end of the dovetail joint, as seen in (**265**). The half-pin must be wide enough to present a strong outer edge, so it is layed out to be as wide as the normal pin. This gives a pleasing repetitive spacing on one face of the joint, and a sense of pins bracketing tails on the other surface.

Pins tend to be made smaller than tails because they are slightly stronger, plus thin pins look nice. We will choose a minimum pin width of 1/4 inch at the narrow end. The reason is that my smallest chisel is 1/4-inch wide, convenient for chopping the waste from the pins and tails.

The rule of thumb is one pin per inch, so our 4-inch wide box has four pins. Don't be bound by rules if you prefer other spacing since it is an area where your

268.   *Marking the pin locations with a dovetailing gauge. Flip the gauge top to bottom to reverse the angle.*

269.   *Make the pin cuts by starting the saw at 45° to the edge, sawing along both horizontal and vertical lines. Slowly tilt the saw to horizontal.*

design freedom is wide open. You can cluster the pins at the ends or spread them uniformly, or place them randomly. Even spacing is likely the strongest, but only by a small margin.

Let's use the layout rule of thumb for this example. Cut the workpiece to exact size and square all the ends on the shooting board. We will designate two of the sides pin-boards and two sides tail-boards.

Using the cutting gauge, set the cutter point to approximately 1/64 inch beyond the thickness of the mating board. Lay the pin boards on a bench hook and score a shoulder line on both faces of the board. You may chose to lighten up the scoring pressure on the face that will show, since the cut will be visible.

With a square and pencil, mark the 1/4 inch pin width evenly spaced across the face of the pin-boards down to the shoulder line. Next take the dovetail gauge and mark the beveled angle of the pins across the end of the workpiece using the lines you just marked. The two end-pins have their bevels sloping toward the center of the workpiece. Note that the outside face will have the thin edge of the pins. It is a common mistake for beginners to get this backwards. (**268**)

It is very easy to lose track of the waste side of the line, so mark an X or scribble in the area between the pins to indicate that this is the wood to be sawn out.

Making the saw cut

Clamp the marked board vertically with about 6 inches of board above the vise, with the layout marks facing you. Place the saw blade at a 45° angle on the waste side of one of the lines and start cutting following both the line across the end grain, and the line on the face of the board. (**269**)

As you progress down the line, loosen your grip on the saw and let the saw blade track the kerf. This is where a finely set saw makes a big difference. If the saw set is very wide, the kerf will be too wide for the blade sides to help track the cut.

Level the saw out as you get close to the shoulder line, stopping before you reach it. Do this for all the pin marks.

Beginning the chisel cut

We switch to a chisel and mallet to start chopping out

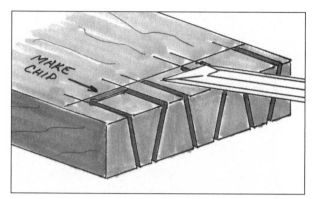

270.   *Make the chisel cuts at a low angle to form small chips that hinge at the shoulder line. Further deepening by repeated chip paring forms the shoulder between the pins.*

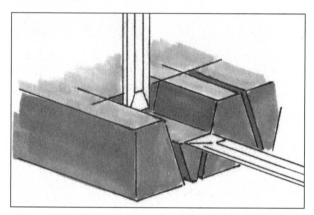

271.   *Use both horizontal and vertical paring to work down half-thickness then turn the board over and start again from the other side.*

the waste. Some craftsmen prefer to use a coping saw to remove the majority of waste, and use the chisel sparingly. My preference is to cut all the waste out with the chisel.

A point about chisel work — when the chisel is cutting across the grain, as in a shoulder cut, use of a mallet is acceptable. When the chisel is cutting along the grain, as in paring the faces of the bevels, use only the strength of your hands or you will risk splitting the wood.

The score line at the shoulder made by the cutting gauge was your first cut, and is termed a stop cut. The

stop cut helps keep the wood from splitting at the surface. We will use this to begin our removal of waste wood by starting on the back side of the workpiece where the pin is the widest.

Lay the workpiece down on a bench hook with the opposite end of the board against the fence and its back side up. Place your sharpened 1/4 inch chisel at a low angle about 1/8 inch to the waste side, facing the shoulder line. Now gently push the chisel into the wood and notice how the shoulder cut is creating a hinge point for the chip that you are making. Push until you feel the chip is loose or until you reach the shoulder line. You do not have to sever the chip at this point. The objective is to create hinged chips all along the shoulder line. (**270**)

Once you have a full line of chips, orient your chisel vertically, with the beveled side toward you, and place the cutting edge into the shoulder cut. You may have to bend some of the chips down to open up the shoulder cut again. Push down on the chisel to sever the chips. (**271**)

With a well-defined line established for the shoulder, we can proceed to deepen the cut by holding the chisel at the same low angle but now placing it 1/4 inch from the shoulder. Create the chips again, and again chisel them off with the vertical chisel, moving the low-angle cut back further from the shoulder until it is at the end of the workpiece.

Treat this as a delicate operation or you will wind up crushing the shoulder wood and moving the line further away from the end of the board. If you see that your best efforts are still crushing the wood, your chisel edge probably is dull.

Paring to the shoulder

Using this procedure, repetitively take small chips out of the waste until you have cut about half the thickness of the board. Flip the board over and start the process again until you have removed all the waste. Note that you will have come to the end of the saw kerf before you reach the shoulder. This may leave a ragged inside corner. Work back and forth between the shoulder surface and the pin bevels to produce a flat, crisp corner between the surfaces.

Repeat the sawing and chiseling for all four pin ends of the pin boards.

Inspect your shoulder line. It should be a crisply straight vertical cut. Your pins bevels should be flat and parallel with the board edges.

Using the joinery check gauge (page 40), set the gauge with its notched surface on the board face, extend the rod down into the cut area and slide the rod up against the shoulder cut to determine if the shoulder cut is indeed vertical. If it is slightly undercut, that is fine. Otherwise, use the chisel to pare the cut vertical. (**272**)

We have finished the pins and will use them to mark their exact locations on the tail boards after we mark mating board ends. Using letters A through D, mark each pin-board end and its mating tail-board end with the same letter. If you mark them on the top edge, you will have the mating code and know which edge is up.

Marking of the tails

Using the same setting used to mark the shoulder line for the pins, score the tail board on all faces and edges with a cutting gauge. This assumes that the pin and tail boards are the same thickness, otherwise gauge the pin board thickness before scribing.

Lay the tail board on the bench top, good face down, and stand the mating pin board on end so it is located on the shoulder line between it and the end of the workpiece with the narrow edge of the pins toward the end of the tail board. Be very accurate in its placement. (**273**)

This short board will stand fairly stable but a long board could be a problem. My solution is to build a 90° corner to cam-clamp to the vertical workpiece. It doesn't have to look like much but if it has a little

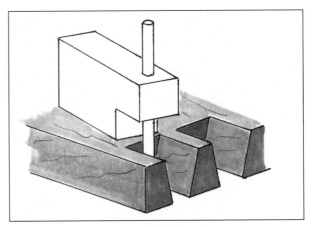

272.   *Using the Joinery check gauge to test squareness of the shoulders.*

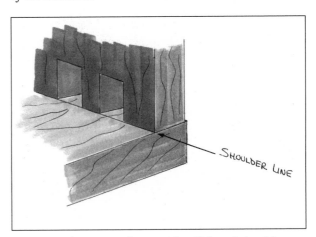

273.   *Alignment of pins with tail-board shoulder line to mark the tails.*

274.   *Using the board stabilizer jig and a clamp, your hands are free to do the necessary marking.*

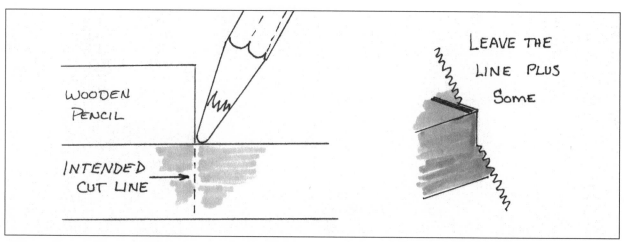

275.   Pencils become dull quickly and the line they leave is unreliable for marking joinery.

weight to it, the vertical board will be held firmly and give good access to the joint for marking. (**274**)

An essential part of dovetailing is to transfer the actual beveled edge locations onto the mating workpiece. For the longest time, this was a point of real confusion for me. Some folks would say cut to the line, others would say leave the line, and others would say split the line. Some would use a knife, some a pencil. When marking mating joint locations, it doesn't matter what tool you use to do the marking. It does mat-

276.   A knife line is crisp and accurate as long as you use them correctly. Tilt a knife edge and hold a chisel edge vertically.

ter that you know what the tool is marking and how to use that mark.

Figure **275** shows an edge of a board sitting on a board surface. The tool in use is an old-style carpenter's pencil. This was a big clunky stick with enough graphite in it to lubricate your car. When sharpened it left a wide line, but when dull it not only left a wide line but one that was far from the point of interest. The good news was it was easy to see.

Using this tool for marking, you can get only a rough approximation of where to make your cuts. I would surely leave the line when cutting. As a matter of fact, I would leave some extra just to be sure.

Marking with a knife-cut leaves a fine line that is excellent in representing where to cut, plus the knifed line is actually the first cut for your joint (**276**). Shortcomings of this method are that you have to apply significant pressure to scribe a visible line into the wood, creating a risk of moving the reference you are using as a scribe edge. Plus, when marking walnut or some other dark wood, it is very hard to see these lines, so rub a piece of chalk over them to make them stand out. On light-colored wood, use charcoal.

A further difficulty is that once you are sawing, you lose your point of reference because that fine line seems to disappear. Heck, it is hard enough to follow

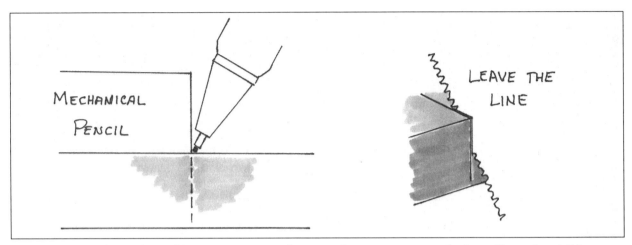

277.   The mechanical pencil line is consistent and narrow. Once sawing starts, the line still remains visible to guide the saw.

the line let alone find such a fine mark amidst all that sawdust. My suggestion for knife-marked lines is to cut to the line on the waste side, and clear the sawdust frequently.

When selecting a marking knife, you have the choice of a blade with a chisel-edge or a knife-edge. The knife-edge allows marking angles to be symmetrical just by tilting the blade left or right. If you choose the chisel-edge, make sure it has two chisel-edges that form a point, like the one described on page 35, so the blade can be flipped over when marking.

My favorite marking tool is the .5 mm mechanical pencil. It requires little pressure to make a mark and it is always at the same level of sharpness, leaving a line just wide enough to see on most woods. If held so the extended point area is rubbing up against the edge being marked, it will leave a line right where the instruction "leave the line" makes sense. (**277**)

Cutting the tails

After accurately marking the tail bevel lines from the pins, clamp the workpiece in a vise vertically. Place the pencil point directly on the transferred line at the edge of the workpiece. Slide the square up to the pencil and extend the lines across the end grain. Mark an X or scribble in the waste area. You now have all the

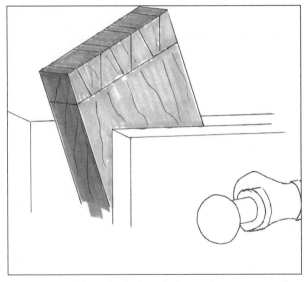

278.   Tail board tilted and clamped in vise is ready for sawing. It is easier to saw vertically with accuracy.

information you need to start sawing.

I find it helpful to tilt the workpiece in the vise to a point where half the lines are vertical. Cutting vertical is more natural and easier to see. Start the cut with the saw at a 45° angle to the horizontal, following both lines and cutting down to just shy of the shoulder. (**278**)

Since the tails are inboard from the edge, we can cut the wood off the end waste area by clamping the workpiece horizontally and sawing about 1/16 inch to the waste side of the shoulder line until the waste is severed.

Use the chisel technique learned while forming the pins to remove the waste up to the shoulder line. Clean the intersection of the tail and shoulder with chisel cuts from both directions.

The cuts we made with the saw to trim the corner waste must be cleaned up by paring to the shoulder line. Clamp the workpiece on edge in a vise or on the bench hook fence. Place the chisel with its flat back toward the shoulder line. Hold the chisel in both hands standing over the work so your head is directly above the cut, and slowly increase pressure as you pare to the line.

Final fitting

Attempt to assemble the joint. If it is too loose, veneer must be glued to the bevel surfaces to build them up. If it is too tight, fitting dovetails can be tedious and confusing. Which tail doesn't fit between which pin or is it all of them that don't fit?

Start out with the joinery check gauge (page 00) and ensure that all the joint edges that were meant to be square actually are. Fix them and try fitting the joint again.

Place the boards back in the position in which they were marked. Clamp the pin board to the board-stabilizing jig and stand it on end. Carefully realign everything as it should have been and study where there are gaps and where there is interference. Pencil a mark on all interfering surfaces.

Start paring the worst area first and check frequently to see if you made improvement. You can all too quickly go from too tight to too loose.

Assembly

When all the joints fit to your satisfaction, it is time to assemble the box. If we were to install a bottom and top, there would clearly be more work. Since this is

---

Making minor improvements

On the off chance that the joints did not come out perfectly, there is an easy fix for gaps between the tails and pins. Once the glue is set and the structure is stable, take your backsaw and cut right on the tail - pin joint line while ensuring that the saw does not cut past the existing joint interface. Locate a piece of veneer of the same species of wood and align the grain direction with the pin-board. Cut the veneer into a small triangular piece, apply glue and slip it into the saw kerf. When the glue is fully set, trim off the excess of the triangular piece and the joint will look markedly improved.

---

learning exercise, we will skip those details.

Place a tail board on the bench hook with its good face down. Locate its mating board ends and slide the pins into the tails. With the assembly looking like a U, place the other tail board on top and slide the tails over the pins. If we had a case-measuring stick short enough to fit between the diagonals, we could check our assembly for squareness before clamping and allowing the glue to set.

Use a bench plane to trim the joints flush, sand or scrape the surface smooth, and get ready for the next exercise because with everything put together, it is time to move on to the half-blind dovetail.

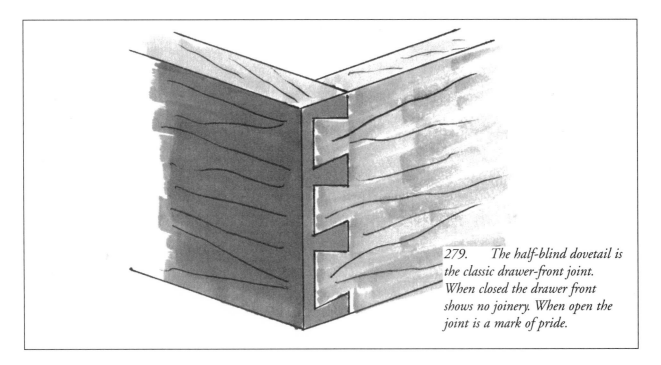

279.   The half-blind dovetail is the classic drawer-front joint. When closed the drawer front shows no joinery. When open the joint is a mark of pride.

CHAPTER 26

Half-blind Dovetail

The half-blind dovetail is most frequently seen holding the front of a drawer to the sides, though the joint is also used in many other case locations.

When you study the drawer-front joint, you notice that the tails of the sides ensure that the wood-to-wood interference created by those beveled surfaces resists the pulling force of the drawer front. Even if the glue has been omitted, the drawer will stay stable. The sides of the drawer opening hold the sides inward while the beveled dovetails keep the front and back from being pulled off.

That observation is important in helping determine on which board the tails or pins are to be cut. If the joint is being used on something other than a drawer, observe if there is a side that must resist force in the outward direction, this side should be where the pins are located so the tails may hold them together.

Once that detail is determined, layout can proceed just as with the through dovetail. The biggest difference in layout is that the tails will be shorter than the thickness of the pin board and the pins will not extend from face to face.

For this project, we will start with the tails first. The pros and cons are about the same but I continue to favor tails first unless the pins are very narrow. We will be attaching 10 inch long x 4 inch high x 1/2 inch thick drawer sides to a drawer front that is 8 inches wide x 4 inches high and 3/4 inch thick.

280.   Mark both sides while clamped together. The increased thickness of the two boards actually improves sawing accuracy and produces identical joint geometry on both sides of a drawer.

Layout of the tails

We will follow the rule of thumb spacing: one dovetail per inch. The drawer front is 4 inches high, suggesting we need to plan for four pins. Since they are bracketed by pins, there are just three tails.

Laying out tails first this time, cut two 1/2 inch x 4 inch poplar boards to length and square them with a shooting board to create the sides, which will be the tail boards. Next, align and cam-clamp the two boards face to face and clamp them vertically in a bench vise. (**280**)

Mark the end grain of the drawer sides with a square, establishing the tail's widest dimension and spacing. Set the fence of the dovetail gauge over the end of the board, place your pencil on a marked line, and slide the gauge up to the pencil. Now use the edge of the dovetail gauge to mark the bevel. Repeat this until your marks depict three tails between two pins and two half-pins.

As a general rule, the half-blind pins will be 75% of the thickness of the drawer front, so locate your dual-beam marking gauge and set one beam to three-quarters the thickness of the drawer face. You can estimate

this since it only has to be consistent, not exact. While you are at it, set the other beam to the exact thickness of one of the drawer sides. Remember which beam is set to which thickness. As a memory aid, my gauges have two different woods for the beams.

Scribe a shoulder line across the board marked with the dovetail bevels. Move all the way around and mark all the surfaces with the line. Mark an X or scribble in the waste area of the joints. We have marked the tails across two boards as if they were just one board. Had we been making the rear joint as well, we would have flipped the boards end-for-end and marked the rear tails.

Now mount the clamped boards in a bench vise at an angle so that half of the lines are vertical. Then place the saw on the waste side of the line and start cutting with the saw tilted at 45° to cut along both the end grain and face. As the kerf deepens, loosen your grip on the saw handle and allow the blade to track the kerf while progressively leveling out the saw. Finish the cut just shy of the shoulder lines. Separate the boards and proceed to chisel out the waste as detailed on page 164.

The drawer-front pins

Mark the location of the mating pins on the drawer front using the cut tails as a pattern.

With the dual-beam marking gauge fence against the back surface of the drawer front, mark the extent of the pins with the same beam setting as you marked the tail shoulders. This line should be about three-quarters the thickness of the workpiece. (**281**)

Next use the other beam setting to mark the thickness of the sides onto the back side of the drawer fronts. This line marks how long the pins will be.

Using the board-stabilizing jig described on page 165, clamp the drawer face and side together while they lie on a flat surface and align the tail ends with the line marking the extent of the pins. Note that the drawer back is toward the jig. Also ensure that the shoulder is flush with the back of the drawer front board; if not,

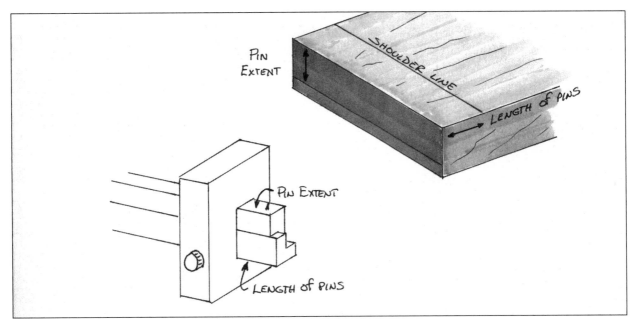

281.   A dual-beam marking gauge is ideal for marking the drawer front.

recheck your markings. With the workpieces secured, mark the pin locations from the cut tails. Do the same on the opposite drawer front end using the other side board. (**282**)

There are several alternatives to this clamping arrangement but this one allows for excellent alignment and access for marking.

Extend the bevel marks on the end of the drawer front onto the back side for the length of the pins, using a square and pencil. Mark an X or scribble in the waste area of the layout.

Cutting the pins

Clamp the drawer front with one end up in a bench vise for sawing. Have at least 4 inches of the drawer front above the vise. Place the saw on the waste side of the line at a 45° angle and saw until the blade reaches the pin line and the shoulder line. Repeat this for all the pins marks. Remember, you want to leave the face of the drawer front untouched while cutting the pins. (**283**)

Lay the drawer face on a bench hook with one end

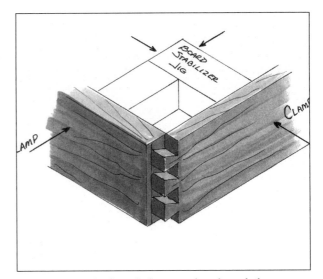

282.   Lay the boards flat on a bench and clamp them to the board-stabilizing jig while marking the pins from the cut tails.

against the fence. Proceed with your chisel at a low angle to create chips along the pin length line just as we did with the through dovetail.

Using a mallet to tap lightly on the chisel, continue deepening the chip cuts at the shoulder, leaving the

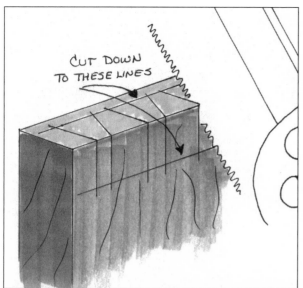

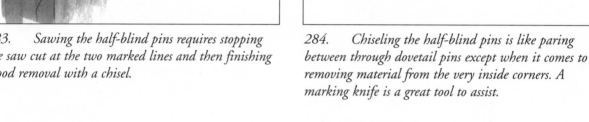

283.   Sawing the half-blind pins requires stopping the saw cut at the two marked lines and then finishing wood removal with a chisel.

284.   Chiseling the half-blind pins is like paring between through dovetail pins except when it comes to removing material from the very inside corners. A marking knife is a great tool to assist.

bevel area uncut. Work down to the pin extent by taking ever-thinner chips because you are nearing the face of the drawer and you do not want to accidentally split the wood. (**284**)

Progress will be similar to the through dovetail chisel work except there is an inside corner below the saw line. This corner is worked by alternating your chisel cuts between defining the shoulder, extending the bevel toward the shoulder, and creating a flat surface at the pin depth line.

Make cuts to extend the bevel of the pin further into the corner but do not use a mallet and risk splitting the wood. Slice thin pieces off the uncut bevel area at the angle of the bevel. Then alternate to chiseling from the end of the board toward the shoulder. Working from two directions will progress your cut toward the inside corner of the pin and shoulder.

As you get nearer the inside corner, you will be wanting for a smaller chisel because the square cutting edge is not able to get fully into the corner. Special chisels called skews can solve this problem, or you can

regrind a 1/4 inch bench chisel to do the job. Another approach to the problem is to use the point of a marking knife.

Refer to final fitting on page 168.

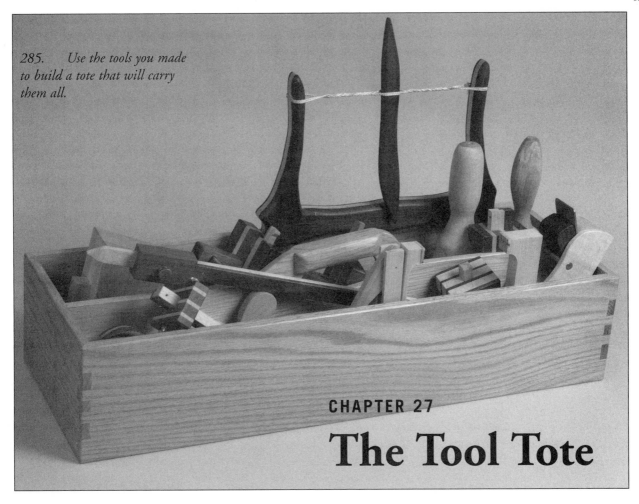

285. Use the tools you made to build a tote that will carry them all.

CHAPTER 27

The Tool Tote

In years gone by, a journeyman woodworker would set out to make a living after completing an apprenticeship. In the Eastern European tradition, besides making many of their own tools, the apprentices were encouraged to build a toolbox that displayed their woodworking knowledge. It would be an advertising device and tool case all in one.

In prior chapters, we have learned to build tools and were introduced to the methods of using those tools to make joints. The tote toolbox project is a wonderful way of putting those talents and tools on display.

When all my shop-made tools are assembled into my tote, it is brim full and there is hardly space for my chisels. We will use the size of my tote as the example. The dimensions listed here are only for guidance since each reader will have built a different selection of tools, thus needing more or less storage.

For materials we have four boards the length and two boards the width of the tote. The bottom is cut 1/8 inch narrower than the inside width of the box to allow for some seasonal movement.

The tote has a center vertical board, called the handle-board, which divides the box into two compartments. The handle board is 2-1/2 inches taller than the side-boards to allow for shaping a handle, and is offset from center by 1 inch to allow the wider tools to be placed in the wider compartment. A unique feature of the handle is that it is sloped to accommodate the natural position of your wrist, which reduces stress while carrying a loaded box of tools.

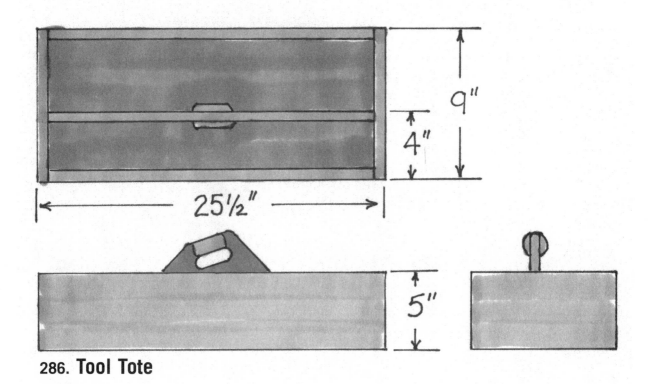

286. Tool Tote

Cut list		
Component	**Dimensions**	**Comments**
Side boards	2 each 25-1/2 inches x 5 inches x 1/2 inch	Tails
End boards	2 each 9 inches x 5 inches x 1/2 inch	Pins and mortises
Bottom board	25-1/2 inches x 7-7/8 inches x 1/2 inch	Tenons
Handle board	25-1/2 inches x 7-1/2 inches x 1/2 inch	Tenons

The stock for the box is 3/8 inch thick for hardwood and 1/2 inch thick for softwoods. We will assume 1/2 inch stock for the tote example.

Note that the specific dimensions mentioned for the joints are only valid if building the exact size tote described. If building a different-size tote, cut the joints as you wish. This keeps to the philosophy of relative accuracy versus measured accuracy. You will see that as long as the second half of the joint is referenced to the first, it will work just fine.

The outside corners are dovetailed while the handle board and bottom board are mortise-and-tenoned into the ends. In addition to the tenons, we may glue optional retainer strips on the sides to further support the bottom.

Before actually starting to lay out and cut wood for the project, read through the following instructions. Knowing what is next to be done will make the project go along smoothly and quickly. Pay particular attention to how the tote is to be assembled

Building the tool tote

Component	Procedure	Comments
Side boards	Lay out and cut tails on both side boards while clamped together.	This improves cutting accuracy and joint symmetry.
End boards	Lay out and cut pins on ends of end boards.	Mark each pin from matching side board tails.
End boards	Lay out and cut mortises in end boards for handle board and bottom board tenons.	Use mortising gauge for layout. Drill mortises prior to chiseling.
Bottom board	Use end board mortises to align bottom board tenon locations. Cut tenons.	
Handle board	Use end board mortises to align handle board tenon locations. Cut tenons.	
Handle board	Lay out and cut handle shape and pads.	

Assembly Notes

— Make trial dry fit, then repeat with glue.

— Insert handle board tenons into one end board, match paired joints.

— Insert bottom board tenons into same end board. During trial fit, scribe pencil lines on bottom on both sides of handle board.

— Disassemble bottom board and drill two holes into bottom board. Reassemble. The holes will allow installation of screws after tote is fully assembled.

— Attach other end board to handle board and bottom board.

— Slide tails of side boards onto pins of end boards.

— Once fully assembled, glue on optional side strips to side boards under bottom. Protect bottom board with waxed paper so it will not adhere to side strips.

— Finish with a water-resistant finish such as polyurethane or varnish.

because this will help you understand the following instructions.

Refer back to earlier sections of the book if you have any doubts about the following instructions since they are abbreviated versions of things already covered.

Marking the joint shoulders

Dimension your wood to exact length, width, and thickness. Four boards will be the length of the tote and two boards will be the width.

Mark all of the shoulder lines at once by setting the cutting or marking gauge to the thickness of the

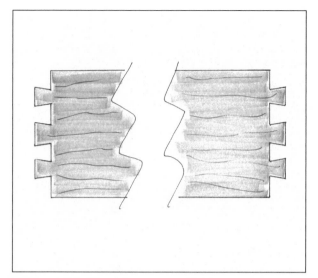

287.   Side board detail shows three tails which are cut first then used to mark the pins.

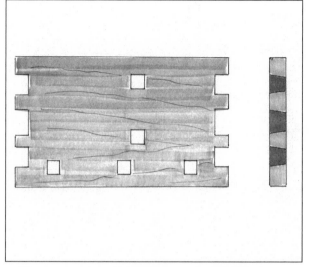

288.   End board detail shows the mortise for the handle board (vertically aligned) and the mortises for the bottom board (horizontally aligned).

wood. Mark all the way around both ends of all six boards.

Cut the tails first

Using the dovetail gauge, lay out the beveled tails on both ends of one of the side boards, which will become the sides of the tote. Cam-clamp the two side boards together and mount them vertically in bench vise with the beveled marking visible. (**287**)

With a square, extend the bevel lines across the ends of both side boards. Scribble or mark an X in the waste area. With the boards still clamped together, tilt the boards in the vise until half of the bevel lines are vertical.

Use a backsaw or bucksaw to cut on the waste side of the lines down to just shy of the shoulders. Tilt the board the other way and repeat, and also repeat on the other end.

Clamp the boards horizontally in the bench vise and saw the waste off all of the corners.

Unclamp the boards from each other.

Lay one side board on a bench hook and use a mallet

to chisel the waste out between the tails right back to the shoulders. Progress to half-thickness, then flip the board over and finish from the other side. Repeat this procedure for the other side board. Trim the outer corners of the tails ends back to the marked shoulder line.

Mark the pins from the cut tails

Mark the ends of the side boards with letters to pair them with the end boards, which will become the narrow ends of the tote. Adopt a marking strategy that will indicate which corners are up. Using the board-stabilizing jig, mark the pins from the cut tails of the mating side board end. (**288**)

Extend the beveled lines down the front side of all the end boards to the shoulder line, using a square. Mark the waste area. Clamp a board vertically in the bench vise and saw on the waste side of the pin lines to just shy of the shoulder line. Repeat for all ends of the end boards.

Lay an end board on the bench hook and chisel out the waste to half-thickness back to the shoulder line. Flip the board over and finish the chisel work from the other side.

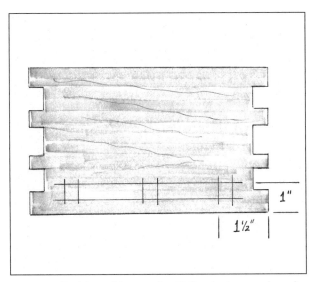

289.   *End board layout detail for the bottom board mortises.*

290. *End board layout detail for the handle mortises.*

Mark the mortise locations for the bottom board tenons

Set the mortising gauge pins to a width equal to the thickness of the bottom board. Set the fence 1 inch from the fixed pin and scribe the dual lines onto the bottom edge on both faces of the two end boards. Set the mortising gauge fence 1-1/2 inches from the fixed pin. Sliding the fence along the end board ends, use the gauge to lay out two mortises for the bottom board. Scribe both the front and back side of the end board. Scribble or mark an X in the mortise holes. (**289**)

Approximately center the third mortise hole between the two mortises just marked. Mark the vertical lines defining the center hole using the mortising gauge. When using the gauge, lay the end board down on a bench hook and use both hands to guide the gauge. One hand will hold the fence and the other will hold the end of the beam. Be sure to reference the gauge to the same end for both "end boards."

Mark the mortise locations for the handle board

Set the mortise gauge to the thickness of the handle board. Set the mortising gauge fence 4 inches from

the fixed pin. Scribe the dual lines of the mortise on both sides of both end boards. This setting will locate the handle off-center by 1 inch. (**290**) Pay attention to the mirror-image effect of the two ends.

Set the fixed pin 2-1/2 inches from the fence and lay out the lower mortise hole in the end boards to accept lower tenon on the handle board. Set the fence against the bottom edge of the end boards while scribing.

Set the fixed pin 1-1/2 inches from the fence and lay out the upper mortise hole in the end boards to accept upper tenon on the handle board. Set the fence against the top edge of the end boards while scribing. Scribble or mark an X in the mortise holes.

Cut mortises for handle and bottom tenons

Drill a hole in the center of each mortise because it is hard to chop these small holes without the relief cut made by the drill. Lay an end board on a bench hook and chop out the mortises to half-thickness. Flip over and complete. Remember to use the mallet only when chopping cross-grain. When paring with the grain, just use steady hand-force. Repeat for the other end.

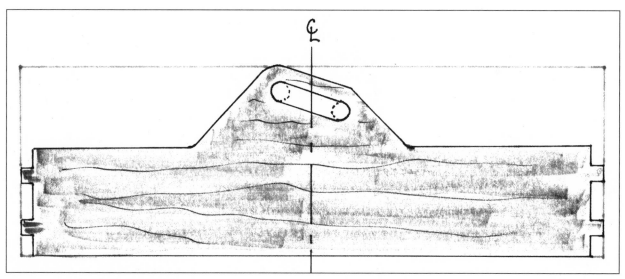

291.   Layout of the handle board.

Mark the locations and cut the tenons for the bottom

Temporarily assemble the sides to one end board. Using the mortise holes as a reference, lay out the ends of the bottom board for the tenons by centering the bottom against the end board. Mark the bottom board tenons to align at the edges of the three mortises. Scribble or mark an X in the waste areas. Mark both ends in this manner.

Clamp the bottom board vertically in a bench vise and saw to the waste side of the tenon lines. Clamp the board horizontally and saw the four corner waste areas off. Chisel the waste out between the tenons and board corners back to the shoulder lines.

We are getting close to the end here. One more joint fitting and we can move on to shaping the handle.

Mark the locations and cut the tenons for the handle

Temporarily assemble the bottom with one end. Mark the handle board tenon locations to match the mortise holes by sliding the handle board next to the mortise holes. Assemble the box at the other end and repeat the locating of the tenons. With a square,

extend the marks around the ends and down the face of the board to the shoulder line. Scribble or mark an X in the waste areas.

Clamp the handle board in the bench vise and saw to the tenon lines on the waste side. Clamp the board horizontally and saw the four corner waste areas off. Chop the waste out between the tenons.

Lay out the handle board

Finally it is time to locate and form the handle. Balance the length of the handle board across a dowel to find the center of its length, or measure to find center. Draw a line vertically at center. Take note that the slanted handle will make this box easiest to carry when the narrow compartment is closest to your body. Slant the handle to take into account with which arm you prefer to carry the tool tote. The handle will slant downward toward the front of the box. **286 (page 174)** depicts a box easiest carried with the right hand.

Using the knowledge we got from sizing the backsaw handle (refer to page 63), we will set the angle (A) and width of our handle. Draw an angled line at angle A (in this design, it is 30°) that crosses the vertical centerline approximately 2-1/2 inches from the top edge of the board. This marks the lower edge of the handle

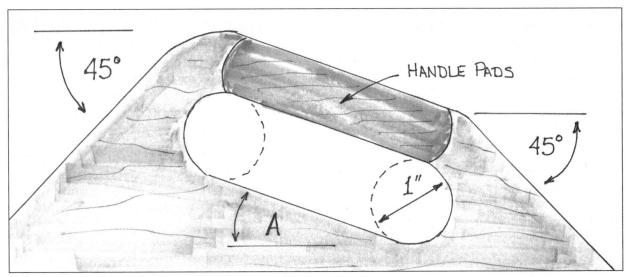

292.   The handle layout shows the tilt of the grip, leading and trailing edges of the handle and the pads. Two 1-inch holes are the first cuts made to define the grip width and location.

opening. Mark the width of the handle plus 1/4 inch centered on the centerline. Draw a line parallel to the angled line 1 inch above it. **(291)**

Temporarily assemble the ends to the handle board. Draw a line at the level of the top of the ends.

Now, from the top edge of the handle board even with the width mark for the handle, draw a line at 45° down to the line defining the top of the ends. This marks the cut lines of the handle. Be sure to leave enough wood to create a strong handle.

Cut the handle board

Using the bucksaw, cut along the 45° lines down to the horizontal lines. Using the bucksaw, rip along the horizontal line to sever the waste. Rip two 1-inch strips off of the waste piece from the handle. These pieces will become the handle pads. Cut them to approximate length of around 3 inches. **(292)**

Drill two 1/16 inch holes through the handle boards to mark the location where we will use a 1 inch bit to define the ends of the handle hole. The two holes should be centered on the slanted centerline. They should be spaced the width of the handle minus 1 inch.

With a 1 inch auger in a brace, or a Forstner bit in a hand drill, drill a hole to half the board thickness at the small hole locations in the handle board. Flip the board over and complete the holes. With a coping saw or jig saw, cut out the balance of the handle. This will create the handle grip.

Shape the handle

Size the length of the handle pads to the just-cut grip. Round the ends and edges of the handle pads. Glue and cam-clamp the handle pads to each side of the handle aligning them with the existing handle holes. After the glue dries, shape the handle to smooth curves and a comfortable grip using a rasp or file. Use the bench plane to straighten out and smooth the top edges of the handle board.

Assemble the box

Dry-assemble the box by assembling the bottom and handle board to both ends then slide on one side board. Flip the box so the open side is up and install the last side.

Locate two holes to be used to screw the bottom board to the handle board after glue-up. With the box

293.   Install tools and gloat.

assembled, select two locations about 8 inches from each end and make two small marks indicating where the handle board covers the bottom board.

Adjust and trim where needed. Shape and fair curves and get the box ready for glue-up.

Reassemble the box as before using glue on all mating surfaces. Work quickly and seat the members to each other with a tap from a mallet. When the tote is fully assembled, clamp across the two ends and use the case squaring stick to ensure that it is actually squared up. Allow it to set overnight.

Add the bottom support strips

Select a piece of scrap to be glued to the underside of the box sides to further secure the bottom. Rip it to approximately 1/4 inch and use the bench plane to smooth and flatten it.

Slide the bottom support sticks into place with some glue on the mating surfaces. Protect the bottom from being glued by sliding a piece of waxed paper between the strip and the bottom. Cam-clamp them to the sides and allow the glue to set.

Trim and finish

Install small flat-head screws by first countersinking and drilling a pilot hole for the screws. Trim any rough joint surfaces with the bench plane, and scrape or sand the exposed surfaces in preparation for finishing.

This time, I recommend you finish the tote with rubbed-on polyurethane to seal the surface from any risk of water or oil penetration. When dried, apply paste wax to the surface of some used 150-grit or finer sandpaper and sand all the surfaces smooth. Buff with a dry cloth or paper towel. Install tools and gloat.

APPENDIX A
Materials and suppliers

The following sources of materials and supplies are provided to hasten locating unfamiliar items, though many are also available locally at better hardware stores. Part numbers are noted are valid as of date of publication. More current information may be on www.creatiere.com, the author's homepage.

3/16" and 3/8" brass or steel rod
Used on bucksaw, joinery check gauge, block plane
  Hardware stores or welding supply shops

1 x 1/4" steel bar
Used on cam clamps
  Welding supply shops

3/32" spring pins
Used on cam clamps
  McMaster-Carr, www.mcmaster.com

Brass thumbscrews
Used on marking gauges, case-squaring stick
Knurled-head washer-faced shoulder screw, 6-32, 8-32, 10-24, 1/4-20
  McMaster-Carr, www.mcmaster.com
Decorative solid brass knurled knob, 1/4-20
  Rockler, www.rockler.com

Frame saw blade
Used on bucksaw
68073 14 TPI replacement saw blade 24-3/8"
  Adjustable Clamp Company, www.adjustableclamp.com
FS-BL Frame saw blade 12" x 1-3/4" x 15ppi Rip.
  Lie-Nielsen Toolworks, www.lie-nielsen.com
KEN63014 Kent miter saw blade 630mm x 14t
  Tooled-Up, www.tooled-up.com

16-gauge sheet steel
Used on backsaw
  Welding supply shops

16-gauge sheet brass or mild steel
Used on backsaw
  Specialty metal dealers and better hardware stores

Connector bolts and nuts
Used on backsaw
  McMaster-Carr, www.mcmaster.com
  Rockler, www.rockler.com
  Woodworkers Supply, www.woodworker.com

Card scraper / Cabinet scraper
Used on backsaw
2 1/2" x 6" blade from .020" to 032" thick
  Dieter Schmid - Fine Tools, www.fine-tools.com
  Highland Hardware, www.tools-for-woodworking.com
  Lee Valley Tools, www.leevalley.com
  Lie-Nielsen Toolworks, www.lie-nielsen.com

  Toolman, www.toolman.co.uk/
  Woodcraft, www.woodcraft.com

Gent's saw
Used on backsaw, 6" or longer blade
  Dieter Schmid - Fine Tools, www.fine-tools.com
  GarrettWade, www.garrettwade.com
  Highland Hardware, www.tools-for-woodworking.com
  Lee Valley Tools, www.leevalley.com
  Toolman, www.toolman.co.uk/
  Woodcraft, www.woodcraft.com

Saw set
Used on backsaw
  Woodworking tool vendors or used tool dealers
  Highland Hardware, www.tools-for-woodworking.com
  GarrettWade, www.garrettwade.com

4" or 5" XX slim-taper triangular file
Used on backsaw and bucksaw
  Dieter Schmid - Fine Tools www.fine-tools.com
  McMaster-Carr, www.mcmaster.com
  Toolman, www.toolman.co.uk/

Shoulder plane blades
These two blades are designed to be used bevel down.
30mm wide shoulder plane replacement iron
  Dieter Schmid - Fine Tools, www.fine-tools.com
07P14.11 1" wide rabbet plane replacement blade
  Lee Valley Tools, www.leevalley.com

Block plane blades
Both the Hock and Finck irons are designed specifically for wooden planes. These blades are 3 1/2 " long x 3/16" thick and come with chip breakers.
  #PI100 1-inch wide
  #PI125 1 1/4-inch wide
  #PI150 1 1/2-inch wide
  Final honing is required. High-carbon steel
  Hock tools, www.hocktools.com

  02PLANEIRON, 1 1/4" plane iron blade
  03PLANEIRON, 1 1/2" plane iron blade
  Edge shaping and sharpening is required. A2 steel
  David Finck Woodworker,
  www.davidfinck.com/irons.htm
The following irons are for traditional metal planes, with a slot for the chip-breaker. Chip-breaker is bought separately
  BL-1 No. 1 replacement blade 1-3/16" x 4-11/16"
  CB-1 Chip-breaker for No. 1 plane
  Lie-Nielsen Toolworks, www.lie-nielsen.com

Flat stock tool steel
Alternative blade material used on bench plane and shoulder plane
  O-1 Oil-hardened
  W-1 Water-hardened
  A-2 Air-hardened
  Starrett Tool Company, www.starrett.com/
  McMaster-Carr, www.mcmaster.com
  Enco, www.use-enco.com

APPENDIX B

Useful information for metalworking

American metal gauges

Gauge #	Mild Steel	Stainless	Aluminum	Brass
7	.179			.1443
8	.164	.172		.1285
9	.150	.156		.1144
10	.135	.141		.1019
11	.120	.125		.0907
12	.105	.109		.0808
13	.090	.094	.072	.0720
14	.075	.078	.064	.0641
15	.067	.070	.057	.0571
16	.060	.063	.051	.0508
17	.054	.056	.045	.0453
18	.048	.050	.040	.0403
19	.042	.044	.036	.0359
20	.036	.038	.032	.0320
21	.033	.034	.028	.0285
22	.030	.031	.025	.0253

British/European metal gauges

Imperial Gauge	Imperial in mm	Metric Sheet mm
10	3.25	3.0
12	2.64	2.5
14	2.03	2.0
16	1.63	1.5
18	1.22	1.2
20	0.91	0.9
22	0.71	0.7
24	0.56	0.6
26	0.46	0.5

Drill size to screw size table

Screw size	Drill size Wood	Drill size Metal	Drill size Clearance hole
6-32	1/8"	1/8"	#27 or 9/64"
8-32	1/8 or 5/32"	#29 or 5/32"	#18 or 11/64"
10-24	5/32"	#25	#9 or 13/64"
10-32	5/32"	#21	#9 or 13/64"
1/4-20	3/16" or 7/32"	#7 or 7/32"	#F or 17/64"

APPENDIX C

Suggested reading

Tool Making for Woodworkers, Ray Larsen
Blacksmithing techniques to include chisels, draw knives, and turning tools. Takes the reader through setting up a forge to forming steel into working tools. Contains an intriguing review of design considerations.

Home and Workshop Guide to Sharpening
Harry Walton
Contains sharpening techniques for a wide range of hand tools plus a good introductory discussion of steel characteristics and heat-treating.

Encyclopedia of Furniture Making, Ernest Joyce
Referenced for a wide range of joinery and techniques.

An Illustrated Encyclopedia of Woodworking Tools
Graham Blackburn
A thorough review of hand tools in a dictionary format grouping families of tools and uses.

The Fine Art of Cabinetmaking
James Krenov
Wooden planes and a philosophy for working wood with your hands and heart. Delves deeply into wood selection.

A Museum of Early American Tools, Eric Sloane
A ramble through rural and pre-industrial era tools. The primitive hand powered tools reviewed present a wealth of alternative design features.

A Reverence for Wood, Eric Sloane
A romantic look into rural labor with significant value in exposing methods of work and tool use.

Understanding Wood, Dr. R. Bruce Hoadley
A technical and practical look at wood from microscope to machining. A must-read for the those seeking a layman accessible understanding of wood.

The Woodwright's Companion, Roy Underhill
The Woodwright's Shop, Roy Underhill
The woodwright series contain an entertaining exposure to pre-industrial woodworking and the major tools of the era. Easy reading that includes how to make tool accessories.

INDEX

INDEX continued